The Problem with Money

by

Tobias Thornes

VOLUME I:
On the Need for a New Economics

WASH HOUSE PUBLISHING

Non-fiction

Published by Wash House Publishing 2018

Printed on demand by CPI Group.
The CPI Group is committed to the prevention of pollution and continual
improvement to reduce our effect on the environment.

ISBN 9781787233454

Produced with the aid of, and available from
www.completelynovel.com

Contents

1. Introduction   **5**

   1.1 An Overview   *5*

   1.2 The Problem with Money   *7*

   1.3 Legacies and Hard Truths   *16*

   1.4 On the Inability to Act   *19*

2. Money   **22**

   2.1 The Capitalist Revolution: A History of Money   *22*

   2.2 Gambling: Addicted to Money   *45*

   2.3 Money's to Blame   *50*

3. A Troubled Society   **74**

   3.1 Selling Ourselves   *74*

   3.2 Materialism   *76*

   3.3 Atheistic Consumerism   *77*

   3.4 Control by Innovation   *80*

   3.5 Capitalist Terminology   *83*

   3.6 Living to Consume   *84*

   3.7 Supply & Demand   *86*

   3.8 A State of Inequality   *91*

4. Respecting the Planet   **98**

   4.1 The Industrial Abuse of Animals   *98*

   4.2 Pollution of Paradise   *103*

   4.3 Changing Climates   *122*

   4.4 Environmental Activism   *125*

   4.5 Living 'in' the Earth   *138*

   4.6 Learning from Nature   *149*

5. The Capitalist Approach to the Environment   **159**

   5.1 Carbon Trading: Capitalist Environmentalism   *159*

   5.2 The current approach of the International Community   *171*

   5.3 'Costs and Benefits': Monetary Approaches to Environmental Problems *202*

   5.4 Beyond the Capitalist Approach: Towards a Better Ethic *213*

Contents

6. The Financial System   **219**

     6.1 Banks   *219*

     6.2 The Problem with Debt   *221*

     6.3 Stock Markets   *224*

     6.4 Insurance   *229*

     6.5 Supply & Demand   *236*

7. Towards a New Economics   **240**

     7.1 Work, Rest & Play   *240*

     7.2 The New Slavery   *242*

     7.3 Employment & Division of Labour   *246*

     7.4 The Trouble with Taxation   *259*

     7.5 New Economics   *260*

     7.6 'Cryptocurrency'   *264*

     7.7 Action Points   *270*

Notes to the Text   **273**

1. Introduction

The clock is ticking. Ever closer draws the hour hand to the midnight of humanity: the time of no return. Our species faces a future of great pain, perhaps even destruction, if that relentless ticking cannot be stopped before it is too late. It did not have to be this way: we must remember always that it was our species that invented this accursed clock. The Earth, in all its splendour, its mountains, its forests, its rivers and seas, would quite happily remain in that timeless lively splendour that existed before the birth of industry. But now, the balance of Nature is in peril, sure to tip against us unless we reverse back up the tracks that the last few generations of humankind have traced. There is no reason to feel bound to what they have done, to feel obliged to maintain that capitalist system of ruthless exploitation that has been allowed to dominate to too great an extent, and has caused them to drive the human world towards its sad end. For before these few generations, mankind existed without the threat of any such disaster, and, though changed superficially and now much more knowledgeable in some ways, it is surely capable of existing so still. A new generation has the chance to change the way things are. We must not allow the only opportunity to reverse the spiral of destruction to pass us by before it is too late. This volume is intended to provide ideas as to how such a shift might be achieved. Primarily it is concerned with the abolition and replacement of a system of thought and way of life that are centred on what has been called proverbially the 'root of all evil': Money.

1.1 An Overview

My aim in this document is not to propose that we immediately instigate a world free of money. Money is essential to the way our societies currently work, and has been a key component in the valuation and distribution of resources in this and preceding ages. But there is a profound problem with money: this mechanism that was invented to simplify the exchange of power and resources amongst ourselves has, in recent times, been transformed into the very focus of society. We live in a society that proclaims itself to be 'capitalist', that is, based to its very foundation upon the idea of capital as the most important measure of success, in business and in life: money has ceased to be a means, and has become an ends in itself.

It is true that money does not, even now, have complete domination over our lives. There has always been a commonly held opinion, best defined by the maxim 'money can't buy happiness', or variations thereof, that there are limitations to commoditisation and that there are aspects of life that should be beyond its grasp. Indeed, this phrase, the origin of which is unknown, has so many variations along the same thread ('money can't buy love', 'money can't buy you friends' and so on) that many people in many diverse circumstances must have seen fit to use it, through the realisation that, again and again, the gain of money is not synonymous with an increase in the quality of life.

The problem here is that, though we do not realise it, all too often money reaches even into those aspects of life from which we wish to keep it. Society has ceased to produce, and to distribute, based upon the needs of its members. The political forces we have put into play to ensure fair and just treatment of all in their transitory existence on Earth are no longer permitted the control that we granted them, as citizens, on our behalf. Government has been demonised and mocked as 'authoritarian' and 'counterproductive' by the proponents of a growing force, branding itself as the champion of the rights of the individual against the menacing control of "THE STATE": the force of the financial market. It is this market, not governments and not the people, that has the real control over today's world.

The last half of the twentieth century, and the start of the twenty-first, have seen unprecedented exploitation of our environment and oppression of our people, by forces claiming to bring freedom where they have delivered only a new slavery; to bring enlightenment where they have only dulled our minds. The problems that we face cannot be solved within this monetary-based system, because the search for profit is fundamentally incompatible with the search for societal prosperity. It is not that profit itself, and private ownership, are to be avoided at all costs: this is one mistake that Marx and regimes following his philosophy have made. The abolition of all privacy and private possession would fail to bring about the equality and freedom which should be at the heart of a prosperous society. But the use of profit and the accumulation of money and material wealth as an ends, rather than a means, to greater wellbeing is anathema to the achievement of maximal fairness and enjoyment of life across society. For this reason, the monopoly of money must be overturned.

We shall start our exploration, which will take us through the history of human society and the myriad new ideas that could be applied to improve it from its current state, with an introduction as to what the problem with money is, and why it is that we should seek to address it. Since its inception in Britain three or more centuries ago, industrial capitalism has spread to much of the world, and now is the time to arrest its progress before it comes to burden yet more heavily the lives of our planet's citizens. We must learn from our history, and from the current and past states of our society. Great change has taken place in recent centuries, but it has in some ways us pushed much too far, and in other ways not far enough. Capitalism seeks to constantly alter the material fabric of society, to disastrous effect. We should seek not to sweep aside the materials and innovations that it has spawned entirely, but to change the ways in which they are used and perceived. A revolution of the mind is what is needed, not a wasteful and oppressive destruction of the material world we have made. The following chapters aim to provide some suggestions as to how this might be achieved.

It has become evident, looking at the various examples of the problems inherent in the capitalist society in which we now live, that part of the difficulty with the capitalist system is that it has inherited some of the tendencies of the societies of our deep past, whilst ignoring others. For instance, like the hunter-gatherers we once were, we continue to shoot wild animals – even when this is no longer necessary – but unlike them we compete with each other and with Nature itself, rather than cooperate, to obtain material goods. The coming of capitalism (as a replacement of the unequal stability of feudalism) has led to a constant focus on this competition, which inevitably results in the creation of losers as well as winners. This is not the same as competition through Natural Selection, as it is often wrongly compared to, because in the natural world, there are no true losers and winners: all species that evolve into being are 'winners' in the sense that they are able to exist for a time, but they are also 'losers' in that they are gradually replaced by something else. Any individual being lives out its own life, naturally, within the context of this much broader picture, and is inherently of no greater or lesser value than any other. The capitalist society, by contrast, gives certain individuals constant power above others, in the form of unevenly distributed wealth. If we are to live in true equality, such that all are able to make the most of their lives, such an unnatural distortion must be abolished.

But these philosophical justifications for change aside, the fact remains that mankind simply cannot afford to live in the way it currently does for much longer: the Earth cannot sustain such ruthless consumption. Why should now not be the time to act t remedy this situation? There is no use sitting back and refusing to change the way things are because we think it can't be done. If we want to change the world, let us just get up and change it. We would each do well to remember that the past does not exist. It is all but history. The present is what we can shape, the place that we can make our own. The current system of inequality is history. The present is the Revolution.

We can ensure that history does not continue to haunt the present only by taking a new look at how we as a society manage our lives and our relationships with one another and with the natural world. This book, in two volumes, aims to address some of the ways in which this can be done, by exploring the history of our society and its financial basis, evaluating how this basis is leading to difficulties, and looking to both past and future for ways of resolving such difficulties by reorganising the ways in which things are done every day so as to make this country more accommodating to life and prosperity. No author is infallible, and these are merely ideas inspired by the limited number of disparate sources that have influenced my subjective experience of this universe. Some may prove more truthful or realistic than others. All ideas for radical change, be they listed here or elsewhere, must meet one key criterion if they are to be adopted. In all our doings, we shall obtain the optimal outcome for ourselves and for others if we love our neighbours as ourselves. Only those ideas that are implemented through loving consideration for all on whom they have an impact, therefore, and which result in a long-term improvement for all, should be implemented. Hold this one idea in our minds, as we go about our day-to-day lives and make those small decisions that have the capacity to change the world for better or for worse, little by little, and we shall not go wrong.

This document will focus largely on how we might transform society in the UK for the good of both people and planet. It is true that the capitalism that dominates our society here is already entrenched – or growing – in many other parts of the world, and ultimately, sustainability and prosperity can only be achieved if the whole world adopts a policy of respect for nature and compassion between all peoples. Indeed, in places we shall touch upon the roles of the International Community and the damage done by the profit motive and consumerism elsewhere in the world. But the best way to bring about change is to start at home – to lead by example – and a single country, unified in its laws and governance, can make radical changes straightaway that would be much more difficult to implement simultaneously across the world. It is my conviction that the UK must lead the way in making this change, today, and my hope that the universally beneficial revolution we instigate here may become the inspiration for movements that will bring about global change. We may fail in this endeavour, but we must at least try, if we are to convert certain devastation into the possibility of sustainable joy.

1.2 The Problem with Money

It is tempting to perceive a timeless quality in the splendour of the 'natural' world. It is tempting to believe, as we escape from the hustle and bustle of the urban existence we have created for ourselves back to an Outside that is more akin to our ancient habitat, that it will always be there, a place to forget those artificial troubles and focus again on the simple needs of pure existence; that, whatever else may befall us, 'they can't take that away from me'. Whom do we imagine this oft-referenced 'they' to be? Hateful tyrants, perhaps, or ignorant bureaucrats; maybe members of the Other Classes, though this is not so fashionable a supposition these days, who are certain to rob us from above or below? If this is indeed what we mean, the statement holds true: *they* have little power to take anything away in the long term, if indeed these demonised phantoms exist at all. For they will undoubtedly lose any misused power they have and be vilified by history.

But it is those much more difficult to vilify that we should rather fear as being capable of taking away what we treasure: we should fear instead the good-intentioned, the 'modernisers' and technologists. They have taken much before, and they will do so again. For these are the slaves of capital. These are the obsessive fanatics of 'growth'. If their societal system is designed always to promote and glorify 'growth' in every sense but the most natural, necessary growth of mother nature's sustaining canvas of green, how can we expect them ever to halt on the path towards a total conquest of that sole uncontrollable, 'unprofitable' domain? Population will grow, cities will grow, and the resources on which they are based will vanish. But this will be done, and, under the present system, should be done, because capital will grow. That is the problem with money. If we are to save what we truly hold dear, society must change, radically and rapidly. Money must be knocked from its plinth.

The trouble is that what generations of technologists and politicians have apparently striven to create, a world where anyone can obtain at once whatever he or she desires; will be able to access all the information they can possibly want in any format they choose; and can be sure that, no matter what the problem, technology will solve it for them, is as alien to ourselves as it is to our planet. Furthermore, it is impossible to achieve universally, because technologies designed to benefit some almost always produce negative effects on others, and often also on the users themselves. We shall encounter many examples of this in Volume II of this work. The car is intended to save time and effort, and to allow long-distance travel from anywhere to anywhere, but contributes to the production of greenhouse gasses that warm the planet and make it less hospitable to life, its most precious asset, whilst at the same time making the user less healthy in body and in mind (see 'A New Species'). The television may be able to educate and entertain millions from the comforts of their homes, but can at the same time be used to control what we know, and isolate us from the people and problems in the real world around us (see 'Journalism and the Media'). Most such technologies are indeed good and beneficial to society if used sparingly, where they can produce real advantages, but become detrimental if they are allowed to dominate whole spheres of our lives. The spheres of travel, education and entertainment are affected by these examples, but new technologies become increasingly pervasive in all facets of our existence.

Yet, under the pressure of capitalist demand for growth, the vision of a future of infinite ease in life and abundance of all things we desire continues to dominate in many respects. We see it in the ever newer mobile telephones, computers and televisions that are supposed to make life easier but which demand continual replacement with the next model (see 'Control by Innovation'); in the idea of robots that act like humans, which it is perhaps supposed will free us of the need to work or at least do chores (see 'Replacing Mankind'); and even in the search for a method to cheat death, that ultimate spoil-sport to a good time (see 'Cheating Death').

All these searches are only bringing us further and further from the natural tendencies of our being, and are failing to make things easier at all. Life without work to do, it seems, is, in fact, boring. Thus, when we invent ways of avoiding manual work through mechanisation, we create new, far less useful, jobs in the so-called 'service industries' and frown upon those who suddenly find themselves out of work because even these new jobs cannot make up the difference (see 'Work, Rest and Play' in this volume). Where once there were cohorts of highly-skilled workers doing useful jobs efficiently, there are now polluting machines doing the work and human beings left with nothing to do, being blamed for not working by certain sections of society.

Life without death is an eternal torture, as either the body or the mind must eventually succumb even if the soul is nailed firmly to the earth. Yet, we ever seek ways of avoiding all physical pain and especially death, by deferring that pain to others, on whom we experiment (see 'Deadly Hypocrisy', volume II). Capitalism prevents us from contentedness in the state we are in, enduring natural joys and pains, and leads us to believe that growth is ever necessary – that the old method will not do and must be replaced – diverting us from the true pleasures of life and fixing our eyes squarely on the magic substance, money, that will feed the flames of our desires and, we believe, satisfy our unquenchable appetite for more. That appetite cannot be satisfied; it is a construct that, though the planet may be destroyed at its behest, will, quite by its design, never end. This world can never be full only of joy and free of pain, no matter how large the 'world economy' grows. But we can be content, even in times of occasional suffering, if we abandon capitalist urges and the cruel inequality of competition, and instead build our society on love and cooperation.

Some may cast scorn on this use of the word 'love'. By ruthless, capitalist standards to try to base a society on love, rather than greed, seems naïve and futile: the assumption is, all too often, that the 'bad' nature of humanity – selfishness and disregard – will trump the 'good' – cooperation and provision for others – and that a cooperative society will fall due to the greedy actions of even a few of its members. But in reality the human species has evolved to be a social species. In truth, it is love that is craved by all, and love that can be so easily given through cooperation. A cooperative-based society would not rely upon the quenching and suppressing of natural human emotions of selfishness and greed; these are traits that we have evolved in order to obtain what we each need to survive. But it would end the distinction, made under capitalism, between the good of the self and the good of society: instead, the best way of each obtaining what they want and need from others, and indeed that love and respect that they truly crave but cannot find in the ruthless pursuit of money, would be to cooperate with their neighbours, as part of a wider society.

In the natural world, rarely are individuals of any species seen to perform actions that are detrimental to the species, for their own selfish good (see 'Learning from Nature'). A species is more likely to survive, rather, if the individual seeks what is good for the species as a whole. So it is, in truth, with humanity: the obtaining of surplus possessions and resources for ourselves fails, we find, to make us happier. But performing a role within society, by doing a job of some kind, and in return obtaining what we need to survive, leads to a much fuller and more joyous life, indeed satisfying in truth what we each seek. Thus, a cooperative society will not be destroyed by human selfishness, but rather will satisfy our desires much more fully than the competitive one could, and will be in the interests of all to maintain. That is also what makes it the most democratic of societies, for it requires the support of the majority of people in order to function. The proof, then, of this hypothesis – that a cooperative society would be preferable from both an individual and a communal perspective – will lie simply in whether it lasts. If the system put forward in this document makes life worse for people rather than better, capitalism will be reverted to quite automatically, but the numerous ills of our current society suggest that this is very unlikely to be the case.

One of the greatest myths pervading a capitalist consumerist society is that of freedom of choice. We are told repeatedly that in a competitive, money-driven world of material abundance we benefit from more choice. Which car to drive, which food to eat, where to go on holiday: the more money we have, the more options are available to us, each competing with the others to seem the best value for our money. But at the same time we are increasingly enslaved by money and the corporations competing to control our lives. Capitalist competition favours technological innovation, but only of the sorts of technology that make money, not necessarily those that genuinely improve our lives and set us free to live in greater peace and tranquillity. The more people 'choose' to heed the automobile manufacturers and drive a car, the less able anybody else is to choose to breathe air that is not polluted or hear the sounds of nature undefiled by rumbling engines. These days, cars are not even owned by the people who drive them: they are rented on credit, remaining in the ownership of the manufacturers or distributers, and after a few years the user will be forced to buy a new one, under a similar credit scheme, if they can't cough up the full cost of the vehicle. Meanwhile, the price of the petrol they fill it with is fixed not by democratic consent, nor to account for the true social and economic cost of extracting and burning it, but rather by the whim of the oil-producing nations and the big businesses that supply it. Yet the price they choose could have a profound influence on how people live and the enjoyment they and those their actions might affect can draw from life.

Ordinary people aren't in control of their own lives in today's world. The public aren't to blame for the pollution their excess consumption produces or the greed, dispute and depression their meaninglessly materialistic lives often engender. It's big business that's in control - forcing people to consume; forcing people to spend their time choosing between bright shiny gadgets and goods and doing their best to prevent them from choosing to opt-out altogether; forcing people to spend so much of their lives glued to the computer, television or telephone and cut off from the natural world, whose enjoyments are freely available and therefore not so easy to profit from; forcing us all to breathe polluted air and mourn over the natural wonders decimated by careless and often needless industry. We can resist some of these things, of course, but we are encouraged not to. If everybody stopped buying new telephones, cars and computers, it would be lamented as a national tragedy - a stymie to the much-vaunted stream of economic growth.

Many people realise this; many people resent the power of the big businesses that have come to rule our lives and the neoliberal political establishment that does too little to stop them. The two most profound and surprising democratic outcomes of 2016 - the choice of the UK to leave the European Union and the election of Donald Trump to the US presidency - represent a venting forth of a frustration that has been simmering across much of the industrialised world for some time. Many of those who chose these options did so, in part at least, on the basis of misguidance. Some wrongly blamed immigration for economic hardship; others wrongly accused scientists of conspiring to 'invent' climate change with ulterior reasons. But most felt that their lives were being controlled by an establishment that was no longer listening to their concerns and that change that they did not welcome was being forced upon them. They opted, therefore, to change those in power in an attempt to keep hold of what they value - be it jobs, environment, way of life - in a world of increasing turbulence and uncertainty that established politicians, bowing to monetary power and not to people, simply didn't seem to have the mettle to take on. That is why people from both extremes of the political spectrum - socialists and nationalists, climate deniers and environmentalists, communitarians and individualists - indeed, anyone who feels their voice is not heard, have united in voting for anti-establishment parties and policies in an attempt to throw off the neoliberal forces of centre-ground politics that refuse to stand up to the capitalist establishment and can only promise more of the same. This demand for change needs to be funnelled into a real, meaningful re-empowerment of the people: it is the only democratic thing to do. The old order is dead; something new must replace it. But we must tread carefully to ensure that the coming societal transformation is positive for all, that it is just, reasonable and environmentally sustainable, and that the wellbeing of the inhabitants of this planet will genuinely improve as a result of it. The later chapters of this document make an attempt to outline the shape that such a transformation could take.

Under the shackles of money we are given more and more choice of how to spend it, but gain less and less joy from the goods we obtain. We are not built for consumerism, not really. If we don't do away with it soon, it will destroy, not enhance, our wellbeing. We need to return to the community spirit we once had; we need to find out what we truly want, what we truly need, and provide these things for each other for the good of society. This is a call for an end to the fake freedom of the capitalist society, an end to superficial materialism, a return to the vitality of cooperation with ourselves and with mother nature that we have known and lost and a step forwards into a new world where everybody has the opportunity to get true value out of life. In this world, all will play a role, with their own individual talents, in the smooth running of society, all gaining according to the true desires of their hearts. It is time for an end to the heartless monopoly of money, time for Mother Nature's finest to stop clawing at the roots that sustain it and blossom into the species she intended.

Money is Power

The key postulate upon which rests the argument to be put forward here is that we are unable to achieve prosperity for all in a society based on the accumulation of monetary wealth. Why should this be the case, you may ponder: why shouldn't it be that this money, which has worked so well for the businessmen and the bankers, in giving them abundance and wellbeing, cannot be the driving force behind such advantages for all? The reason lies in a divided society. Reliance on money as the key focus gives rise to a society that sees individuals sleeping on the streets relying on money from passers by. A society that sees generations locked in soulless housing estates, not with so great a material need as the poor of the past but nevertheless treated as second-class, without the comforts, security and added luxury that others enjoy. A society in which disparity reigns, from birth, between rich and poor. A society in which citizens see fit to rise up, as they did in the United Kingdom in the summer of 2011, to steal goods that they do not need to live but which they are driven to desire, and which the other half of the population has come to take for granted.

1. Introduction

Such riots are not the result of 'sick' individuals. They are the result of governments of recent years failing to do their job properly. They have failed to provide the same level of useful education to all who are born, as equals, into our country, regardless of whether those people go on to further study or feel better placed with manual work. They have failed to ensure that everybody, no matter how much wealth they have accrued (which will depend upon the job that they hold) has the same access not just to the basic necessities of health and food, but also to the community, family, culture, art and understanding that make life worth living. These things should not be bought by those who hold a more prominent job: they should be provided by society's collective efforts – not by reliance on the good-will of some private charity – for the good of society, to all. Government is the tool with which society regulates itself, and it follows that government should be responsible for doing this.

Money, which was originally invented for our convenience is, conversely, what fundamentally gets in the way of this fair, prosperous society, when it comes to be applied to all our resources – natural and manmade – to our art and science, and, in the most worrying of cases, even to our religion. To money is given power over these staples of every life, and because they lack sufficient money, many come to be denied access to them. It is unfair that in the only Earthly existence each of us has, we should, because of natural weakness or choices that we or our parents have made, sometimes be unable to experience the rich, inspiring beauty and diversity that the Earth and human culture have to offer. It should not be that some are able to enjoy the fascinations of art and science, and the best of the world's resources, whilst others are too busy to enjoy the gift of life, slaving away to get the money they need simply to survive because their jobs are considered so much less important or because they simply have more mouths to feed. In the present society, money is required even to obtain basic goods and services, which are not provided according to need, and it is this that gives rise to inequality and inhibited wellbeing for many.

There are, though, two potential solutions to this problem. Either the disparity in monetary income must be overcome, so that whilst some higher-demand jobs are higher-paid than lower-demand jobs, which tend to require less training, all wages move into a similar bracket (since an hour's work is, after all, an hour's work, whatever that work entails) and all are given at least the 'living wage' required to lead a good life. This wage would have to be adjusted to suit the needs of the person in question: a larger family to provide for would mean a larger wage, for example. The actual wages given would have to be set according to the prices of commodities, which in turn would have to depend upon the amounts of resources available sustainably to us, so as to avoid damagingly degrading the environment. This scenario would still be based on money, but not in a

14

free market: the power of money would, in turn, be subject to the power of the democratically elected government. Alternatively, a more radical but more straightforward change could be brought about, whereby the power – and lure – of money is removed altogether. If money is indeed the 'root of all evil', rooting it out would indeed produce great gains. In reality, money is but a catalyst to existing forces of greed and selfishness inherent to human nature, but by removing it and re-forging the natural connection between what is good for oneself and what is good for society (see 'Learning from Nature'), it is the aim of the present work to show that we can make our society a much more fulfilling and sustainable place in which to live.

To break the power of money, we must make access to the arts and the sciences, to sports and leisure, free of charge for all to enjoy. Why should a monetary value be imposed upon these natural human endeavours in the first place? Good houses, which are designed to shelter people, not to make money for builders and building societies, should be provided to everyone, as they were in previous societies long before capitalism. All should be cared for and care for one another: the homeless given homes, the hungry given food, at no expense. We have the resources to provide these things; why should they be denied to some? There should be no such outrageous waste as we see at the moment: no houses standing empty because they have been repossessed from their rightful inhabitants by the merchants of money or because they belong to one of the few rich enough to possess multiple homes. No food thrown out by supermarkets, perfectly edible but too old to sell, which a hungry soul could be arrested for 'stealing' from the bins.

Through gradual programmes of brining industries back into public ownership and the active redistribution of real wealth, this ideal of maximum equality of wellbeing – not just equal opportunities, which are no good to the unlucky or to those who make mistakes – can be brought about. When all the basic needs of life are made free of charge, money will become worthless with regard to what is truly important. It may still be used by some, if they choose to use it to swap between themselves superfluous privately-owned goods. The world will not become perfect, but we will all share, together, in its imperfections, and each work in our own way to keep society going and bring each other through. There need be no end to privacy, or private possessions: indeed, personal freedoms – of speech, of politics, of religion – will be made more obtainable without the barrier of greed for money to hold us back. We shall all be released from the shackles of capital and come to appreciate life for what it really is, so that justice and prosperity can exist for all, where now it truly exists for none.

1.3 Legacies & Hard Truths

As we attempt to progress towards the more prosperous society, moment by moment trying to make this world a fairer place, there is nonetheless a hard truth that we must face. The world in which we find ourselves, whose future we can shape, is a world that our forefathers, through their decisions, created, and it is far from ideal. We are unfortunate in that so much of what was good – communities, traditions, sustainable methods once employed – has been swept away, and so many of the Earth's resources have already been plundered. Forests have been destroyed, and fossil fuels burnt. Worse, we have been from our births locked into this cycle of excessive consumption and destruction, in which the very infrastructure of our society is entwined. These facts we cannot escape from, and no good will come of wishing the damage undone: rather, we must take the world as we find it today, and do what we can to make it better.

The chief obstacle to a better world for the future is not the physical damage done in the past, which in many senses can be reversed, but its accompanying behavioural legacy: increasingly ingrained practices of the present that perpetuate the harm done. The Industrial Revolution, accompanied by the advent of capitalism, set in motion cycles of destruction and customs of carelessness were passed down and swelled through the following generations. A mind-set directed always to look to short-term fixes rather than long-term wellbeing has arisen, and can only be escaped by casting aside the ways of doing things that have come to predominate over recent decades, and learning instead from the instincts and practices that we honed for centuries before the technological revolution. From Mother Nature herself we learned how to live in a state of stability and cooperation so as to thrive as a species over millennia. Now, though, we have come to trust instead in our own ingenuity, to focus only on immediate comfort and ignore the long-term future of our species and our planet. This change runs against the grain of evolutionary development, and indeed threatens to destroy us through the depletion of the environment on which we depend. The only way to achieve a better future for our descendants, then, is to abandon the consumerism and material emphasis that we have so recently adopted, and restore the balance with Nature that we once possessed.

It has been said, truly, that any government we put in place legislates not only on behalf of the citizens of the present, by which it is elected. It is bound to the actions and decisions of those of the past, and will be responsible also for the wellbeing of those of the future. All the dwellers on this land, whether or not they have a present voice and vote in our democracy, must be taken into account. To throw away the hard-learned truths passed down by previous generations, as is increasingly common it seems, is surely foolish, and can only lead to a repetition of those problems from which we once escaped. But at the same time, former practices should not be perpetuated just because they are there.

We can take the example of household chores. Over many generations women were taught how to clean and how to cook, exerting physical effort to produce the desired result in a more natural way than with the modern appliances that have taken the place of these old practices. More recently, the trend has been to save on effort as much as possible and have machines perform the hard work for us. To obtain a free, sustainable society, we must reject those parts of these twin legacies that make life worse, but simultaneously embrace any valuable skills that they teach us. There is no reason that women should be confined to performing household tasks and men confined to going out to work, so the tradition of gender-based restrictions on useful activity is clearly one that should be discarded: both men and women are equally capable of doing household jobs and going out to work, and should have ample time outside of their work to look after their homes and families. But so also should the laziness of more recent decades be dispelled: the energy-intensive, 'time-saving' reliance on electronics has surely gone beyond its logical limits. People are becoming less physically healthy as a result of over-reliance on modern devices, and a partial reversion to manual washing, cleaning and drying techniques would be beneficial to the health of ourselves and our environment. Education, here, is key: let us educate ourselves in the old arts of our ancestors, and in when to use them to maximise the benefit. But so is societal time-management: we must give all people ample time away from their main jobs to do important household chores and look after their family.

The balance is a difficult one to strike, but a necessary one: all that we can predict about the future is, after all, based upon our knowledge of the past. Over the course of the present work, we shall explore ideas about either changing, preserving or restoring currently held and past ideas, so that those that spring from Nature are preserved, and those that derive from materialistic tendencies are discarded. This will be beneficial for the survival of our species, in health and prosperity, as an example from the Boxing Day 2004 Indian Ocean tidal-wave most powerfully illustrates.

The disaster struck over a wide area, killing more than two hundred thousand people in total, mostly in Indonesia and Ceylon[1]. But a much larger proportion of the population died, not in the less-'developed' islands of the Indonesian archipelago, but in the more technologically advanced regions, where western-imported mobile telephones and other communication devices abounded. Just 50 kilometres from the epicentre of the earthquake that struck the region, triggering the tidal wave, the island of Simeuleu might be expected to have been devastated by the event. But here the local people still led their traditional lifestyle, handing down traditional poems and stories. They had known, through these 'Smong' stories, that the receding of the seawater and the flight of the birds would lead to the inrushing of water, and had put their faith in the wisdom of their ancestors, who had witnessed such events countless times before, and fled to higher ground as soon as the waters disappeared. Just seven of the thousands of inhabitants on the island died[2]. Meanwhile, a comparable earthquake not having struck the region for centuries, people in the more 'developed' parts of the region, such as Aceh on the mainland, did not heed the warning signs, and many thousands of people perished as a result, for all their supposed technological advantages. The effect had been made worse by the destruction of natural coastal habitats, which would otherwise have provided a buffer to the ocean, to construct modern cities and infrastructure. Trees provide the best haven from a tidal wave[3], but here all too many had been cut down.

The problem with today's society is that policy-makers are unlikely, under the lure of capitalistic growth, to heed the message of such disasters: that the more technologically advanced suffered more greatly, not because technology in and of itself is a bad thing, but as a result of the modern-day human disconnection from the patterns and protection of Nature. Human ingenuity is not sufficient to sustain us, and human inventions often fail to anticipate potential dangers and drawbacks that only become clear after much suffering or loss of life. The capitalist world is, alas, unlikely to attempt to re-engage with the natural world, for just as it hankers after short-term gains rather than long-term prosperity, it is likely to look to the methods of recent years rather than the distant past.

Our ancient ancestors lived in what was in some ways a far superior society, in that it entailed a more stable and sustainable way of life extending over centuries, not changing every decade in such a plethora of ways as ours is often found to do. We must re-employ some of the methods of the ancients, alongside our modern-day scientific findings, so as to understand the natural world fully and work alongside rather than against it to produce a prosperous and safe society. We should not seek further technological solutions such as early-warning systems that rely upon more resource use and more destruction of the natural world to defend us against nature as if we are at war with the very forces that created and sustain us. Choosing to construct walls to hold back rivers as though we have the ability to tame the elements instead of avoiding building on floodplains, as our forefathers did, is an example of this. We should follow instead the example of our ancestors, set long before they constructed the first cities and towns, and acknowledge that we are part of the natural world, respecting and cherishing this precious foundation upon which our species stands.

1.4 On the Inability to Act

None of the problems set out here are newly discovered. For decades mankind has been aware of the devastating impact we have on our environment and the social and spiritual depression which it engenders. For centuries the unending process of industrialisation and commercialisation has been bewailed. And yet, even as the repercussions of modern life have become more and more pressing, still humanity has seemed unable to change. The temptation to remain with what we know, with what seems comfortable in the short term, is too strong. The danger of removing the capitalist system in which we have come to trust in order to give ourselves a collective purpose – the religion of economic growth – seems too great. The tendency of mankind is to adopt a philosophy that will allow us to make sense of our place in the world and to avoid despairing in the face of the purposeless decay of time, a decay that is invisible in the slow alterations of Nature but that is made clearly visible by the inventions of art, science and technology that so quickly change.

In order to change, and to adopt a new way of life, we therefore need first to adopt a new collective philosophy. To simply remove the capitalist philosophy of materialism and growth without replacement would be to starve humanity of its basic need for purpose and fulfilment. This explains, perhaps, why the change to a more sustainable way of life is so difficult to bring about: before we remove wasteful practices, we first need to remove the desire for these practices, which can only come about by switching our aims from material accumulation and success in resource-intensive cultural activities, back to the much less demanding satisfaction of the need for fulfilment in life that comes from an appreciation of life itself, in all its forms, that we formerly possessed. Change the mind-set and the drive behind man's activities, and we shall change his practices.

Still contentious, however, is whether this change in mind-set is desirable, even if we accept that it will precipitate the creation of a more sustainable society and hence the continuation of the comfortable (albeit with a comfort less dependent on material wealth) human society we have devised for ourselves. We all know that our current practices cannot continue indefinitely, and that we and our descendants would benefit directly from their abandonment. But to therefore choose to abandon them requires an acceptance that the continuation of our existence and that of our descendants is itself an end towards which we should aspire. Is there any purpose even in existence itself? Is there any gain in endless reproduction? Perhaps we are reluctant to change our philosophy, because joy in life itself is no longer sufficient to fulfil our need for purpose: because we realise that everything, even the continuation of our own species, is itself fundamentally purposeless, and that therefore there is no point in moving away from a mind-set that, although it will destroy us all the more rapidly in the long-term, at least allows us to place a shallow faith in something that pretends to give us fulfilment and purpose in the short-term, and distracts us from the despair that might otherwise engulf us.

In an attempt to mitigate this despair, many have attached themselves to the capitalist myth that growth – in a wide variety of forms – is the purpose of human life and society, and should be achieved at the cost of all else. The notion that growth in material comfort, population and energy use is unsustainable is brushed aside by the proponents of capitalism, under the notion that technologists will invent away the problems with resource scarcity, land use and climatic change associated with such increase. But regardless of whether or not technology can – in the short or long term – allow society to grow in these and other ways, the capitalists appear to be relying all to unquestioningly on the assumption that such growth, whether or not it is sustainable (which, in the opinion of this author, it is not), is in itself desirable. Again this is highly dubious.

For what purpose do we each find ourselves, existing within this society upon this planet? Is it for the creation of works of art, or the discovery of laws of science? Each of these cultural 'achievements' is pleasing to the human mind, for a time, and appears to give some creative purpose to our actions. But all the paintings, plays, works of music we produce, and all the scientific discoveries we document, will before very long fall away into dust, like the city of Shelly's Ozymandias, except that not even a signpost of their former existence will remain when humanity has fallen and all its works are finally forgotten. So the use of resources in pursuing these ends does not give us reason to live, for they are futile.

So are art and science, then, not ends in themselves but means towards a greater goal, that of the improvement of material comfort? This seems to be the argument of the capitalist society. Markets assume that more and more resources should be used to sustain a higher and higher population in a state of greater and greater material comfort because this comfort itself is valued, as if it had some purpose. Yet we shall all still die, even if medicine extends our lifespans beyond their natural limits. What, then, is the purpose in short-term material comfort? If it could give our lives fulfilment and true well-being, then it would indeed be a good end in itself, but in truth material comfort does no such thing. Technologies deny us the satisfaction of achieving the things that we need to do in order to exist for ourselves, with our bare hands, as we used to. In former times, at least we had the struggle for bare existence – obtaining food, water and shelter – as an aim in our day-to-day lives. In a world freed of physical pain by innovation and resource extraction at an ever-increasing rate, we are introduced to the psychological pain of no longer having provision for our own and our families' existences as a daily achievement. It has become all too easy to exist, and existence for its own sake has thereby lost its charm. Growth in material wealth divorces us, furthermore, from the natural world around us, condemning us to live in an environment of sterility.

Hence development of the material world cannot be the purpose in life, for it is a false well-being that it engenders. In fact, the only true purpose in life is life itself: the joy of existence for its own sake, that of ourselves and that of the fellow-creatures with which we share this biological planet, and that joy is most thoroughly realised not through the creation of art or science, or the production, sale and accumulation of goods, but through struggling, each day, to obtain what we need to live from the world around us. Materialist capitalism leads us away from fulfilment in life, not closer towards it: the Towers of Babel that we construct for ourselves and the industry that we perform, divorce us from the purpose of life as we develop more and more. It is with pity that we look upon those who live without the material comforts of the modern world: those who came before us and those that live in less wealthy parts of the world. But our pity is erroneous, for it is we that have sent ourselves spiralling into a crisis of futility and depression, by creating a world both unnatural and unfulfilling, by removing the purpose of our everyday existence, and trusting not in ourselves or in the goodness towards one another encouraged by religion, but in the myth of 'progress' of a scientific, artistic and materialistic kind.

This would not matter, if it was we alone who suffered as a result. But by exporting this terrifying culture to other parts of the world currently living in stability and still blessed by the gift of purpose that we have squandered, we condemn other humans to the same fate of despair; and by treating the world around us as if it were filled with resources for ourselves to extract as part of the quest for materialism, we are destroying the habitats and well-being of myriad members of other species. We are living in depravity at the expense of others' well-being, and thereby achieve the worst possible scenario: it is our task to have joy in existence and allow other living beings to do the same, but we are denying it both to ourselves and to those around us. We would do better to mimic them, the birds and the flowers, and seek only the joy of love and of life. This is what will require a fundamental shift in mind-set to achieve. The following chapters will provide some suggestions for what shape such a shift might take.

2. Money

2.1 The Capitalist Revolution: A History of Money

Money can be defined as any commodity, with a generally agreed (though usually variable) value, that can be used as a basis for trade: the exchange of goods and provision of services. It is, in effect, a single quantity by which the respective merits of human labour or Earthly resources can be measured. The concept of money is a human invention, but one which has been with us since the dawn of civilisation and has, so far as we know, been essential to the successful functioning of advanced societies. Today, we associate money with coins and notes: pieces of metal or paper to which is assigned a value by society, which are used through a general agreement as to their worth, always trusting that the notes or coins we receive from one person in exchange for goods or services that we can provide will be equally acceptable to some other person whose goods or services we require. But coins and notes have very little intrinsic use in themselves. The electronic form of coinage, visible only as numbers on computer screens, still less. We cannot survive on, cannot eat or shelter under money. We survive, in a monetary society, on trust in the acceptability of coinage as a medium of exchange for the things that we do need.

The trend through human history is for money to have become less and less useful in itself and more and more of a mere token of value. The earliest societies to use money did not possess coinage, but relied on anything from slaves to pigs' jaws to provide a measure of each person's relative wealth and standing. This sort of money was too bulky to provide a means of exchange, and was more about ostentation than convenience. The same remains true in parts of Africa today: the mark of wealth is the possession of a large number of cattle, which are in themselves useful for the milk they provide at the same as forming a rudimentary currency.

But in the first millennium BC, as social groups became more sophisticated and trade between specialised producers of more advanced wares more necessary, it was necessary to adopt a more portable currency. Money became ornamental, composed now of precious metals – gold and silver chief amongst them – which were difficult to come by and easy for the powerful to control supplies of. Only then could money as we now know it be realised, in its inflatable and depreciable form, because for the first time it was able to fulfil the three primary requirements of modern-day money: it could act as a medium of exchange, a unit of account by which products could be priced, and a store of value. In this way, it eliminated the inefficiencies associated with bartering goods for goods by ensuring that a fixed quantity of any particular product could be bought and sold at a fixed price. Precious metal coins were chosen to facilitate trade and valuations in this way, because they satisfy the six key criteria identified by financial historians as necessary for the fulfilment of this role: they are at once available, affordable, durable, fungible, portable and reliable[4].

The earliest coins that have been discovered date from 600 BC, from the Temple of Artemis in Ephesus, an Ancient Greek city in modern-day Turkey. Soon the concept spread to other civilisations, with the coins named by each people according to the weight of metal they contained – hence the 'rouble', 'lira' and 'pound' – or the quantity of stuff they could buy, as in 'drachma' ('handful')[5]. In the ancient world, money remained firmly fixed to physical, material worth, and was handled in a manner quite different to how we handle modern day currency. Under such circumstances, the amount of money in circulation – and hence the price of goods – is automatically limited by the amount of precious metal available. The sovereigns who monopolised the production of coins both profited from their manufacture and were able to use their supply and valuation as a means of control. Monarchs in the ancient empires or in medieval Europe could 'debase' the currency by reducing the amount of precious metal put into each coin, which enabled them to mint more coins and thus to spend more, usually on wars, whilst at the same time reducing the value of existing coins by making them more common, which could have negative impacts on the rest of the population. It was up to each government to weigh up the advantages and disadvantages of such actions, and they enjoyed control over prices except when natural calamities or bumper years caused the supply of produce to collapse or explode. It was the surplus or lack of stuffs of real value – most importantly, grain for food – that dictated the health of the economy, not the availability of money. Such coin-based monetary systems were relatively stable in the long-term, therefore, and conducive to stable ancient and medieval societies in which technological change was rare and production and consumption remained largely unchanged over generations, with very little inflation of prices over many decades. Only war tended to produce considerable financial constraints on such governments.

One of the ways in which a medieval European monarch might finance their wars was to take out a loan, the concept of which was invented by the Ancient Babylonians. It is not surprising that it was they, one of the most vicious opponents of the Jews recorded in the Bible, who also invented that most uncharitable notion – interest. Interest is expressly forbidden in Jewish Old Testament law because it involves charging your neighbour for borrowing money, which even certain Babylonian kings decided amounted to an unfair disadvantage against those already out of pocket, leading them to enforce debt forgiveness after three years. Borrowing and lending are, in themselves, acts of cooperation and can help those in difficult situations to revive their fortunes. But to profit from this business was seen as so morally repulsive in medieval Christendom that usurers – generally defined as those who charge interest above the legal rate, which was at that time zero per cent – were declared excommunicate from the Church by the Third Lateran Council of 1179. This had the effect, however, of discouraging lending amongst Christians, who though they might be willing to lend a few pennies to a neighbour saw little incentive in allowing large sums of their money to be borrowed if, for example, the monarch wanted to wage an expensive war.

The first banks originated from this, because of a loophole in the Old Testament Law whereby Jews were allowed to lend with interest to non-Jews. So, whilst Christians were prevented from charging interest to anyone, certain wealthy Jews, who did not regard the Christians whose religion had evolved from their own as being Jewish in the strict sense, were willing to lend vast sums of money to monarchs, including many of the Kings of England. This was a risky business, however, as was proven when Edward III defaulted on a loan from Italian creditors, who were left with no means of regaining their money.

The stable and natural system of metal-based money served medieval Europe well, but towards the end of the medieval period things began to change. The Spanish Empire was eager to expand its conquests, and greedily gobbled South American gold as it did so in order produce enough money to pay for them. More money, after all, was needed to facilitate more economic activity (such as war), and by the sixteenth century there was a shortage of the metals with which to make it in Europe itself. So the greed for money was already fuelling one of the worst atrocities in human history – the Hispanic enslavement of South America to extract its wealth, which simultaneously destroyed its native people. Back in Europe, other ways were being devised to overcome the money supply problem. Aside from minting coins, another way of increasing the amount of money in circulation is to gather up the savings of one group of people and lend them to another. This is the business of banks: if one person puts £60 of savings into a bank, and the bank then loans £40 to another person, there is in effect now £100 in circulation, because the saver still owns their £60 but the borrower is able to spend their £40. The problem arises if both these people want to spend this money at once, and the bank is unable to reclaim the £40 it needs to fully reimburse the saver. That is why the early creditors went 'bust' when the likes of Edward III took out huge loans and refused to pay them back.

This problem was surmounted by creating the first big businesses in history, the big banks, whose formation essentially marked the beginning of capitalism. For from now on money would begin to decide more and more the course of society, rather than government. This is where the real 'problem with money' begins. The inventors of the big bank were the Medici family, who lived in Florence in the fifteenth century. They worked out that it was possible to profit by providing large loans – with interest – to wealthy customers whilst minimising the risk of collapse by loaning to a large number of people at the same time. The chances of any one person defaulting on the loan were relatively high, but the chances of most people defaulting were low, and the costs of the small number of defaults could be covered by the profit made from the loans themselves and by buying loans from other creditors. Controlling so much money made the Medici extremely wealthy, and for the first time money directly (and undemocratically) produced power: the Medici became so powerful that they began to have an undue influence on Florentine policy, to the extent that they were expelled by the angry citizens in 1494[6]. It was a scenario that had been and would be repeated many times in medieval Europe amongst the wider Jewish population: because members of their community lent money and charged interest, they quickly became unpopular amongst those forced through financial hardship to take out loans, and were unfairly blamed, all too often, for the ills of society, and even expelled or massacred.

It is not without reason, then, that it is said that money is at the heart of all evil, because greed for money and the fear of those in control of it or who threaten to take it from you lead to acts of unrivalled maliciousness. It was their early association with money that led to hostility rising against the Jews in much of Europe over the coming centuries, which then produced the vindictive theories of anti-Semitic social Darwinism and of a Jewish 'conspiracy' to destroy economic prosperity in the twentieth century, in turn leading to genocide. At the root of it all was resentment about money.

Gradually, money began to take hold of the countries of Western Europe, and the love of it spread from them into the empires they would create. In 1609 the first central bank, the Amsterdam Exchange Bank, was set up, largely as a place where money could be saved. It kept almost as much gold in reserve as it had deposits, being careful not to engage in credit creation by loaning vast sums. The same was not true of the Stockholm Bank, set up in 1657, nor the Bank of England, formed in 1694. By then, money had become mostly invisible, outgrowing its physical manifestation in coins: the 'total liabilities' of the bank, which included all the loans it had made, far exceeded the cash it had deposited. These banks had created money in order to increase economic activity, as capitalism began to demand a growth in material production and consumption, supposedly with the aim of making life better through technological innovations: the start of capitalism enabled the start of the industrial revolution, because the steam engine, which the Romans had invented as a mere curiosity, would be put to work using invested money to make more money. This is how the banks remain to this day – credit-creating machines that produce economic growth by loaning out almost all the assets that are deposited in them, and leaving relatively little cash in stock. But it remains a dangerous business. All the fake money that they pedal would come crumbling down in a heap if everyone tried to withdraw their savings at once. Being big, and trusting that not everyone will withdraw at once, is still essential to the stability of any bank.

In the nineteenth century, the potential for disaster that this presented was mitigated in the UK by setting the Bank of England, which acted as the lender of last resort in Great Britain with a monopoly on the issuing of bank notes in England and Wales, to the gold standard, which meant that all of its liabilities had to be matched in gold within its vaults. Thus arose the ridiculous situation that vast quantities of this precious, beautiful metal, which took such effort to extract and purify, would lie unseen and unused, securely locked in the vaults, because most money would no longer need to be manifested in gold coin. The private banks, which were not on the gold standard, facilitated the economic growth that capitalism clamoured for. Although the banks have continued to hold on to huge stores of gold, denying it its sole use to us (its beauty) by hoarding it, the trend since that time has always been away from the gold standard; when President Nixon closed the 'gold window' that allowed dollars to be exchanged for gold under certain circumstances in the USA in 1971, he ended western capitalism's partnership with the gold standard for good. This, under a system under which the actual material worth of currency – be it paper money, electronic money or modern coins, which contain little precious metal – is close to zero, is very dangerous. It means that banks now have the unchecked power to literally make (i.e. create) money through the creation of loans. This leaves the whole of society at the mercy of the richest, who make the decisions about where to invest. When their confidence in the banks is high, everyone has access to this money, much of which has been invented out of thin air but treated as though it were real, and the capitalist economy is kept moving by their spending it. If confidence collapses, however, for whatever reason, suddenly there is a 'financial crisis', everyone becomes worried about their money and tries to withdraw it, and the bank, which does not have sufficient reserves to pay everyone, collapses unless the government physically creates more coins or bank notes with which to bail it out. Then, society can be brought to a halt, all because of a lack of confidence on the part of the rich.

The first step towards this harmful situation was taken with the invention of paper money – a note through which originally the bank 'owed' the bearer the stated value in real gold – in France in 1716. With the abolishment of the gold standard, these notes became and remain essentially worthless: they only have value because people put their faith in such pieces of paper, acting as though the paper is worth the goods exchanged for it, so that capacity for trade can be created simply with the printing of more notes. This solves the problem of coin shortage suffered by medieval governments, which led the Spanish to conquer lands in South America in the search for gold, but at the same time leaves the monetary system at the hands of rich financiers and their sureties and doubts.

The banks began creating money in this way because it suits the interests of capitalism, interests which involve the maximisation of productive and consumptive capacity and the multiplication of money. By continually creating more money, the banks make money worth less and less. This reduces the incentive to save money except within the banks themselves, where they will pay interest to the saver to counteract the inflationary effect. Meanwhile, the means by which this money is created – loans – is highly profitable because the banks collect even larger interest payments on these. The bankers multiply money and make themselves richer, at the same time forcing all the activities of society to take place through them as mediators, increasing the power of money over everyone's lives. 'Credit booms' are created, whereby the economy appears to be 'flourishing' in that large amounts of production and consumption are occurring, but only on the basis of debt for ordinary people who have to take out loans to meet the rising prices of everything they are encouraged to buy. But when confidence collapses so do some of the banks, and this is why so many banks fell during the nineteenth century when this stratagem had just been created. Nowadays there are far fewer banks, and because they have so many customers they can rely on the government to give them financial support in time of crisis and protect them from collapse. The government supports them because the government itself, under a capitalist system, needs to retain the confidence of the wealthy.

It was with the creation of the bond market, which had its origins in fifteenth century Florence, that government became beholden to the confidence of the rich. Bonds were originally invented so that Florence could pay for its costly wars without having to resort to unpopular taxation. Essentially, wealthy contributors lend the government money by buying 'bonds'. If the investors lose confidence that the government can pay this money back, interest rates rise and the bonds are worth less. Faced with 'public debt' of this form, the government may have to cut public spending or raise taxes to avoid default. Otherwise, it is unlikely that they will be able to raise any more bonds in the future. Thus, government policy ends up being dictated by the bond market. Investors had an incentive to buy into bonds because interest could be paid by the government without usury technically being committed, because it could be argued that the government was paying compensation for using the investors' money. From Florence, bonds spread across Europe, helping the Dutch to finance their war of independence in the seventeenth century and coming to England during the eighteenth.

2. Money

The motivation behind the rise of market economics lay in a philosophical shift brought about in the eighteenth century by a number of 'liberal economics' thinkers, the most famous amongst them being Adam Smith. In the centuries before this, a realisation of the fundamental worthlessness of money was commonplace in philosophical literature, and money remained, by-and-large, the servant of governments: a useful means through which goods and services could be exchanged and wealth could be accrued by the powerful, but one whose value could be controlled and regulated to suit political ends. Money was a means of directing and controlling the masses, but remained a force at least nominally under the control of governments and wealthy families. It was laws and customs, decided by such people, that were used to determine how much was produced, where and by whom. Good government would cause these decisions to be made well, and sufficient money would be injected into society by the powerful to ensure that the economic activity mediated by money could be carried out efficiently, leading to high employment and productivity. But a bad government might mean that money – the imposed means of exchange – was not circulated properly, that the country's resources were not efficiently exploited and that many people became unemployed.

In 1705, observing just such problems crippling his own land's economy, the Scottish economist John Law published a highly influential book, *Money and Trade*, in which he blamed a lack of circulating currency for economic hardship and called for more money to be supplied to support more trade and hence more employment. Law was highlighting a danger prevalent in money-based economies up to that time: if money is made to be essential to drive production and consumption, these activities become restricted not by availability of resources or need for goods and services, but by how much money there is to facilitate them. The crops may be ripe and the forest may be thick, but with no money with which to employ labourers to reap the fields and chop down the trees, these assets will not be realised, all will go to waste and the people will starve. Hence, the government always needs to step in to provide enough currency. Of course, the same problem also arises when all the currency is hoarded by a few individuals, who refuse to spend it and make it available to others, a point that we shall shortly return to.

Law recognised that money is not a commodity in and of itself – it is not something to be treasured of its own accord, nor need it require any effort to produce. He criticised the use of gold and silver as bullion, since shortages of these precious metals would lead to shortages of currency. Rather, Law was an advocate for paper money that could be supplied in whatever quantity was needed. Like Thomas More, he recognised that all money is fundamentally worthless, so there is no point in using items with fundamental worth – difficult to produce metal coins – to represent it. There was purpose in this originally, for when money was first introduced this was the only means the government had of ensuring that nobody could usurp their power by duplicating it. But by the seventeenth century the use of money was so long accepted and the trustworthiness of an official signature sufficiently assured, that a bank note could be used instead. In this view, if society chooses to have a money-based economy at all (and it is argued in this book that it should not), the government's role should be to supply enough currency for the economy to function healthily, regulating to ensure that money does not end up coalescing in the hands of a few to the impoverishment of the many.

But there are few signs today of governments redistributing money from the wealthy to stimulate the economy and avert the man-made 'financial crisis', which is arguably caused by their refusal to do so. This is because of the new idea of money invented in the eighteenth century, an idea that sees money as a force of its own, capable of self-regulating the markets in which it is used without the need for interference by the government or anybody else. This is the 'invisible hand' idea of Adam Smith, the linchpin behind financial 'liberalism' – 'chaos' might be a better term – and the 'neoliberalism' that followed it in the late twentieth century. Proponents of this idea would resist the forced redistribution of wealth and the printing of more currency to give to the poor (though they seem to have little objection to wealthy banks multiplying their money through skilful manipulation of digital markets), arguing that the 'natural' laws of demand and supply will lead people to produce what's needed where and when, and will encourage people to work and enable them to consume.

This philosophical shift has had profound consequences. It means that monetary markets must not be manipulated, as this would muddy their power to naturally direct the economy. Manipulation by governments to redistribute wealth and by big business cartels to monopolise the market or artificially drive wages down and prices up are, alike, anathema to this market-liberal view. Over the centuries following Smith, it is this philosophy that has been increasingly dominant, but not because it is correct. Indeed, market liberalism has led to exactly the sorts of problems Law might have warned us of: a shortage of capital leading to unemployment and impoverishment for many, cycles of boom and bust and the driving out of small businesses in favour of the large. This is because Smith's theory is flawed, both in principle and in practice. The principle that destroys the theory from the outset is obvious. 'Letting the market decide' translates inevitably to letting the rich decide, as they can choose where to put their money. This leaves the economy vulnerable to the whims of rich investors, who have the power to bolster or destroy any part of the market according to their confidence levels and personal preferences. They – like regulating governments – are only human, and there is certainly no guarantee that they will act in the best interests of the country as a whole.

The difference with the government is that at least it can be democratically accountable and has an expertise in public policy, which rich investors lack.

On a practical level, this problem has manifested itself in a whole host of ways that Smith himself warned against. The rich have formed cartels, driving up prices – just as the 'big six' energy companies do in the UK today. Monopolisation has occurred on a huge scale, with a very few large corporations dominating most markets and preventing any real 'competition', paralysing the 'invisible hand'. One need only look at the rise of the aptly named 'supermarkets' to see this in action in the physical world. In the new digital world of computers and the web, the likes of Amazon, Google, Facebook and Apple have taken up all the pie, leaving very few other players in their markets. These companies all have holdings worth billions of pounds – in other words, the richest companies and individuals are holding huge amounts of currency, preventing it from being used as oil to the monetary-based economy's wheels. It is little wonder that everything is grinding to a halt. The 'invisible hand' has given the rich an excuse to hoard wealth whilst claiming that it's the market that's directing where it goes.

So it was that, under this new 'liberal' economics of the invisible hand, banking, bonds, debt and, after its legalisation in 1854[7], usury became more and more prominent, and a new class of people began to develop: the wealthy bankers and investors who clung to money far in excess of that available to their poorer, hard-working labouring contemporaries and who began to threaten the power of the aristocracy. In a capitalist society, after all, it is those with the most money that wield the most power. Families such as the Rothschilds, who made their fortune out of determining the outcome of historical events such as the Battle of Waterloo before anyone else could know it, and buying or selling shares appropriately, became a power unto themselves, feared more than loved by the people of Europe whose governments they could influence through the threat of controlling market confidence. At the pinnacle of their power, it seemed that the Rothschilds were even able to decide whether or not wars could take place[8]. In 1841, the poet Heinrich Heine marked society's transition from the Christian faith based on morality to the Capitalist one based on monetary greed when he satirically proclaimed, in a parody of the Muslim affirmation of faith, 'money is the god of our time and Rothschild is his prophet'[9].

The Rothschilds, and other rich families, continue to pull the strings of power, if not always so visibly, in today's society, and may still be able to hold capitalist governments to ransom (it is difficult to ascertain how much power such wealthy interests really have). During the last quarter of the twentieth century, the trend towards nationalisation of public services that had briefly developed in the middle of that century was rapidly reversed, and the privatisation of much of what society depends on (services which, by their very nature, are and should be monetarily 'loss-making'), together with the decline in power of the Trade Unions, led to an increase in confidence in the government's ability to pay off its bonds, and this market has therefore become more successful. In essence, the power of the government has been decreased, which pleases those who profit by manipulating the economy and sometimes jeopardising the smooth operation of society by speculating on and thereby controlling the prices of goods.

The rich are at their most powerful when combined together in the form of private companies which, unlike the state, do not act primarily in the interests of the public, but in the interests of their own profit. The first big company was created in 1602, when several wealthy patrons came together to found the Dutch East India Company to trade in spices from the East. No longer would small merchants be the ones to buy and sell exotic goods; soon the market was entirely monopolised by this single corporation, which by strength of sheer size was able to outcompete everyone else, including the smaller, later established British East India Company. In many ways, these companies and the huge number of corporations that would follow in their wake became like miniature governments of their own. They only operate, usually, within one area of the economy of the countries where they do business, but within this sphere they are each able to have a huge influence on society. A company or group of companies that achieves a collective monopoly on a particular trade can, through advertising, persuade the public of what to desire within that trade, and provide goods or services just as the government ought to do. Competing companies are like separate political parties, for which the public votes by shopping at one or the other, which gives the false illusion of freedom of choice. In reality, though, the choice of parties is limited, because these parties commune together to decide what choices they will offer so as to maximise all their profits. This is how energy companies are able to make so much profit in the United Kingdom today, for example: a few big companies monopolise the market, and decide together what sort of prices to charge their customers. Just as the confidence of the wealthy in the government is decided in a capitalist system by the price of bonds, the confidence of investors in a company is decided by its stocks or share prices.

The stock market can be likened to a constant referendum of the rich; when they decide that the company is doing well, many rich people try to buy shares and the shares increase in value; otherwise, everyone tries to sell their shares and their value decreases. The poor have no say whatsoever, except to choose which of the competing companies within the cartel to shop at. Their need to shop in the first place is stimulated by this cartel, which also determines what exactly is on offer. These decisions are made only with the rich investors in mind – those who can afford to buy shares – just as politicians will keep constantly in mind the need to please their constituents. The ordinary public, in other words, is left powerless when it comes to privatised industries, because the companies that run them listen only to the rich. This is what makes capitalism inherently undemocratic, because it takes power out of the hands of the democratically elected government. Ordinary people are made to suffer every day by this unfair situation: they are cajoled into buying things they don't need, and the products they purchase are often not as good as they could be.

Take, for example, the collusion between mobile telephone companies to improve each successive model only one small bit at a time, so as to sell multiple inferior devices, or the collusion only to let devices, from laptops to light-bulbs, last a certain amount of time before wearing out, forcing the buyer to replace them. But the situation is made far worse for the ordinary person when the rich suddenly decide to lose confidence in the market. Stock prices almost universally fall, companies lay off workers and poverty and unemployment result. This is exactly what happened with the 1929 Wall Street Crash, and successive 'financial crises' culminating with the post-2007 'credit crunch'. In most cases, such crashes are followed by periods of depression, when people who have been forced to take out ludicrous loans to pay for the things they have been persuaded by the capitalist companies to buy or the homes they have purchased that have been horrendously overpriced by the market are suddenly unable to pay them back. This 'boom and bust' cycle hardly affects the rich, playing their little games of investment, but is devastating for the working poor.

The Development of Modern Capitalism

'Capitalism' is defined in the Oxford English Dictionary as 'an economic and political system in which a country's trade and industry are controlled by private owners for profit, rather than by the state'. Under this definition, in the strictest sense capitalism is not and has never been implemented in an absolute sense: no country in the world has all its trade and industry entirely in the control of private owners. But where any particular trade or industry have been in private, profit-making hands, we can speak of a capitalist tendency within a society, whether or not it is restricted to small parts of the economy, and whether it is engaged in actively by many or by few. In this sense, 'capitalism' has existed for thousands of years. Yet the modern 'capitalist state', in which capitalism is the dominant force across most the economy, is something quite new, emerging only in the quarter-millennium since the Industrial Revolution, and possesses a very different character to the smaller-scale capitalism that existed before. This shift in style was very important as both motivator and enabler for the proliferation of modern-day capitalism, and is worth briefly dwelling upon here.

It was Max Weber who first described the existence of a new 'Spirit of Capitalism' and, in his 1904 work *The Protestant Ethic and the Spirit of Capitalism*, demonstrated a connection between its inauguration and the Protestant reformation which, because it changed pervasive religious worldviews so radically, had implications for the way in which we act and order our society reaching far beyond the pulpit. A religion is not, after all, a passing occupation or amusement. It is a way of living and of thinking about the world and the wider universe, and Weber makes a convincing argument for the role of the Protestant religions – in the plural because Luther's breakaway protestation against conventional Catholicism soon split into many doctrinally distinct sub-sects – in the development of modern-day capitalism. This is not the place for a detailed discussion of this connection, but it is impossible to explain how the god of money could come to be so highly revered in European societies without alluding to the shift in mind-set that Protestant doctrines brought about.

Outside Europe, and within Europe before the industrial revolution, capitalism existed only in what might be regarded as a 'primitive' form. As we have seen, money existed, and was used to make transactions and to trade. Interest and usury existed, and were means by which some could grow rich at the expense of others. Opportunistic traders – who might be called 'entrepreneurs' in modern parlance – took advantage of the economics of supply and demand to make money out of fulfilling others' needs for goods or services that they could obtain or find the means to carry out for less money than the customer was willing to pay for these products, thereby making profit. But this money was used to buy luxuries, to live in plenty, and perhaps to pay members of the Catholic Church or another religious institution to pray for the deliverance of one's soul, and atone for the sins one had committed. Money was not an ends in itself; in many traditions, to regard it as such would be a sin. In many societies, those who possessed a lot of money were expected to use it to help the poor and destitute; the rich gave dinners in their houses to which the poor were invited, and so on.

What Weber calls the 'Spirit' of capitalism only entered the picture after the Protestant Reformation, first in Europe and subsequently in all places of the world subjected at one time or another to the European yoke. For the Protestant's 'work ethic', the duty to serve God throughout their lives by working as hard as possible for His kingdom, could be all to easily co-opted by the false prophets serving Capitalist gods into an ethic to work all hours of the day for the good of the capitalist organ and the making of money. The Christian work ethic is not exclusively associated with what is commonly called 'work' today by any means: one's vocation, the 'work' one does from day to day, is good to the Christian only insofar as it brings benefit to others or opens the Christian's mind to God and His creation. In medieval Catholic Europe, 'good works' were a means of atoning for one's sins by helping one's neighbours, as much a means of proving one's worth before the earthly Church as an act of love or duty to God. The post-medieval concept of 'good works', which the Christian is called to practise continually, evolved from this ultimately self-centric idea to an arguably more God-centric concept, encompassing the service of God in myriad forms, from volunteering to help the poor to taking regular time for prayer and meditation to taking rest so as to refresh the 'temple' that is one's own body that God has given. The job that the Christian does is one of their 'good works' among many; just one part of their wider vocation.

But in the Methodist churches of the nineteenth century, the working classes were urged to adopt a still different meaning for 'good work', by placing their particular job so much at the centre of their lives that it should consume every possible waking hour. Under this doctrine, working for God meant working, and making money, for your employer. Only by making 'productive' use of every hour, and suffering in the process, the workers were taught, could they obtain salvation and release from their suffering in the life to come. Life was hard, but it was meant to be hard, and to spend time away from one's money-making work – giving one's time to family, friends, other (perhaps in truth more useful) tasks or even to private prayer and contemplation – was painted as a sin. So it was that feeding the capitalist machine with one's labour was reconciled with Christianity, which demands whole-hearted service to God. God's will and the profit of the factory-owner were artificially but conveniently aligned by those who would exploit the religious working classes. Such could only be achieved against a reformed, Protestant religious backdrop where the Catholic concept of good works no longer applied. Meanwhile, the factory founders, innovators and industrialists of the eighteenth and nineteenth century were inspired by a similar Protestant view, namely the need to increase productivity, maximising human industry to provide goods in abundance for society, and, if God favoured their work, monetary profits for themselves to boot.

Capitalists subverted and utilised reformed Christianity to divert Christian energies for their own worldly profit, and, remembering just how closely tied the lives of everyone in the kingdom and the justification for the power and policies of the government were to Christianity and the real or supposed will of God at this time, the Reformation was an essential element in the unfolding of a technological and industrial revolution that had its roots in sixteenth century Europe and has continued to transform the world at an ever-increasing pace to the present day. It was through this industry and technology that individuals and businesses made profits and grew and capitalism was able to thrive. Therefore, the history of capitalism from the Reformation onwards is intimately connected not only to religious transformations, but also to the history of industry.

It is no coincidence, then, that industrial capitalism first took root in England during the reign of Queen Elizabeth I, whose then recently deceased father had inadvertently initiated the English Reformation in the break with Rome that resulted from his infamous divorce scandal. It was then that new industries such as zinc mining and brass production, aided by the invention of new technologies such as the blast furnace, first began to demand relatively large troupes of workmen to become involved in ongoing large-scale manufacturing and mining enterprises. England become a world leader in coal mining, and was becoming increasingly advanced at metal refining. At this early stage of industrialisation, new labour-saving technologies that helped with these processes were offset by the vast increase in production – which required more workers to both mine and process raw materials – so that more and more workers were employed in the new industries. This was, again not coincidentally, also the beginning of the consumer capitalist age: now that goods could be produced in such large quantities, it was no longer only the rich elites that could be provided with household goods and luxuries; increasingly, wealthier members of the lower classes were also able to afford them. The early stage of industrialisation in Britain lasted from Elizabethan times until the Civil War, after during which it slowed but by no means disappeared, only to be reinvigorated in the eighteenth century[10]. From the late sixteenth century onwards, then, England's people have been assaulted by continual technological change and consequential social change and uncertainty.

The most profound change that industrialisation brought about was a movement away from self-sufficient, agricultural lives in the countryside to lives oriented around work for money, and the need to purchase goods, in the cities. The worker, who had previously been – whether peasant or craftsman – the master of their own life and trade became, as Marx put it, the 'appendage of the machine'[11], a faceless part of the machinery of the factory, which took raw materials in and put identically manufactured goods out with no place for individual skill or creativity. In the countryside, the old ways and common lands were swept aside in favour of larger, less labour-intensive, enclosed farms run by rich farmers; agricultural production rose to feed the growing cities, at the cost that the self-reliant peasantry was destroyed and dispossessed, pushed into migrating to find factory jobs in the 'treadmill cities' where they must be 'prepared to work like a slave and live like a slave-master' according to the historians John and Barbara Hammond[12], accepting long hours and low wages in exchange for a few material luxuries. The way of life we experience today is a consequence of this change: gone is the stable, sustainable stability of centuries of life on the land; in its place – for better and for worse – is an ever-changing, technology-based society with the city at its focus. We are still reeling from the unaccustomed uncertainty and alien environment that such a change has created, and the many instances of mental illness witnessed today as compared with past ages may partially be accounted to a transformation made not with the specific aim of making life better, but rather with the Capitalist aim of making life more profitable, more productive, regardless of whether it makes life better or worse.

Such an utter reorientation of our society took place, as was inevitable, gradually, but insofar as it has rendered our surroundings and lives so very different from those of most of our forebears, it surely well deserves the label 'Revolution', as employed in the terms 'Industrial Revolution' and 'Agricultural Revolution', a term which in its truest sense refers more to the enormity of the magnitude, not the speed, of the change. The fastest-paced stage in these revolutions took place in the late-eighteenth and the nineteenth centuries, when making money by mechanisation first took off and new technology brought new opportunities for the landowning classes to expand their estates. No longer need they rely on tenant farmers to till the soil: new machinery such as the steam plough could do it quicker with fewer hands, so there was no need for peasants to own their own land. Instead, the smaller farms were consolidated into fewer, larger ones; common fields were repossessed (after all, the peasants who had been farming them had no papers to document their right to own this land); and crop rotation could then be practised over a wide area, something that was not possible when individual small-scale farmers tilled individual, small plots of land. This was all taking place in the early eighteenth and nineteenth centuries, the acceleration of the process of land enclosure by the wealthy that had been underway for hundreds of years, but now took on a much larger scale with official governmental backing in the form of parliamentary acts.

Peasants themselves had very little power over such acts, brought by wealthy landowners, which demanded the repossession of land formerly held in common, with compensatory land to be provided to those dispossessed as decided by a commission. Such commissions were composed of people appointed, often, by the landowner themselves, and made decisions always in his favour. The plots of land re-allotted to the poor were, in consequence, almost invariably too small in size, and the peasant was no longer able to sustain himself and would in many cases choose to sell up rather than continue to try to farm in such diminished circumstances. This was, in fact, the aim of the landowning class: to squeeze out their poorer neighbours, to grow their own estates and profits, to further their own prestige; in short, to embrace the spirit of ruthless capitalism in the countryside. Farming was no more to be a way of life. It was to be a business, and one for which profit and productivity replaced people as the primary concern. For the capitalist landowners, there was no point in 'breeding men' without profit[13]: men were only useful insofar as they could be used to make money; and for that, work in the factory was more suitable.

So small farmers left the villages, and the craftsmen that served them, with no repairing or equipping work to do, followed. With the arrival of the railways, bringing fast travel and new technologies and ideas ultimately to every corner of the country, this process sped up still further after 1840. Over the space of a few decades, the villages were depopulated while the towns expanded and an agricultural feudal society became a industrial capitalist one.

It was not that the poor were left completely destitute; indeed, millions of pounds were spent on poor relief to allow impoverished yeomen to purchase goods they could previously have at least partly provided for themselves[14]. Helping those harmed by the enclosures of the early nineteenth century was costing the government so much by 1832 that a commission was launched to enquire into the Poor Laws, first established under Elizabeth I with the aim of helping those unable to work and preventing begging because it was a threat to civil order. In Elizabeth's time, everyone within a given parish could be assumed to know one another, making it very unlikely that people would obtain benefits that they were not eligible for. Most relief took the form of handouts of food, clothing or money to people living in their own homes. To cut expenses, the 1832 commission recommended that the Tudor laws be replaced by a much harsher system more suited to an industrial capitalist world.

Firstly, so-called 'out-relief' should cease: the poor were now only to receive relief in 'workhouses', where they would work to earn the help they were receiving and would be devoid of the comforts of their own home. This was supposed to make the receipt of relief unappealing to all except those that genuinely needed it, and would further hasten the migration from the countryside into towns and factories to work for capitalist masters. These workhouses were exactly those lampooned in many of Charles Dicken's famous novels, such as *Oliver Twist*, and the conditions could be genuinely horrific. Second, different classes of poor were to be separated into different workhouses, with husbands separated from wives, and – just like in Dickens – orphans in a workhouse of their own. Third, a central body should ensure uniformity of practice across all workhouses. Finally, support for mothers of illegitimate children – who often had no father to provide for them – should be withdrawn. These recommendations were based more on principle than on empathetic engagement with the poor, inspired by Malthusian ideas about the dangerous of population growth and the notion that giving aid to some undermined the wages of others, and they did not therefore bode well for the welfare of the poor. Not all the recommendations were incorporated in the New Poor Law Act that followed in 1834 – notably, 'outdoor' relief was continued in some circumstances – but this was nevertheless harsh enough to provoke widespread opposition from workers and some politicians, and was condemned as unchristian by some religious leaders. It encouraged maltreatment so cruel that conditions in some workhouses were found to be unacceptable, and the Act was quickly amended and eventually (in 1948) abolished entirely in favour of a welfare state.

The Poor Law represented another victory of capitalist industry over citizens' lives, which are treated in a capitalist system as assets to be utilised and, if necessary, abused for the pursuit of profit. Then and now, only government regulations and stipulations can curtail the exploitation of the public by big business, and it was in the nineteenth century that the acute necessity of such regulation was made painfully apparent by the appalling working conditions suffered by so many. To begin with, factory workers could be made to work (on pain of losing employment altogether) for an unrestricted number of hours in the day. There are stories of children from the towns as young as seven being exported to Lancashire mills where they would be made to work alternating shifts so that when one batch was sleeping the other was working – it was said that the beds never got cold.

A life in the factories was one of unrelenting drudgery, devoid of leisure, interest, and even education as the factory owners feared that educated workers would be more distracted and less productive. The holidays, saints' days and festivals, those happy stage-posts marking out each year for as long as anyone could remember, were swept aside, no longer regarded as important by some strands of the new religion and seen as a hindrance to productivity. Workers' imaginations were starved and their self-respect crushed by the removal of leisure time and the freedoms of holiday and sport: now, everything was under the control of the factory owner; to resist or protest was to risk dismissal on a bad reference and perpetual unemployment, and, so the new work-ethic had it, eternal suffering as punishment for a refusal to suffer in this world instead. There were no gardens or parks, no flowers or trees or even sight of the sky; only the factory for work and the back-to-back hovel to sleep in. Slum-standard housing was built on purpose as it was more profitable. Beauty, colour, happiness, leisure, learning: none were profitable, and all were denied in a world where 'everything turned to profit'[15].

Some have called into question the role of capitalism in what was undoubtedly a state of utter depravity – the conditions that the factory workers of the early nineteenth century had to endure were worse than those endured by any workforce in England before or since. If harvests had been uniformly good, if the 1811 and 1816 Corn Laws had not interfered with free trade by forbidding the milling of foreign grain except in near-famine conditions, if there had been no Napoleonic war, says Thomas Ashton, the results of the Industrial Revolution would be hailed as universally good [16]. All of these factors are blamed for increasing prices of goods, driving up profits for the factory-owners and driving down living standards and employment rates. What we see here, however, regardless of the catalysing factors, is the beginning of a cycle of boom and bust typical of all forms of capitalism – both the industrial capitalism of the nineteenth century and the commercial capitalism that followed it. Boom and bust have never had serious consequences for the rich, who simply gain or lose a proportion of their monetary wealth accordingly. But for the poor, a bust can mean a descent into starvation, homelessness or worse, and to make the pathetic claim that an increase in the availability of material goods, spurned out by factories and sold to rich and poor alike, can in any way make up for this is to entirely miss the point. These products were unavailable to the unemployed, and, although they may have helped to alleviate the terrible conditions of factory life, the new consumables were hardly beneficial substitutes for what these workers had lost in their migration from pastoral to industrial life. In place of fresh air and fresh food, they now had coal smoke and processed wheat and meat; instead of open spaces, back-to-back slums.

Capitalism didn't arrive without protest. Facing chronic underemployment, and recognising that certain technologies had begun to cause worker redundancies in order to increase industrialists' profits, members of the Luddite movement staged a nationwide rebellion in which they smashed machines such as power looms between 1811 and 1816. In August 1819, in the midst of a deep period of 'bust' following soldiers' return from the Napoleonic Wars and poor harvests, protesters gathered to demand electoral reform so that they might have their voices heard in Manchester's St Peter's Field. In an attempt to arrest the speakers rousing the crowd, the local magistrates called in military assistance. The cavalry charged on the swollen crowd, killing tens and wounding hundreds. This 'Peterloo Massacre' caused public outcry, but it could not stop the tide of capitalist development, as the continued cycles of boom and bust thereafter testify. Indeed, money was made from the massacre through the sale of commemorative plates and handkerchiefs. The government's response was not to listen to ordinary people's concerns about a world turned upside down and the relentless pace of change and enslavement that they had little desire for and no control over, but rather to clamp down on reform and arrest the journalists who had reported the events. This all goes to show how hopelessly out of touch the capitalist establishment was from its people.

Gradually, laws did come into place to water down capitalism and stymie its worst effects. But these were only brought in during the worst years of depression, when the cries of the suffering poor were loudest and the negative effects on capitalists' profits of introducing these changes were the least. When unemployment was high, after all, it didn't matter so much to the factory owners if working hours were reduced, since there were surplus   to fill any gaps and demand for goods would be lower anyway, so that production was in excess. Hence, it was during the troublesome times of 1819, 1833,

1842 and 1847 that the Factory Acts of Parliament were introduced, culminating in the limiting of employment to ten hours at most per day in 1847[17]. On the other hand, in the boom years laws designed to repress the workers tended to be relaxed, since at these periods there was little discontent to be vented through the likes of unions: hence the abolition in 1824 of the Combination Act that had banned unions since 1799. In all cases, the laws were not allowed to get in the way of the great pursuit of the age, 'progress', which is to say the development of capitalism; either they were weak (even a ten-hour day is hardly generous to the worker and no form of minimum wage was suggested) or they were not enforced. Commissions enquiring into the state of workers' living and working conditions repeatedly called for the abolition of back-to-back houses; again and again these were banned on paper, yet they continued to be built throughout the century.

The growth of industrial capitalism, continuing apace through the nineteenth century, saw the gradual de-skilling of the workforce as more and more advanced machinery replaced hand-crafts and products were produced ever more cheaply and in ever greater quantities to sell back to the impoverished masses. A simultaneous revolution in agriculture saw traditional countryside lifestyles abandoned and the number of hands required on farms steadily diminishing, and devoid of their traditional communities and rural pursuits the new populations of the town needed something new to occupy their leisure time when, at last, legal restrictions on working hours and the swelling population of workers available to fill the factories meant that allowing workers more time off was no longer necessarily unprofitable. Indeed, it was realised that by paying workers slightly higher wages and giving them space for leisure, the economy could be made to grow by having them purchase superfluous goods and pay to be entertained.

New technologies soon became the essential ingredient in this novel recipe for economic growth. Because frivolous goods and bought entertainment are not very good surrogates for the fulfilment obtainable from nature in less artificial surroundings, they do not give lasting satisfaction and always leave the 'consumer' eager for something new and better. This desire drove the development of consumable technologies through the nineteenth and twentieth centuries alike, with goods and entertainments becoming ever cheaper and less long-lasting. Any invention, seemingly, could be adapted to this purpose. The telephone was invented in 1876, and was at first a trinket of the rich. Gradually, though, every household then every person was encouraged to own one, until we arrived at the state of affairs we have now, with mobile telephones in almost every pocket, rendered repeatedly redundant by the invention of newer models with more features every year. In the twentieth century, ways of producing cheap meat by lowering standards of animal welfare were developed; soon, unhealthy, processed 'fast food' meats that came to proliferate, pumping people with junk that leaves them hungry for more and contributing to a fast-food-fuelled obesity crisis. And while at first people paid to see entertainment shows in the flesh, they were later persuaded to see black-and-white films in the cinema, then 'talkies', then colour films, then television, HD television, internet television: a continuing progression of technological development leading to more and more ways to sell something new, and make money. It's how the modern world works, and the vast majority of people have no choice in the matter whatsoever.

All the consumer goods of today – everything that people buy that is non-essential – are part of this web of manipulation, using new technologies to make money by driving people to consume. The industrial revolution has created a society addicted to material things, addicted to novelty, addicted to pointlessly over-produced products that make big business a lot of money. Precisely because the rich and powerful could make money by selling this materialism to the poor – 'lifting them out of poverty' is the expression usually used, though what is happening is nothing of the kind – the burdensome working hours were relaxed, wages were increased and the absolute poverty of the poor was lessened, even as their relative poverty continued to increase. It was only with the election of a Labour government in 1945 that national policy was altered out of a genuine concern for the welfare of the public and a genuine vision for a society of universal prosperity rather than primarily on the basis of economic, monetary factors. But before this came the most flagrant illustrations of just how devastating industrial capitalism and rampant competition could be, in the form of the First and Second World Wars.

The two atrocities perpetuated in 1914-1918 and 1939-1945 can leave us in no doubt of the terrible effects that industrialisation has had on the world. The first killed around sixteen million people; the second over eighty million (counting those who died as a result of famine and disease because of the war) including more than fifty million civilians. Both conflicts involved an extraordinary amount of suffering, which could only be brought about by the sheer weight of industry used to maim, frighten and kill in a manner that was inconceivable before. It is true that one reason for the increased death tolls relative to previous eras is that the world's population was much smaller before industrialisation, but nevertheless around ten per cent or more of a country's population being killed in conflict (as happened to Germany, Poland, Russia, Belarus and Ukraine to list only five) was entirely without precedent. The industrialised murder of 'undesirables' in the Holocaust could not have happened with the technology available at any era prior to the industrial capitalist one: pogroms in which Jews were murdered and attacks on gypsies have sadly had a long history, but never was the unwarranted hatred of these scapegoated peoples translated so brutally, extensively and effectively into a campaign of mass murder than under the shadow of the Second World War.

Capitalism caused the devastation of the World Wars in two different senses. First and most obviously, it powered technological advances that allowed machinery such as aeroplanes, tanks and machine guns and deadly weapons such as poison gas and – most disturbingly of all – atomic weapons to be developed and deployed. New technology meant more troops could be sent to the battlefield, and more civilians transported to their deaths at concentration camps, than would have been possible a hundred years before. But at the same time capitalism also enabled – indeed encouraged – people in power to use this technology in an assault on humanity that might never have been countenanced in former times. No matter how war-hungry some of the medieval kings, Roman emperors and Greek tyrants had been, codes of conduct and chivalry had usually held back a passion for slaughter. There have been massacres in every age – from the Roman rape of Jerusalem to the Christian crusades – but these were usually carried out under the spell of momentary anger, as a cruel retaliation against a people specifically considered to have done wrong. Ordinarily, civilians were raped and pillaged out of lust and greed but not murdered on mass out of racial hatred; soldiers were killed in the heat of battle but there was no desire to obliterate one's enemy or to kill as many as possible by whatever means possible until they ran out of men. A fair fight, hand to hand, with capture favoured over killing, was the chivalrous medieval mode of warfare in Europe. After all, the combatants claimed to be Christian.

There was no chivalry involved in the two World Wars. These were wars born out of ruthless competition, imbued with a capitalist lack of concern for the individual dignity and wonder inherent in all human beings. In the early years of the twentieth century, Germany and Britain were scrapping for a fight, competing with one another to build the biggest and best navy. Although such huge losses in human life – which could not have been foreseen – were undoubtedly not the intention of those who pushed for war, from the point of view of the capitalist establishment as a whole the war was a profitable enterprise. It saw munitions manufacture ramped up, technologies propelled forwards that could be adapted to suit the civilian market in peacetime, and women entering the workplace in greater numbers than ever before. No longer would the push to produce and consume be so restricted to men; the woman's achievement of working and spending power comparable to that of men would render her, too, grist to the mill of the capitalist machine. Cleaning up after a war is also a costly and potentially profitable business, and the economies of the victorious powers were helped by so punishing a suite of reparations payments from their defeated enemies that those counties were crippled.

Meanwhile, the great European empires continued to expand and flourish. They had won the competition, and reaped the resulting financial fruits.

The Second World War, provoked by those same reparations payments, saw a defeated Austria and Germany eager to reassert themselves, to reignite the competition and prove their armed forces and economic prowess superior to that of the countries that had so humiliated them in the First. Again, such competition was encouraged by capitalism, and again capitalist industries profited from the eruption of conflict. The development of computers, aeroplanes and nuclear energy was hurried on by concentrated wartime effort; no holds were barred when it came to conjuring machinery that could crush the enemy, culminating with the successful completion and tragic detonation of the atomic bomb by the USA. The result was the Cold War: a nuclear-armed stand-off between the competing edifices of capitalist America and a Russia that called itself 'communist' but was in truth almost as committed to competitiveness and the achievement of economic growth. This time, these were the two winners, monetarily: whilst Britain and France's empires crumbled away, the USA took its position in the centre-stage of world politics, and the heyday of consumer capitalism was inaugurated. Britain was, in the short term, the real winner, in that the spirit of pulling together occasioned by the war at last provided a context into which the Labour party's vision of socialist equality could be popularly introduced. But that, as it transpired, proved short-lived, and from the 1950s onwards it was consumerism that spread, like an undiagnosed disease, across the western hemisphere, with the capitalist emphasis on mass consumption and economic growth becoming ever more engrained. In this way, the two World Wars can be seen as accelerating factors in the campaign of global conquest waged by capitalism.

It is a campaign that continues to this day, with the spread of capital as a means of measuring people, of materialism and of industrialism advancing across the globe under the benign title of 'lifting people out of poverty', a myth as powerful as any nineteenth-century religious opiate was in persuading the peoples ruled by the capitalist powers from calling this spread into question. But there is no reason why the wheels of capital – which become a law unto themselves once they have started turning – could not drive war, once again, to be a means of spreading capitalism's influence, spurning on new production and consumption and increasing global profits. Next time, the human suffering involved will most probably be even more acute. It seems insane, to any onlooker blessed with the barrier of years to separate them from the heady days of conflict past or future, that any power should use such a horrific means to do anything, let alone to generate more of the worthless substance that is money. No sane society practices war, for war involves causing each other – our own brothers and sisters – to suffer and die. But capitalism is not sanity.

The World Wars were its children as much as are the skyscrapers and the sweatshops, the shopping malls and the barren wastes being created under its supervision across the world today. The weapons of world war, the mind-set of war, the willingness to kill in a mechanised manner without thought exhibited in the trenches of the First, the concentration camps of the Second and the drone strikes of today's war: all are products of the capitalist industrial revolution. Make no mistake: it is preposterous for us to live in a world with nuclear weapons that are capable of destroying all life on Earth; these devils of destruction would not exist were it not for capitalist industry. The history of the worst crimes committed with human hands – the slavery of the factories and sweat-shops, the needless murder and dismemberment of world war, the denigration of man to an expendable implement whose time in Earth can be bought as if it were the richer man's to own – is written with the pen of industrial capitalism, driven by the desire to manufacture money.

This is not to say that all the industry and new technology brought about under capitalism are negative developments. But the pace and scale at which technological evolution took place and continues to take place is what is at fault, for the consumer revolution is neither environmentally sustainable nor motivated by a genuine need for genuinely better ways of doing things. Quite the contrary, since the technological progress of capitalism is motivated by the desire to make money for its own sake, the actual needs of the people and the optimal degree of technological change and deployment are not important. Instead, the public need to be persuaded to buy as much as possible, pushed to the limits of what they will accept as worthy of their cash – even what they can't afford (there are people going hungry who nonetheless have mobile telephones) – and the long-term environmental and social costs of this are ignored except where capitalism is tampered with by governmental intervention and forced to take these into account. The rampant pace of change spurred by capitalism over the past two centuries and more is not driven by social necessity, and in many ways has been and continues to be contrary to the well-being of most people. With the digital revolution underway and the robotic revolution set to sweep away jobs and diminish human importance in favour of unconscious electronic copies of ourselves, this is set to become ever more blatant: unless, that is, we choose a different path. For why should we invent technologies that remove what is pleasant and meaningful in our lives and replace it with digital substitutes divorced from reality? Why should we rid ourselves of meaningful, useful jobs and let machines make their feeble imitations of human studiousness? Only because of money, the idolised tyrant of the modern capitalist world.

2.2 Gambling: Addicted to Money

Gambling is a phenomenon that can only come about in a society that is to some degree capitalistic – one that at least measures wealth using some form of money. Through gambling, people seek to increase their monetary wealth by taking risks with the wealth they already have; sometimes, they are putting the currency reserve that they need to live on the line in the hope of 'winning big' and getting much more money that they could in principle spend on much more luxurious living. In other cases, the gambler's fortune is sufficient that the risk to their real welfare is small. But gambling is a fool's errand, which is why the companies that facilitate this 'game' are able to make so much profit. The origin of such profitability lies in the human condition itself, and our natural responses to gain and to loss, which conspire to prevent a gambler from ever ceasing to gamble. If the gambler has risked and lost a lot of money, their natural inclination is to recover these losses as soon as possible, which drives them to risk more money. Once they are winning, on the other hand, their natural inclination is to win yet more, confident in their own ability to be successful. Luck can be callous and deceptive: it may remain with a gambler for long enough for their gains to be great at first, then suddenly desert them. Gambling is an addiction, and it is the gambler's inability to stop, especially when they are winning, that causes most gamblers to lose more than they win.

Gambling is, therefore, extremely harmful to the wellbeing of the gambler, especially if it is likely to render them unable to pay for their basic needs or send them spiralling into debt. But the very presence of gambling within a society also illustrates that that society suffers from much deeper evils than the addiction of gambling itself. Gambling is motivated by greed or by necessity: a society in which many people gamble must be one in which people are encouraged to be greedy for more money, as though money were an ends in itself; one in which people are driven to risk what little they have in order to get what they need to be equal members within that society; or both these things at the same time. The problem of gambling is, therefore, intricately linked with the problem of money and the unequal distribution of resources in the modern world.

There are many different types of gambling. At the bottom of the range are the small investments and the extremely unlikely possibility of very big returns of the National Lottery, which is open even to those on very modest incomes and depends entirely on luck. Then there are the betting shops and casinos available to those willing to risk larger amounts on the basis of their own luck or ability to predict an uncertain outcome for the promise of slightly more likely but less copious returns. Finally, there is the risking of huge amounts of money speculating on the financial markets by rich capitalist corporations and individuals, who at least profess to have the expertise necessary to know a safe from a toxic bet. All of these are based on the premise that multiplying your money is very beneficial and that taking risks and speculating successfully deserves great reward, as though it were somehow useful. In truth, these risks and speculations are useful only to the profit-books of the organisations that preside over such scams.

Certainly no form of gambling is beneficial to the poor. The man who has less access to money than most is 'poor' in a capitalist society, because in such as a society he or she is unable to afford to own or do the same things as their richer neighbours, making them feel inferior. They may even have so little money that they are literally unable to afford their basic needs – to rent the roof above their heads, to feed their family and so on. Our society is not entirely capitalistic, so that people who find themselves unemployed or earning too little to meet their family's needs are not left entirely to themselves, but nonetheless a large contingent of our society remains 'poor' in this way: they face the threat of eviction, they cannot afford nutritional food or they simply feel inferior to their better-off neighbours. Such a person is in a state of desperation, either because they or their children face homelessness or malnourishment or because, in a society that teaches that money and possessions are the measure of one's worth, they count themselves of little worth indeed. Because the government does not guarantee housing, food and equal access to life's true joys for all, the poor in our society may therefore be forced to seek a loan to cover their needs and wants, or may turn to gambling.

It is for this reason that the poor partake in the National Lottery. The promise seems great: the winner will receive millions of pounds, enough to pay off all debts, meet all needs and live in a degree of luxury. But nobody needs a gift of millions of pounds, and what's more very few who try for it will get it. Week after week, pound after pound, the poor will waste what money they have contributing to the very jackpot fund they hope to win. But the vast, vast majority will lose almost everything they put in; only a very few will be given far more than they need, so much indeed that they are likely to waste it. The National Lottery therefore constitutes a tax on its participants, who are mostly relatively poor, and its purpose is to take from the many and give to the few. It is the very opposite of equal wealth redistribution, and an extremely inefficient way of helping the poor. If any government were to emulate the lottery, in gathering up a small sum from the entire populace each week to bestow upon one particular individual or some few individuals, there would quite rightly be general outrage. The lottery does fund various artistic, sport and scenic projects that are of potential benefit to all, but it would be far better for the government to organise public resources into facilitating these projects rather than taking money from those who, in a capitalist society, need it most to fund them. The Lottery is, in fact, a cruel ruse dressed up as 'fun' but designed to trick members of the public into thinking that they can win life-changing amounts of money to save them from desperate situations that, if it were really to serve its purpose, the government should not allow them to fall into in the first place.

Most every high street in the towns and cities of Britain has a betting shop. Casinos, it is true, are more difficult to find here than in that heartland of capitalism that is the United States, where an entire city – Las Vegas – has built its reputation upon gambling. But obscene amounts of money can be won and lost in both these arenas, and almost always the ordinary person who comes in off the street to place a bet will lose. Such is the nature of the business made from gambling. In essence, gambling shops and casinos play on a larger scale on the same human traits exploited by the National Lottery, except that it is less common for most people to gamble in these establishments on a regular basis. For many, the Grand National horse race or another such sporting event represents the only time at which they will stake money upon an outcome, because everybody knows the risks and few are willing to take them often. Yet the very fact that we collectively allow such establishments as betting shops and casinos to exist shows that we have been, fundamentally, wedded to an idea of money as an ends in itself, one that would have been foreign to our forefathers in ages past when religion was all-important and gambling almost universally frowned upon.

There is nothing especially wrong with playing a game of cards, or with trying to predict an outcome. Indeed, such games and flirtations with triumph and disaster can bring great enjoyment to life: it is important to have time to play and to take risks and try out our strategizing, and we should all be free to do so with our friends and family if we so desire. But it is when such games and frivolities become associated with monetary stakes that the problem arises. For some, yes, they probably remain simply games, but the attachment of money to the outcome introduces an extra thrill and gravity to the activity. This shows that these people place great importance in money, and yet are not afraid to risk it – the currency that they depend upon to obtain what they need in a capitalist world – on a game, because they are at some level greedy to obtain more. In a society where the basic needs of everyone are provided for by everyone without recourse to money, this motivation to gamble would be removed, because money would cease to hold its cherished position within our hearts and the glory in winning the game could not be heightened by association with monetary loss or gain. For these people, then, games and speculation would return to being simply games and speculation, and gambling would become automatically undesirable and unnecessary.

Others, though, gamble more frequently and suffer from the addiction of gambling. Whether winning or losing, they will always seek to gamble more, and will undoubtedly lose more than they win. They do not gamble only occasionally, or to sharpen a game they enjoy playing, but gamble from necessity and sometimes as a career or second career in an attempt to improve their lot by increasing their wealth. It is rare that they will be able to do so. Meanwhile, capitalist corporations benefit from their attempts. Gambling dens of whatever kind can only do harm to society in the long-term, by making the poor and desperate even poorer and encouraging less desperate occasional gamblers to value and seek out money to an excess. They should not be welcome in a prosperous and happy society, where there will be no need to gamble to satisfy one's needs, and no added excitement in doing so. Spectator sports and participatory games can continue to flourish without the added element of gambling, which has been encouraged in our society for far too long.

Gambling is not restricted to those with little money aspiring to climb up the social monetary hierarchy that is imposed by capitalism. Many of those at the top of this hierarchy seek to increase their riches still further by gambling with their own or somebody else's money. These are the speculators, the investors and the bankers. Within a capitalist society, to some degree the role of one of these groups is essential: under capitalism, it is difficult to produce change and innovation, sometimes, without the investment of capital from an investor, which could take the form of an individual or corporation. Investors tend not to gamble their money on high-risk ventures, preferring instead to place it where they know it is very likely to multiply. They are rewarded, through profits on their investments, for the small risk that they are willing to take and for having enough money to invest in the first place. So the system of investors needing to contribute capital to produce innovation and profit thereby is not good for society: it creates inequality, and hence unhappiness, by multiplying the wealth of those who are already rich and rewarding them with money – which is power under capitalism – for doing very little.

But investing in this way is not much of a gamble when compared to speculation. Speculators – including bankers – speculate on the prices of goods and the outcomes of political decisions, essentially betting huge sums of money on the outcome and thereby making huge profits. These profits again constitute a reward for doing very little at all, and nothing that is useful in any way to society. It does not help anyone in society to make a prediction of the future prices of goods on the market; in fact, it hinders society because these predictions – the 'confidence' of the market speculators – can affect those prices. The price of food may be manipulated to be higher so that those wealthy people who have placed a bet that it will rise win out, whilst the ordinary people that the food has been produced to feed find it more difficult to buy. This is a real travesty of capitalism: rather than producing as much as we need for everyone to live a happy lifestyle and distributing those goods according to need, we produce and price our goods according to the speculations of a wealthy few.

These speculations extend to the political sphere. In 2014, the Scottish vote against independence from the United Kingdom was predicted by a wealthy ex-banker, who placed the obscene amount of £900 000 as a bet on the outcome. That one person should have so much money in the first place, in a society where money is power, is ridiculous. In an ideal society where money is divorced from power because the basic needs of everyone are met automatically and money buys only superfluous material luxury such an accumulation would not be quite so worrying. But in the state we are currently in, for a person to have such a vast amount free to bet with illustrates that they have been paid (or have inherited) far more wealth than any amount of work they have done could deserve, a situation that is as harmful to them as it is to everyone else. In the case of an ex-banker, we can see that this wealth must have come from doing very little at all that is useful, but in spending a huge amount of time simply making investments and speculations on behalf of the bank with no good done whatsoever to society.

This person, who wishes to remain anonymous, won more than £1 million because they were already rich, and so had the funds both to investigate the likely outcome of the vote and to put down the initial £900 000. In a capitalist society, there are many people with far more need of this money: those who struggle with homelessness and starvation and would consider £900 000 beyond their wildest dreams, let alone an amount to be expanded upon by betting. The book-makers made a profit of some £10 million from the referendum result as a consequence of gamblers[18] – most of whom were much less wealthy and were betting far less money than this particular ex-banker. Had the result been 'yes' to independence, which the book-makers had not predicted, they may have made a loss. But the book-makers rarely if ever make a loss because they gather all the evidence available with regard to a particular result and make as certain as possible that they can themselves predict the outcome correctly.

Much worse than this betting by individuals through a book-maker or gambling at casinos is the institutionalised gambling that pervades the 'financial sector' – the 'City' that wins so much praise for the 'economic growth' that it produces. In the 'City', traders employed by banks and other financial institutions are paid extraordinary amounts of money for working very hard doing something of very little worth, which is buying and selling assets according to their predictions of which prices will rise and fall and thereby making their employers vast profits. The 'City' is the very epitome of the problem with money, and that of the capitalist society: there, money is everything, profit is everything and gambling with the finances and fortunes of society at large is done as a matter of course. The traders care little what implications their speculations will have through the

2. Money

rising and lowering of the prices of goods. They care little whether their profit-hungry tactics will bring the whole capitalist enterprise grinding to a halt when the bubble bursts, confidence is lost and investment ceases altogether. This is what happened in the 2007 financial crisis: the professional gamblers lost their confidence that there would be 'economic growth', and so there was none. Ordinary people's money, which they had put for safe-keeping in the banks, was risked on ventures that failed, and lost. The governments of the capitalist world, being intricately entangled with the capitalist system, like the private corporations, were no longer able to invest and laid off workers. The result was great harm to society, where in a system that is unchained from the shackles of money and gambling is worthless everyone would have continued to be in employment and with their needs met by the state. This institutionalised gambling must be stopped: we must build a society based on goodness and reason, not on gambling and greed, if we are to obtain relative equality, sustainability in place of continual cycles of growth and decay, and greater emotional well-being for all.

2.3 Money's To Blame

In the later chapters of this document, we shall come across numerous examples of the failings of our present industrialised society: ways in which it has failed to provide true joy, equality and fulfilment to its members; ways in which it has endangered other animate beings by engaging in unparalleled environmental devastation; ways in which it has failed to provide a sustainable basis upon which future generations will be able to build prosperity and ways in which, contrary to the 'never had it so good' mantra of post-industrial popular opinion, through its very success in creating vast material abundance for some, it has in fact made life much less happy for the majority than it was in former times, far from ideal as those times were. But how can we be sure, one might ask, that this is the fault of capitalism itself, as opposed to a failure to implement capitalism properly, or some other factor altogether – perhaps even the fault of Nature? What evidence is there, in other words, that the problem with society as a whole is, fundamentally, a 'problem with money'?

Truly, human nature does have something to do with our current problems: for it is human nature, and our inbuilt urges and fears, that capitalism has played upon to brace us to its yoke, acting as though it were some hideous Leviathan, autonomous in and of itself, an emergent intelligence coordinating its many human elements like ants in an industrial colony and playing us all with its Pied Piper tune. Yet on a deeper level, human nature comprises compassion, love and grateful joy more fundamentally than it does greed and fear, and we shall explore here how it is Money that distracts and debars us

50

from these truer and better emotions; Money that is, unless we cast it off, dragging us towards Malthusian catastrophe; Money that is, indeed, to blame.

Money is worthless. It always has been – whether it comprises numbers on a computer that record the size of a bank account, paper notes or metal coins. The very fact that these things, even when they are physical objects, are being used as currency prevents us from employing them for any other purpose and so renders them useless. The 'value' that is attached to money is entirely arbitrary and dependent on the continued consent and confidence of those who use it; it is a fiction, not grounded in any real, practical value. Therefore it can fluctuate unpredictably and at the whim of those in power: money is used by the rich to control the poor. Emperors, kings and modern-day 'democracies' have since its inception been able to set its worth, to some extent, by deciding how much currency to make and how to distribute it. When the scarcity of precious metals – in themselves almost worthless but given value by their very rarity – meant that rulers could not mint as many coins as they wanted, they were forced to invent paper notes and then electronic money to circumvent the problem and keep the economy 'growing' and people trading. Yet even the will of these highest authorities can be undermined by the private interests of other, rich individuals whose greed and games of speculation can cause the value of money to pass out of government hands and out of all semblance of democratic control. In today's world, the 'value' of money is set by banks and investors who can make ideas, technologies, public services, policies and entire ways of life rise or fall according to where they put their substantial hordes of money. But it's all just empty air. Pieces of paper. Scraps of metal. It's fundamentally worthless.

No phenomenon illustrates this truth more clearly than that of hyperinflation, when the worthlessness of money becomes painfully evident in the colossal acceleration of prices to ludicrous heights because governments (or, potentially, banks) for one reason or another feel themselves compelled to create vast sums of currency and pump it into society. Suddenly, money is abundant. Is this not the dream come true of those wedded to the idea of money-making, working all hours at what will make them the most money so that they can become rich and purchase what they are encouraged to want? Not so, for the worth of their new-found funds is relative, and what is superficially given is quickly snatched away. Money's supposed value lies in its scarcity, and it's only worth having if some others have it not. That's what makes it so unnecessary, and so conducive to a state of inequality. In hyperinflation, everyone has lots of money and none of them can do anything with it unless they do so very rapidly, because prices must soar to prevent the poor from gaining the luxurious living of the rich.

That money in itself is worth living one's life for is therefore shown spectacularly to be a lie during a period of hyperinflation, and that real objects and services have real value that money only superficially can capture is made painfully clear. These things retain their value to society, and the cost in real resources, time and effort on producing and delivering them remains as it always was, yet their monetary 'cost' sky-rockets. This only illustrates the purposelessness – except to rich elites who wield the illusion of the allure of money as a means of control – of giving anything monetary value at all. Doing so is merely a means of oppression and control.

And yet things are given monetary value, and the effects on society during a period of hyperinflation are catastrophic. Under the pressure of the greed and vengeance of victorious powers following the First World War, the Weimar German government found itself printing so much money to meet reparations payments that prices doubled every few days; workers had to be paid twice daily so that their wages could increase rapidly enough for them to afford food and the wheelbarrows used to carry cash were of more value than the thousands of notes they contained. It took the establishment of a new currency to stabilise the situation, rendering the 497 billion billion old 'marks' in circulation completely obsolete. When the crisis peaked in 1923, inflation had been at 182 billion per cent per month and unemployment had hit a quarter of trade union members. Germany's internal debt had been written off, but the reparations payments – fixed in dollars, not marks – were unaffected. The richest weren't hurt much; they could simply buy dollars or real estate with their marks when hyperinflation began. It was the ordinary people – professionals and labourers alike – doing proper jobs for society who lost out when their savings were obliterated and jobs disappeared, alongside the benefits to society that those jobs would otherwise bring. All because they had trusted in the myth of money, and its peddlers had heartlessly fooled them.

Nor was this the worst case of hyperinflation history has seen. The unenviable honour of hosting the second worse case ever recorded lies with the country of Zimbabwe, which has been reduced from prosperity to poverty through the follies of a greedy elite. Governmental corruption and spending on the Second Congo War in the early 2000s, combined with a declining ability for the country to manufacture or produce food because of mismanagement, caused confidence in the Zimbabwean dollar to collapse. In November 2008, inflation reached nearly eighty billion per cent, and prices doubled daily. In 2009 the currency was abandoned entirely, another testament to the fact that money has no lasting or absolute value. The daily inflation rate was 98 per cent at peak, worse than the 20 per cent experienced in Weimar Germany. The very worst inflation rate ever experienced, of 207 per cent per day or four quadrillion per cent per month, fell upon Hungary in July 1946, when the government attempted to stimulate production by printing money. Real wages fell by eighty per cent, pushing many into poverty. Yet Hungary, like Germany and Zimbabwe, survived: evidently the obliteration of the 'value' of money didn't prove so devastating that society completely collapsed. Hyperinflation teaches us that money has no real power; to put our trust in such an entity can only cause disappointment.

Why, then, do we continue to use money? Because of power and pride. Money is the cause of inequality, and more importantly it is the means by which one group of people is able to raise themselves up above another. By counting the monetary 'value' of each person, the rich can be enabled to feel superior to the poor: their bank account is bigger, so they must be better, more successful people in capitalist eyes. In this way, the secular need to feel superior to others and the desire to be regarded as better than our neighbours can be satisfied. And once, in their pride, people begin to judge each other using the artificial and meaningless measure of money, life becomes a ruthless competition: to the monetarily rich, a competition to maintain their social place and 'success' by preserving or expanding their monetary hordes; and to the monetarily poor, a competition simply to survive and obtain some form of joy – however superficial – in a world where everything has a price, all our wants and needs cost money and they haven't got it. Of course, the real joys of life – joys of helping others, of giving love and comfort to one another, of the natural world around us – are free of any monetary charge. But the rich promulgate the myth that money is needed for satisfaction in life, and price the basic needs of the poor so that they cannot afford those things that ought to be shared amongst all and thus cannot feel satisfied. Without the basic things our bodies need to live healthily, how can anyone experience the higher joys in life? They cannot live out a purposeful and happy existence, cannot devote themselves body and mind to a fulfilling and useful profession, and cannot experience the freedom to live in a way that they have chosen, free from distracting and debilitating material cares.

Distraction

So we come to the first allegation to be lodged against money: that it distracts us all, whether we are monetarily rich or poor, from what is truly important in life, and by creating false illusions of freedom such as that of 'consumer choice' enslaves us into an obsession with unimportant concerns and vain lusts. What we ought all to occupy our minds with is what gives us lasting purpose in life: how we can best serve each other, enjoy the gifts of this life that we are given by man and by Nature – and indeed the gift of life itself – and make the most of the opportunities we have to generally increase the peace and contentment of ourselves and our fellow beings. Some of the gifts we enjoy are material things, and some of what we give to society might be material – we might cook food, make clothes, manufacture goods for example – but our aim in making and receiving them should be to foster joy and increase prosperity in the long term. In other words, gifts given and received are only truly valuable if they have some value beyond the material. When we are not performing some service to others, some job or vocation, our joy can only be complete if our minds are free to wander to other ideas and thoughts about the phenomena that surround us in our fascinating world.

But pricing everything we make and every item we use in terms of monetary value prevents us from giving of ourselves freely at time of work, and from allowing our minds to be happily occupied in time of rest. It prevents us from truly enjoying life at all. We can see this when it comes to the selling of goods, though the same arguments also apply to the provision of services, or even intellectual products such as works of art and science. Once the goods we make have prices, alongside competitor goods, and the maximisation of money becomes the ends of society, we have to spend our efforts convincing the 'consumer' that our goods are better 'value for money' and should be purchased instead of rival goods, which should be wasted – discarded as the losing product. This therefore drives the purchaser of goods not to focus on resource efficiency and utility in what they obtain, but to look for the item amidst rival items that will give them the most short-term sensual pleasure.

If the shopper is really to make use of the advantage of competition that capitalism supposedly provides, they must spend copious time and effort in carefully choosing between rival products, or purchasing they don't really need or want at all but which they buy because the competing producers work hard to convince us all that their product represents the best value for our precious money through careful campaigns of advertisement and manipulation. In this way, both the producers and consumers of goods waste their time buying and advertising pointless items, or having to make choices, listening to the persuasive voices on either side, that we needn't make at all. In fact, to save time the shopper often simply follows their immediate sensual desires: desires to get some satisfaction from the process of purchasing goods whilst saving as much money as possible. They go for the cheapest or most immediately pleasing option. For capitalist competition to really function as it claims to requires the shopper to make a considered choice, finding precisely the best option for his or herself from a range of rival possibilities, which requires a lot of unnecessary time and effort.

We all recognise this drain on our time, and that it could be much better spent doing more interesting and fulfilling things than shopping. That's why we often give in to the advertiser that shouts the loudest, following the call to opt for, say, cheap and unethical foods rather than seeking out nutritious, less processed options grown with the welfare of the grower and the rest of humanity in mind. Everyone ultimately loses out in this situation – in this case through poor health and obesity on the part of the buyer and the land-degradation, greenhouse gas emissions and animal suffering that afflict us all in the end as a result of their 'choice'. The situation is somewhat of a 'catch-22': either the advertisers distract us from the choices we really want to make, causing us to choose options that are not for the long-term good of ourselves or others; or else we have to spend a lot of time investigating the choices that are on offer and what their real implications are.

It is the use of money that causes this. Adding the dynamic of 'saving' and 'making' money into the equation of buyers and manufacturers upsets the balance of genuinely important factors in our decision-making. Pricing everything imposes upon us all the burden of a choice: a choice of what to spend our money on. After all, under a capitalist system we have a duty either to spend it or to invest it; to destroy our money would be a sacrilege in the church of capitalism akin to blasphemy amidst religious believers. We are burdened with the need to get as much as we can for as little money as we can, whether that be in terms of material volume or quality of product, because buying one thing prevents our spending the same sum on something else of equal 'value'. If one tries to be as 'ethical' as one can in a money-based society, one becomes quite paralysed, unable to make any purchases at all before reading up on the ethical implications buying any one of the competing products in the market, for every purchase amounts essentially to a vote of approval in favour of the company one chooses to buy from and its means of production.

All of this is a result of the individualist nature of the money-based society, which puts the burden of responsibility upon every 'consumer' to make the correct choice of how to spend 'their' money. By contrast, a logical and caring society, freed from the shackles of money, would only require each of its members to ask a few simple questions when it comes to the acquisition of goods: 'what do I need?', 'what do my dependents and neighbours need?' and 'what would it be useful – rather than harmful – for me to acquire so as to be of service to my family, friends and neighbours?'. There would be no question of choosing the most ethically-produced product over another, for though there would undoubtedly be a range of choices available, all would be produced in an ethical manner by local people. The democratically-elected government – local and national – would determine the resources required to make each product, and provide them as is necessary to satisfy the demand that accrues from each of us answering these three questions. We should then be able to make use of what we need, and return it when finished, without having to worry about having enough money. If the tool is available and we can use it do good work for society, why should we need to exchange worthless papers or coins before we can have or borrow it? Nobody would need to fear not being able to feed their children at the same time as paying the rent, and would be freed from this great distraction and mental weight.

Take the example of clothes. We would not, in such a society, need to waste time choosing between the latest fashions in clothing, since clothing that is comfortable, attractive and hardy enough to meet our needs would be provided. When it reached the end of its useable lifetime – which should be several years, perhaps with repairs – it would be replaced, likewise without payment. If we only take a logical perspective and produce and use what each of us needs, there is no need for surplus alternative 'choices' that are not as optimal to be presented to us, wasting time and resources, and no need for pricing with money. Money only distracts us from important matters, making us think about pointless material cares and causing many to spend their days in worry and fear.

This distraction matters because it makes us less happy and healthy people than we would otherwise be. That somebody should delight in shopping for its own sake, in food solely for its flavour rather than its utility, in clothes and shoes for their appearance rather than their long-term usefulness and durability, must imply that meaning and higher purposes have been taken away from their life, so that they feel compelled to seek meaning and gratification in the immediate sensual pleasure of having things. Such a person cannot see the gifts of food, clothing, shelter, gadgets and everything else that we have as but small components to help sustain us in the great adventure of living a meaningful life. Furthermore, by focussing on money and the things that it can purchase, we become selfish, keeping the money for ourselves or spending it on things for our own immediate satisfaction and grudging to give up very much of it, by and large, as a proportion of what we have, to others who have not 'earned' it but might need it – not unless they can give us something else in return. That is why charities have to organise cake sales, jumble sales and sponsored activities to raise money, for few will give it for nothing in return.

We are prevented from being altruistic and giving others what they need, because to do so would require expending money, which would score against our personal account – that is, the bank account that is both the measure of our 'success' in the capitalist world and the means by which we shall meet our future needs. We obsess about keeping our money, if not in physical notes or within the account then lurking within the 'value' of the items we have bought, which could in principle be sold again, and are reluctant to simply give it up with nothing to show for it. So, money distracts us from generosity, distracts us from being truly useful to one another and leaves us all less happy and more self-centred as a result.

Why is it that we fall into this state? Why is it that rich and poor alike become transfixed so easily by the religion of money, and come to see little greater purpose in their work than the accumulation of money and the spending of money on sensual pleasures? Why are we unable to transcend this sorry state of affairs and view money as simply a convenient tool? How is it that the filth of money rubs off onto our fingers and penetrates deep into our hearts? Partly it is because money takes the place of other, declining religious traditions that once gave us higher ideals and provided us with meaning. Humans have always possessed the need for a goal and purpose and beliefs transcending our day-to-day existence, and if we cannot satisfy this need through the one God that most faith traditions worship or other gods of human making, it has to be through idols of other sorts. Money is, essentially, an idol. The reason why it was able to become such an all-pervasive and powerful idol has to do with the second of its great crimes: that of the perpetuation of drudgery.

Drudgery

When everything has a monetary price, and money must be worked for, we soon find that work becomes less and less about passion or vocation – about using natural and learned talents to serve society by providing for others' needs or making cultural contributions for oneself and others to enjoy. These are the things that should be the aim of work, something that we choose to do to make our lives worthwhile. Instead, work becomes primarily about making money, through which we are enabled to live and 'succeed'.

Our work is what occupies the best hours of our lives. It may be difficult or tiring, and a small part of our working lives may involve doing things that nobody enjoys doing but which have to be done. But overall, surely our work should be enjoyable and rewarding to the spirit, not a source of depression or something to be endured. Perhaps, as the twentieth-century philosopher Herbert Marcuse put it, we should even look upon work as a form of 'free play'[19]. The reward for the work done by each of us should be a happy society in which all needs – including our own – are met. When we have to work – or choose to work – for excessively long hours at something we don't enjoy or feel to be meaningful, in order to maximise our monetary income, work becomes drudgery rather than fulfilment, and it is then that we turn to the idols of money and materialism in the search for superficial meaning.

This applies to the 'working class' person who, rather than learning and practising a craft that they value and manufacturing useful items through their own skill and ingenuity, is forced to work in a factory or sweatshop as a replaceable part on a conveyor belt, in a system whose goal is the production of many goods to sell at profit (whether society really needs them or not) with no happiness, meaning or sense of value in their job. But it applies equally to the wealthy slave of the 'service economy', the rich banker or big business employee who has an equally purposeless or destructive job but who spends nearly all their time working and very little of it living and appreciating the world because their goal is the maximisation of money. Now, between these two extremes there are many people who genuinely enjoy the job they do, and many who don't. The former find meaning and purpose perhaps because their job involves serving some extant need amidst the populace: the farmer, baker, artist, electrician, postman, and perhaps even the shop assistant, alongside many more, may sometimes fall into this group. But in insisting that they take certain hours and must be salaried for their work as though it were about money rather than service, we devalue them and reduce the enjoyment they can glean from their jobs.

Without money, we could simply share out the work that needs to be done in society amongst those capable and willing to do it. Pointless work could be avoided by doing away with competing products and the need to advertise them, with the financial sector entirely, and with the producing or importing of boatloads of unnecessary 'consumer' goods. There would then be less work to be done in total, and with the currently unemployed given an equal share, that would leave everyone able to do only a few hours of work per week as are necessary by obligation, with additional hours taken by choice. If there are essential jobs that nobody wants to do, these and these alone are the sorts of jobs that ought to be mechanised, and in the meantime shared between all who are able to contribute.

Money's crime is to prevent this happy situation from arising; to debase the work we do; to create pointless, superfluous work in the name of 'consumer choice' and in the wholly anti-democratic, unfair and manipulative dark art of advertising and marketing; and to create lives of drudgery not only in factories but in all sorts of workplaces up and down the country, prevent people from enjoying their jobs. Money renders lives that could be full of joy and purpose into a state marred by depression, over-work, over-consumption and non-altruistic, selfish waste. All of that comes from paying people monetary wages rather than allowing all to share in the common wealth.

Inequality

Drudgery and over-work for no good purpose afflict all echelons of a monetary society, but money's third great crime is to perpetuate what is the primary reason for unhappiness in societies – inequality. The most equal societies, not the richest, are those in which the citizens report themselves to be the most content in the world today. But money creates inequality, by vice of two simple facts: that some people have more money than others; and that, in a monetary economy, those with more money have more power, material wealth and opportunities, which often allows them to get still more money and to maintain the imbalance. The inequality gives rise to unhappiness because we are at heart a species that wants to share – in joy, sorrow, experience and material wealth. People who cannot afford to buy, say, a car are not unhappy because they do not have a car – countless billions have survived quite well without one over the millennia. They are unhappy because others around them can afford to buy a car, whilst they are denied the experience of using one and visiting easily the places it can take them. That's why people in less-industrialised parts of the globe are rapidly building roads, buying cars and learning to drive in spite of the overwhelmingly negative impact these vehicles are known to have – they are trying to catch up with the industrialised 'West', desperate not to be denied access to something that others have.

`By insisting that everyone has to earn money with which they can buy personal copies of all the 'must-have' possessions of the modern world, but making it that some earn more than others, and so have more or better possessions, we encourage the rich to try to stay ahead by 'earning' yet more (or investing and profiting from their money itself, without any more work), and make the poor feel inferior, no matter how many goods they purposelessly acquire and replace according to the latest fashions, because they can never catch up with the richest, always remaining a few steps behind. Even the beggar on the street has a mobile telephone these days, but they are nonetheless poor because they have no power, no opportunities, no home and no companionship – and worst of all in a money-obsessed society, they have no means of obtaining money except by begging. These people are considered to be 'failures' because they lack the means to make and spend money, but in reality they are just as entitled to have joy in life as everybody else.

It could, of course, be possible to create equality even in a society based on money, by distributing that money evenly. But this fact does not let money off the hook – for the simple reason that money, by its very nature, resists equal distribution. 'Money has its favourites', they say. Its entire purpose is to move perceived wealth from one person or group to another, which means that even were we to begin with an equal amount of money each – and there was no time in history in which that state of affairs existed – the person who was able to sell the greatest volume of the fruits of their labour and to get by on the fewest resources from others – they might, perhaps, have a sedentary low-energy craft, live close to natural resources and produce something difficult to make – would soon begin to gather a surplus of money, and therefore a surplus of power. They, after all, would have the power to loan to those who, by mistake or bad fortune, had little and perhaps to charge interest; they would have the power to bribe for favours and to make or break producers competing with one another for their custom by buying in bulk from one and not the other. Theirs would be the power, and they would use it to accumulate.

Only through regulation by some outside force can the rich be prevented from acting in this way and taking excess power, but since they are the ones with the capacity for power in the first place it is unlikely that they will allow regulations to stand that would force them to give up their wealth; this, they will quite rightly point out, would dis-incentivise the whole economy: in a society based on money, for which the purpose and measure of life is the acquisition of money, inequality is essential to keep the workers incentivised and to keep everyone producing and consuming.

Furthermore, money corrupts: once one devises a numerical measure of success in life that can be earned and must be exchanged for anything that is desired, the increase in this measure instils feelings of pride in those that attain it. The rich feel proud to be rich, and come to believe that it is through their own skills and abilities that they have become so, and although they may give a portion of their wealth to the poor, they will not give so much as to lower their rank in wealth or induce monetary equality. Once elevated above others, they will do what they can - for the most part - to retain this elevation, even avoiding taxes that would help to fund the very state and society that enabled them to obtain their money and rank in the first place. These rich are the powerful, and without their cooperation monetary equality cannot be imposed. Therefore, monetary inequality continues to rise, and all through the corrupting influence of money.

In the absence of money, this inequality - and the associated inequality of power and opportunity - simply would not exist. There would be no measure by which one person could be ranked as more important than another; all would be equal members playing their individual roles in society, so long as their government was democratic. Everyone would have what they needed and the opportunity to pursue any vocation they felt drawn towards, and there would be no need for 'class' to distinguish them. Once the allure of all their money and power has been removed from them, the rich can be seen to be just like everyone else.

The resulting state of equality would be to the benefit of all, because inequality causes unhappiness across all invented ranks. The rich person has to worry about staying rich, and about what to do with his or her surplus goods; the poor person has to worry about how to get richer, and suffers from feelings of envy or inferiority. The evidence that these feelings abound in our society is clear: even those without much money continue to accumulate consumer goods where they can, often falling into debt; they suffer obesity and ill-health because they try to live the high life with cheap, tasty but unhealthy food and sedentary entertainment such as television and gaming, that was once the preserve of the rich. Without the inequality caused by money, they would no longer need to make themselves feel successful in this way and could concentrate on more important things in life. Furthermore, all the excessive waste associated with rich and poor alike trying to prove themselves wealthy – everyone having a computer of their own when, except in computer-based professions, we could easily share; children receiving mounds of cheap plastic toys at Christmas; copious amounts of every type of food going on display at supermarkets only for one third to be thrown away because eyes are bigger even than burgeoning stomachs and supermarkets over-dress their shelves to impress – could be eliminated. That would allow us to create a sustainable society, which will be to everyone's benefit in the long-term given that every single one of us is utterly dependent on the finite resources of our planet to survive, however much money we have. Without the need to compete on a ladder of inequality, we could share much more and make do with less and yet be much more contented. It is only money – invented and preserved by the rich and powerful to keep themselves rich and powerful – that prevents us from banishing inequality and reaping the benefits for rich and poor alike.

Violent Crime

The feeling of inferiority and powerlessness that accompanies a lack of money in a money-based society, and the lust for more money, more success and more power that come with it, also underlie a whole host of violent crimes, which constitute the fourth great problem with money. Perhaps Thomas More goes too far in his *Utopia* when he has the narrator claim that without money 'fraud, theft, robbery, quarrels, brawls, altercations, seditions, murders, treasons' and so on would be entirely eliminated: there is not sufficient scientific evidence to support such a strong claim, and stresses, strains and temptations will always persist, even in a happier, money-free society, that could provoke such deeds. But undoubtedly, money is a major source of crime, and providing everyone with all they need to live without charge would remove nearly all incentive for those deeds.

If you have access to all the food, clothing and other goods that you need, and machinery and technology is held in common – an economy of sharing – what purpose is there in stealing? Nobody need be pushed into burglary, robbery or mugging by the need to feed themselves. If nobody has any more wealth than anyone else, and money is just metal, worthless except by its prettiness, why would anyone cheat, murder or brawl to get hold of it by force or premature inheritance? If everyone is housed, but houses are not assigned monetary worth and instead judged by their ability to provide adequate shelter and comfort for the number of people inhabiting them, maintained sustainably to high standards by society in a common effort, why need anyone lust after a larger or more comfortable or valuable house and defraud, blackmail or murder to get it? If work is shared so that everyone has a job and purpose in life, where would be the place for the disillusionment and emptiness that accompanies unemployment or drudgery and causes many youths to turn to drugs or crime? Sharing property, education, resources and work according to need instead of using money will resolve all these problems, because everyone will feel of worth to society and will have an interest to respect their fellows, with nothing to be gained by selfishly taking for themselves alone.

If most property – excepting our basic personal items such as clothing – is held in common, essential needs are met for everybody and even all non-essential valuable items are equally accessible to all to loan and share at no 'cost', there will no longer be a need to protect private property using alarms and closed-circuit television. Indeed, if the demise of money brings about the near demise of violent crime, there will be no need for the 'CCTV' that surveys us all as we go about our lives and can prevent us from enjoying privacy, or lead us to fear that we aren't as individuals trusted by our fellow citizens or our government, since they feel such a need to watch us. Such monitoring leads to distrust and fear of the government and is corrosive of democracy. It is only necessary where there is no other way of protecting private property from theft and people from violence, and therefore only in a society where these are considerable problems.

Without money, there will be no need to guard any physical object, since there will be no incentive for anybody to take or deface it. Least of all will we need to guard gold, silver and money itself, as they are all inherently so worthless that it will not matter who takes these glittering icons or what they do with them when such things are stripped of their power. Nobody will have much interest in hoarding gold when we already have all we need – all that is truly useful and pleasing to us – without it. It is only money and attachment to monetary worth that have caused us to jealously guard property; the rich have invented, historically, money precisely so that they can use it to impose inequality, accrue wealth themselves and glory in the light of their own pride by showing-off their gleaming gold ornaments, clothing and stores. Such showing-off provides no lasting well-being to anyone. There should be no place for it in a society of equals. That greed, pride and the violent crime that sometimes accompanies them exist at all today is a symptom of the persistence of money's rule over our lives and thoughts, and money is a ruler that it is high time we deposed.

Worthless Jobs

Money is also to blame for wasting a huge amount of time and resources through our doing things that give no lasting good or, worse, cause harm, and yet are lauded as 'work' in the capitalist society. Most importantly, associated with the making of money are a whole host of worthless professions whose slaving labourers could do so much good for society if only their efforts were directed elsewhere. The entire 'financial sector' comes under this bracket: all those involved in investing money, 'risking' money, providing monetary loans and mortgages, running stock-exchanges, protecting monetary assets, deciding bonuses, banking, detecting fraud and so on – all are doing essentially pointless jobs that add nothing tangible to anyone's enjoyment of life and are only of any purpose at all in that they increase or secure the monetary wealth that can bring only superficial pleasure.

Some of these jobs – for example, fraud detection – do provide real benefits within the current capitalist system to real people, because at the moment everyone has to use and rely upon money; no doubt those that do such jobs are just as well-intentioned and compassionate as are people in other lines of work. But remove money from the picture and we see that they are all a waste of time and energy. All these people could be employed crafting or repairing useful objects, farming real food, providing others with their needs and enhancing their lives in some way, instead of shoring up fictitious financial fences and fishing for gold. They could be doing art, science and culturally significant things of that kind, yet instead they push sums of money from place to place, protect it, help people to hoard and accumulate it, or – in the case of debt collectors – even deprive people of things that they genuinely need to be happy because such people do not have sufficient pieces of metal or sheets of paper to 'pay for it', their very house and home. Such people should not be supported in this destructive activity by society. Terrorising the poor by bombarding them with notices of their debt, turning our families from their repossessed homes and condemning the needy to lives of mental torment and shame is a despicable crime. With the demise of money, debt collection, debt collectors' threats and the repossession of homes would be at once abolished.

There are only a very few finance-sector-related jobs that could be useful top a money-free society, were they to be directed to better purposes. The design of fast computer algorithms for financial transactions, for instance, could be considered in some way a science in itself and detached from its debauched current application and put to better use in science and societal organisation. Accountants, too, may be of use if only they cease putting monetary values to 'assets' and instead count which resources are needed for which task, as part of the process of managing society efficiently and effectively.

Financial sector jobs, though, in general either give nothing at all or they give misery to the rest of society and the world. They create a whole plethora of work that merely exists to further greedy interests and drive society into a less equal and less efficient state. They lie at the core of the capitalist monster, and help to maintain its market-driven trends of over-production, over-consumption and misery for the majority of people tossed around by the whims and mistakes of the few highly-paid employees of this most wicked sector. The 'financial crises' provoked by the decisions and temperaments of the rich market-traders and the careless mistakes of bankers and estate agents cause havoc in a society controlled by money and the markets that they sustain. These 'workers' and everybody else would be much better off if they abandoned their 'work' entirely and devoted their lives to something more helpful to the sustainable, happy, compassionate society. Without money, we do not need to invest or trade in markets. We need simply produce what we need and anything above this that we can sustainably provide, sharing the gifts of the Earth and investigating new ideas and technologies when they are proposed to see to what extent they might help us to do this. Technologists, scientists and those who work day to day in producing food, goods and services that are genuinely needed and wanted, are in a much better position to decide which new ideas ought to be adopted than are rich investors who care primarily for making money.

Environmental Destruction

Associated with worthless jobs is a waste of energy and resources – all jobs require some material input, and these provide no output by way of justification for the spent resources. The sixth problem with money, then, is that it causes environmental destruction both by its very existence and because of the jobs connected directly with it. Energy is wasted heating the offices and powering the computers of investment banks and so on, when much more good would be done leaving the fuel unburnt and the bankers at home. The production of money itself, at the same time, is a waste of vast resources, in whatever form it is made. Coins require metal to be mined and processed or recycled from old coins, all of which needs energy input. Notes have to be printed and trees cut down or oil extracted to make the paper or plastic notes on which they are printed. These then have to be transported and distributed, and efforts must be made to ensure that they are difficult to forge and that fraudulent copies are taken out of circulation.

Fraudster criminals fight to stay one step ahead of the authorities, and a lot of time, energy and resources is wasted in the course of a purposeless battle to maintain the integrity of inherently worthless currency while the state struggles to ensure that every person only has access to the money they are 'entitled to'. How much simpler it would be, were we simply to distribute resources to where they are needed, without money in the equation at all. All that wasted energy and the associated damage to our environment would be circumvented. Real resources such as food, water and homes, of course cannot be faked, nor is there any incentive for criminals to pretend that they have them when they do not.

Nor does the credit card relieve us of the environmental burden of money, for it requires even more resources to make than several notes and is replaced every few years. Indeed, resources are wasted when we represent real goods and services with monetary values even when physical money is not involved at all. These days, much of society's money takes a form no more tangible than numbers on a bank's computer system, detailing how much of this magical substance – the 'snake oil' for which we sell our time, our goods, our very lives – each person or company possesses. This is a substance that somehow doesn't need to be physically observable to be 'real', and yet, though imaginary, can be counterfeited and is considered invalid if it is dreamt up by unauthorised persons instead of wealthy banks. Electronic money removes the need to mine, mint and print, it is true. But it is even less inherently valuable than physical money, and still more of a deceitful trade.

Furthermore, the ecological damage that the conjuring of such non-existent money wreaks is far from negligible. The supercomputers that sore up all the information regarding where we all rank monetarily in society need to be powered, again leading to the emission of greenhouse gasses or the guzzling of renewable resources that could otherwise be deployed elsewhere. Plastic and metal are wasted in building such machines for such a purpose, and of course in building the equipment at banks and cash machines that allows people to access their accounts. This is not to mention the powerful machines of investors and stock markets, used to make lightning-fast trades around the world. All such infrastructure essentially exists to maintain inequality. Were everyone to be treated as equals, with an equal share in the resources sustainably available to society, there would be no need to keep a record of how much everyone possessed or for banks to store it in. We should only need a record of which house each person lived in, how many people need to be served by each goods-distribution centre and what their wants and needs are, and so on. Undoubtedly, money is not to blame for all bureaucracy, for we need some record-keeping to run society efficiently. But money makes society less efficient, and thereby adds unnecessarily to the burden of bureaucracy. Were we to rid ourselves of the financial sector, we should simultaneously remove its direct ecological footprint and could redirect its resources, infrastructure and effort into much more useful jobs, saving areas of land and reducing pollutant emissions by eradicating unnecessary tasks that only serve an industry that causes harm.

Closed Creativity

Not least among the harms of the industry of money is the seventh crime of which it stands accused: the metaphorical pollution of more enlightened human pursuits, stymying and encasing them to prevent the full flow of human creativity from being realised in the realms of science and art. Money turns these most delightful, useful and fascinating cultural endeavours into 'intellectual property'. Because of the need to 'make money' to survive in a world where making science and art for their own sakes and the useful insights and emotional responses they beget is apparently not enough, practitioners have to be paid for their discoveries and creations, whether by a university, trust, corporation or customer. The scientist and artist are not permitted to treat science and art as their goals, despite the fact that it is for love of science and art that they choose enter these fields and thereby draw meaning and fulfilment for themselves and others. Instead, money has to become the goal, and only that science and art that can be 'sold' in some way and proven to have 'economic value' can be funded. So, often, the 'success' of a work of art or scientific investigation is gauged by how much money it has brought in from the public visiting the art or through practical applications of the science.

It is no bad thing that many people are able to see and appreciate a piece of work of art and that there are good uses to which science can be put. But there should be no need to quantify these happy outcomes in terms of some arbitrary monetary quantity (one that could of course be influenced by other factors than the actual enjoyment or practical use of art and science, such as advertising or coincidence); nor should art and science be supported or not on the basis of some preconceived notion of its future monetary value. When people talk of these sectors being 'of value' to the British economy, they miss the point entirely: science and art are ends in themselves, and the British economy is in fact of service to them, in that it provides the resources by which such cultural heights can be climbed. In any case, many works are not appreciated at the time of their composition but loved by future generations; and many scientific findings tell us something profound about the universe that is only later realised or have much later practical applications undreamt of when they were first made. If only short-term monetary returns are considered, society is denied all these. Babbage's mechanical computer didn't receive the monetary funding it needed to be built in the nineteenth century; the Victorians had no way of conceiving what great uses the computer would, in later incarnations, be put to.

So it is that money is guilty of limiting our culture's creative sphere of the arts and sciences. Ironically, only those who have so much money that it becomes no object even in a money-based world can provide their own materials and equipment and (like the Victorian amateur-scientists) pursue their creative instincts without restraint. Other, perhaps initially more enthused and inspired, individuals have this enthusiasm sapped by the need to do work that is seen to make money. If their creative pursuits are not deemed to generate sufficient funds, they must waste their time performing some other, more menial task, and push what they are truly passionate about to the periphery of their lives. We are fortunate that money's hold over culture is not yet complete, and that 'blue-sky thinking' is still supported by some institutions in our world. But, little by little, money's power grows, and universities around the world become more and more like businesses, more interested in monetary profit than enlightening thought.

As well as cutting off creativity for artists and scientists, money also hinders the enjoyment of culture by the wider public – thereby undermining the very reason for its existence in the first place – and diminishes the possibility that others might be inspired into building on cultural creations, by making art and science the 'property' of its creator or funder, and preventing anyone else from widely disseminating or copying such creations. Scientists have to pay huge sums of money for their reports to be published 'Open Source' for anyone to view; this means that most papers are instead accessible only to those at rich universities or who can afford to pay expensive subscription fees to the profit-making journals. Technologists have to 'patent' new inventions so that others cannot copy and sell them and they can be paid for their work and any future applications it finds – even if the invention would do far more good for society were it to be widely and freely replicated and distributed. Works of art such as paintings, books, films and musical recordings are made subject to 'copyright' so that nobody can copy and share them for others to enjoy without explicit permission. All of this is born of the need to make money in a money-based world. The artists have to make money; those funding the scientists haver to make money; technologists have to make money. All of them have to have a way, therefore, of saying 'this is mine – I made it; you must pay me if you want to use it'.

The result, of course, is that the prime cultural advances of our society are not shared equally between its members. Even though the paper, paint, ink, computers, electricity, tools and buildings that the artist, scientist or technologist utilised in their work were provided from the resources of a shared world – and indeed a small but certainly not negligible quantity of harm to others may have been done, through resource depletion or climatic change for instance, in the course of carrying out that work – the end result is marked out as private property and the poor are denied access. Usually, the publishing company, record label or commissioning company assumed ownership of a work of art, and denies its use to others unless they pay sufficient money. This would only be fair if this magic ticket, money, was equally possessed by all, which it is not.

Of course, it is right that an artist, scientist or inventor should be given credit for their work and acknowledged where it is reproduced if possible. But that is no reason why such work, if it is of genuine benefit to society, should not be shared equally by all who want to use it. Only money holds us back from equal access to and enjoyment of cultural achievements. Only money keeps works of art in private collections and restricts music, literature and research to those who can afford them. Only money holds back the use of beneficial inventions and medicines at the whim of those who first patented these particular ways of combining Earth's elements and powers together. Without money and the need to earn it, the fruits of creativity can be made free, with artists and scientists supported in their creative work – wherever it leads them – by the public, with no need for profit, competition and private ownership. Then, these fruits can act as seeds strewn as widely as possible, for further trees of creativity to sprout up, sometimes in the least expected of places.

The greatest crime of all to be perpetuated by money, though, may be the corrupting influence that it has on those in power who, under the misconception that the country itself must be somehow profitable, in times of financial stress carry out spending cuts that leave public services decimated and needy people suffering – not because we lack the resources or people to run the services and support everyone, but simply because we are supposed to lack the money, and in a monetary society those services and people cannot survive easily without it. The capitalist government strips back what is good and praiseworthy in our society, all in the name of cutting the budget deficit and bringing down the national debt.

This only occurs because money is allowed to hold a grip upon the very reins of our country, driving decision-makers to neglect the needs of the majority in favour of the profits of the rich. Under 'austerity' policies such as those imposed by the Liberal-Conservative coalition that came to power in Britain in 2010, or by the European Union when it sought to call in the debts of countries such as Greece and Ireland that had apparently 'overspent' in recent years, the monetary funding that was being used as a proxy for real resources to feed doctors, nurses, social carers, police, firemen and all sorts of other public servants was cut, alongside support for the unemployed. Across countries affected by austerity, public health has declined, families have lost their homes and had to resort to food banks to survive – around one million people relied upon these in the UK alone in 2015 – and unemployment has soared. Public libraries, hospitals and even forests have come under threat – all the things that people really value in life, facing destruction for the sake of saving a few imaginary pounds. Everyone except those rich enough to 'weather the storm' of the financial 'crisis' has become in some way less happy, with less of what they really find fulfilling in life available to them. But materialism, and the capitalists' encouragement of everyone to consume more and more has not abated. So, society continues to wastefully indulge in material goods that are not important, while the rich continue to gather in their precious money and the poor slide further into debt.

It is through debt that the rich hold the poor to ransom. The 'national debt' is used as an excuse to sweep aside care for society and the environment in the name of this falsely-valued commodity that is money, because it is not 'economically viable' to maintain it. Personal debt is used to haul families out of their homes and unfortunates into the courts, simply for spending what they needed to spend to live or were encouraged to spend by the very same capitalist society that drove them into such desperation. All of this makes life much worse for everyone in the long-term, and all comes from the pointless desire by thoughtless governments to 'save money', spurred on by the liars who claim that money is important, usually because they have garnered so much of it themselves.

Lack of money did not prevent the creation of the welfare state in Britain in the 1940s. Lack of money did not present us all from working together, making the best use of everyone's talents rather than making them sit around unemployed. We have more than enough food to feed everyone, more than enough expertise to teach everyone and off good healthcare to all. Money has no value; it is unnecessary, and in the main harmful. It need not enter into the picture, when it comes to deciding what we can and ought to do for one another. It commits its greatest crime when its allure persuades politicians otherwise.

Gambling

Even those committed to running society as a capitalist 'free market', who deny against all sense and evidence the other crimes of money, must admit to one of its most long-established faults – money's precipitation of ruin through gambling. It is probably a human trait universal to all societies that we seek to play and game – indeed, friendly competition is important in the development of social skills and play is a vital part of learning. Many of us, because of this, like to 'try our luck' in games of chance. This only becomes significantly harmful when people choose to stake their entire means of living and their family's material well-being upon such games. Such recklessness is only possible because of money.

In a money-free society in which everyone's needs are met by society itself through common endeavour and sharing, nobody can gain by gambling for those essential goods themselves, because there is no incentive to accrue more of something that you already have – and always will have – all that you need of. If more luxurious items such as computers and household appliances are also shared communally, they do not belong to any single individual to gamble with at all. Therefore, in such a society, gambling could not possibly undermine anyone's access to any such things.

The same is not true, of course, when money is used as a medium for exchange that is necessary for the purchase both of basic goods and of luxury items, which are not held in common. In those circumstances, the desire to convert the enjoyable activity of playing a game into a means to gain more privately-owned goods – or, indeed, in a world where money has become an ends in itself, simply more money – becomes too strong for some to resist. Perhaps they feel themselves unable to become 'successful' by any other means, and where 'success' is measured by the size of one's bank account, 'skilful' play with chance might be considered a worthy way of obtaining it. These poor victims begin to gamble their money, which is their means of sustenance and determines their family's well-being in a cut-throat capitalist world.

Gamblers may be pushed into this activity by desperation: perhaps they are at the bottom of the ladder of capitalist inequality, and are desperately seeking for a means of fulfilling needs that cannot otherwise be fulfilled because they have too little income. Or, they may be quite wealthy and simply seeking amusement, like the rich aristocrats that gambled their fortunes away in the earlier decades of this capitalist age. Either way, money is precious to them, and they are greedy for more. But because money is, in this world, allowed to be the master of all things, the gambler, once they have begun, can seldom stop. Either they begin to win, in which case the sheer thrill of taking such a risk and having it pay off inspires them into believing that a lucky streak can continue and that that this plan will actually bring them the success they crave; or else (more likely) they begin to lose, in which case they become possessed by the desperation to undo this misfortune and the ruin and shame it may cause them and their dependents if they do not win back their losses. In both cases, they are driven to gamble more and more, even though most gamblers lose much more than they win – for how else would book-keepers and casinos make a profit? The only likely result is the destruction of the perpetual gambler's enthusiasm, self-esteem, means of living and love of those they care for. It's only because of quantification of resources through money that this can happen. Indeed, the only cure for the broken and dispirited gambler who had so much and has lost everything, is to enlighten them to the truth that money is, in fact, worthless, and that they have not really 'lost' anything at all: it has been taken from them by a society that demands money in exchange for things that we need to live.

If money were to be stripped of its power and divorced from the supply of the fruits of society's labour to its labourers, it would perhaps not be possible to obtain such a 'thrill' from gambling with it. But actually, friendly gambling would perhaps become the only use for this unmasked and dethroned currency. Money, when made to be worthless in the eyes of all, could still be gambled, but the only gain achievable by winning it or sorrow caused by losing it would be the thrill or disappointment of winning or losing the game, just as is the case with fake money used in board-games today. This could remove some of the appeal of gambling altogether, but would certainly render it a harmless pastime, and the gain to society would undoubtedly outweigh any loss in the form of fun were gambling to become in this way an infinitely less risky but much less thrilling occupation. Games and sports would then all become more about the appreciation of a long-honed skill and the thrill of good fortune than about the chance to win funds to satisfy material desires. It is to be hoped that, living meaningful lives free from the tyranny of money, we should all find plenty of excitement and amusement in life without the need to draw anything more than this from gambling, a need that is sadly ever-present for a minority in the capitalist world, who in this respect suffer from a profound misfortune, whatever their success rate at card games.

Hampered Innovation

The last in this list of charges to be brought against money is that money hampers and constrains the technological development of society, in addition to the restrictions it imposes through closed creativity. This means that solutions that ought to be available to certain problems are not, and that people are made to put up with faulty goods and infrastructure that could easily be rectified were it not for money. The reason for this is that all innovation in society must, in a money-based world, make money. Innovations that we have the resources to bring about sustainably but that do not make money are not able to occur, because the rich investors that have power in such a society will not support anything that will lose them money. In order to introduce a new technology, the cost of the raw materials, labour and ingenuity required to make it must be exceeded by the money that can be brought in by selling it.

This causes problems when a technology is very difficult and therefore monetarily costly to create and cannot be sold for a large return, and yet could be of great benefit to society. The most important example of this, perhaps, is that of pharmaceuticals. Private companies that develop and manufacture drugs are only willing to do so if they can spin a profit. Antibiotics are an important class of drug that is essential for the treatment of a whole range of conditions caused by microbial infection, but because of human mismanagement and antibiotics' over-use in the pursuit of profit, bacteria are largely developing resistance to the existing forms of these drugs. It would be of great benefit to millions of people to develop new antibiotics that can fight infection by bacteria resistant to all other treatments. But developing new antibiotics is not profitable: in order to prevent widespread resistance, antibiotics must be used very sparingly, and if they are successful in killing off harmful bacteria quickly they will not need to be used by a patient for very long, restricting the revenue that can be gathered in selling them. Meanwhile, developing a new antibiotic might involve a great deal of research, searching for bacterial resistance in Nature and trying to synthesise the necessary chemicals to bring it about in a medicine. This all costs a lot of money, and the necessary chemical compounds themselves may also be expensive to obtain, in a capitalist world. As a result, drugs companies are unwilling to invest in the search for new antibiotics, and even if they were to do so, they would probably have to charge huge sums for medical practitioners to use them in order to make a profit. Without the need to make money, this restriction would of course be lifted and the drugs we need could be made by researchers passionate about and skilled in developing them, without the need to worry about fundamentally meaningless monetary costs. The millions that suffer because of the lack of research into new antibiotics suffer, therefore, only because of money.

Once we realise that this is the case, we can see that the claim often put forward by proponents of a capitalist system – that this competition-based, monetary way of doing things is the only way to stimulate innovation, cultural development and technological improvements – is false. Rather, capitalism always encourages change and development that is monetarily profitable: indeed, we have a great deal of change and development in today's world that is profitable, as a result of capitalism, but not all of this is positive change. Much of it is very destructive – of cultures, people and the natural world, as we shall explore in later chapters. On the other hand, a society that is free of money is by no means devoid of change and development, but the difference is that the change and development therein can be directed by the needs of society, not the desire to make money. There may or may not be less change overall in a money-less society, but this question need not be cause for concern, because any development that does come about will almost certainly be positive, as the true human and environmental costs and benefits of change can be more effectively taken into account.

The development of new antibiotics is one example. Others might include the advancement of renewably-powered vehicles and other devices in the interests of society, without needing to worry about the apparent profitability of using fossil fuels instead; the manufacture of better-lasting, more pleasant and more meaningful goods by passionate craftspeople rather than cheap tat churned out by inanimate machines or factory slaves; and the construction of better buildings in place of the cheap concrete edifices erected under capitalism.

Money even undermines the ways in which we are each able to interact with and understand our society and surroundings. It is by money-hungry corporations that we are flooded by advertisements whenever we try to use the web, slowing us down and diverting us from the best search results to 'sponsored ads' instead. It is by money-hungry map-makers that faults are intentionally introduced into maps we use to navigate ('map traps') in order to prevent them being copied without this being noticeable[20]: obviously, knowledge of the true lay-out of streets is not something that any one company can have a monopoly on, so their maps have to be made faulty – and less efficacious – to ensure the manufacturer can trace 'their' map. In all these ways and many more, our lives are directly hampered and sometimes endangered, and our time is wasted, by others' pointless pursuit of money.

Conclusion

Money stands accused – and there can be little doubt of its guilt – of at least nine terrible crimes against society. These in themselves do not prove that the influence of money is negative overall or that there necessarily exists a better alternative, although it will be the purpose of the rest of this document to argue that it is a negative influence and that we would be better free of it. But they do show that the paradigm that puts profit and monetary wealth at the pinnacle of society's aspirations, which is known by all of us to be fundamentally misguided, is responsible for a great deal of avoidable harm. From desperate gamblers to governing politicians, many are corrupted by money, and its use to facilitate the conversion of work done into resources 'earned' devalues both our purposeful labour and the goods we depend upon to live. There is, therefore, a great deal of promise in abandoning our obsession with the worthless paper, metal and computer digits that form modern-day money and seeking a way of running our society without it, as we shall now begin to explore.

3. A Troubled Society

There are a great host of ways in which our current capitalist society, which has grown from strength to strength over recent decades and centuries, is having a negative impact upon our wellbeing as individuals and on the relationships we enjoy. We are the same species that we always have been, with the same innate desires and tendencies as we would have under any form of social organisation. But these have been exploited by the machinery of capitalism, which has begun to act, as this chapter will show, as a slave-driver, perpetuating longer-term misery and inequality where there could be joy and prosperity. In the next chapter, we shall witness the damage that this way of doing things is having on our precious environment, on which we all depend for our ultimate wellbeing, compounding the problem for ourselves and future generations. Capitalism is not what it was in the nineteenth century, and some of its ills have been remedied even as others have been allowed to become yet more acute. But never before has man been made so subservient to money as in this present time.

3.1 Selling Ourselves

Something has changed in society over the last few centuries. Somehow, rather than acting as a conglomeration of individuals, combined in our collective desire to survive, together, as a species, as we always did, we have become a nation of slaves. This modern slavery is not, of course, by-and-large of the sort that plagued the societies of the past, whereby one person physically forces another to work against their will. Today, we are enslaved not by one another, but by the agent that has somehow been allowed to become the master of society: money. Everybody now has something to sell, and their sole purpose, it seems, has become to persuade others to buy it.

Inevitably associated with this obsession with buying and selling is the continual increase and proliferation of modern technologies that we have seen over recent decades. In the past, it was sufficient to live, as well as we could, using the tools we had access to. But today, it is not considered sufficient to remain stable, using the same technologies to perform the same tasks in the manner they always have done. Once a static technology is bought, it need not be bought again, and by continuing to use the same mechanisms that were formerly employed we should thereby deny the chance of another to sell us something new. So, the misconception that has arisen that everybody must provide some product or service that would otherwise be lacking in some place or at some time, in order to be accepted and helped by society as a whole, and that each is likewise expected to use the money they have obtained through the sale of their particular contribution in the purchasing of others' goods. This has inevitably led to an increasing rate of change, in the world, in order that all can be kept employed in continually innovating and replacing, rather than making do with what we already have.

No sane society should feel any need for the creation of advertisements to persuade others of the need to purchase one particular product, or the careful manipulation of 'brand names' to make that product attractive to the 'consumer'. In a sane society, one that exists for the mutual benefit of all its members, each would choose what was best for themselves and those surrounding them – the product that was best matched to their purposes – perhaps with the aid of external expertise and information, but certainly not needing to be *persuaded* in one direction or the other. It would be better, therefore, to abandon the whole idea of competing and advertising, constantly trying to persuade everyone else that they want what we've got. For our labours to achieve the maximum good for our neighbours, we must refrain from viewing as everybody as having something to sell, and our peers as people who might potentially buy. We must instead think of ourselves as being capable of bringing something to *provide* for everyone else, if there is need, and of our comrades around us as those with whom we can work, in unity, to make life joyous and fulfilling for all.

Nor should any sane society be wedded unquestionably to change. Change, indeed, needs to take place in a healthy and satisfying society. But by creating corporations whose goal is not to provide the change that is best for society but rather to persuade everyone to make use of their particular product or service, bringing about change solely for the sake of profit, we are enslaving ourselves to change and to innovation, preventing ourselves from obtaining stability, and chaining ourselves into the desire to want always more and better than what we already possess. Furthermore, we are enslaving our own planet, extracting more and more resources to fuel greater and greater innovation simply for the sake of money.

There is no need to have ever more sophisticated computers, and ever higher-definition films. These things are only desired because it suits the capitalist system that we do desire them, so that, by their creation, more people can be kept in employment. Employment for the sake of employment, rather than for the sake of society, is utterly useless, and only serves to squander precious resources. We must reject this diabolical state of affairs, reject the need always to be selling ourselves, and buying from others, and focus on what is more important: life itself. Life has existed for countless millennia, without any requirement of these modern peripherals to sustain it. Where they can truly do net good, they should of course be endorsed. But my plea is that we do not allow ourselves to become enslaved by innovation: if the old way suits, let it linger. Ignore any message propagated through advertisements, which are by their very nature designed to lead us away from what we would naturally choose, to fulfil our needs, for the good of some other agent, not of ourselves. We must not be afraid to reject unnecessary innovation, or to turn down the salesman's offer, whatever tactics of persuasion he may use: for we will find that life is fuller without superfluous goods.

3.2 Materialism

It is true that mankind has always sought to gather and make use of material resources, fashioning these resources into a growing array of devices as the sophistication of our species has progressed. But of late this trend has become something of an obsession; items which are not really needed are bought for the simple enjoyment of buying them; money is spent because we have it – or are able to borrow it – not because we need to spend it. Indeed, even the very universe in which we live, one in which we have long appreciated a dimension beyond the physically observable, has been reduced in the minds of many to a purely mathematical, divisible and exploitable creation whose components can be simply assigned a value, bought and sold. Religion and spirituality have been thrust aside by many, intent as they are on gaining wealth in the form of the money and material possessions by which 'success' is apparently measured. Where our natural spiritual tendencies survive, they are often kept alive only to be exploited for the purpose of profit, with for example such superstitious nonsenses as communication through mediums and horoscopes being allowed to continue as a form of paid entertainment. Most people recognise that there is more to the universe than the material, which is why such practices continue to be popular. But these superstitions, these empty ghosts of our former religiosity, are a far less threatening – to capitalism – alternative to a true understanding of what is beyond the material, which might undermine a person's willingness to put production and consumption at the centre of their lives. They are employed by the capitalist world to silence spiritual longings without engendering the discontent with materialism that a deeper understanding might invoke.

Such spiritual repression in the capitalist world is not the fault of science: indeed, science is but another of its victims. The noble sciences of the material world, so useful to us through their ability to explain the workings of the universe we see, hear and touch, are misused by the capitalist society in which we live to provoke endless material innovation. The 'blue-sky thinker', exploring the universe regardless of any technological developments that spring from their work, is either mocked or weakly tolerated according to the promise that 'real applications of the work will arise later'. In other words, in order for the capitalist world to allow, through its mechanisms of competition and monetary investment, a scientific investigation to continue, that investigation must lead ultimately to some material technological gain. The curse of materialism is the curse of always wanting more and better goods which are often unnecessary and always being hungry for more precious resources. Whilst the rich world satisfies its materialistic hunger by pointlessly wasting resources, the rest of the present world and the future world are left starved of what they need. Modern-day materialism is nothing other than a form of society-wide obesity, squandering and stockpiling resources that are needed elsewhere, swelling the arsenals of superfluous goods.

Like literal obesity, it is not surprising that this technological obesity, sustained nowadays by the likes of electronic devices and lavish ornaments, has come to pervade our society. Both are born of an earlier survival instinct: the instinct to obtain whatever we can get in order to survive as individuals and as a species. But such hoarding, once so useful, is not applicable to the modern lives we live. We have already obtained a standard of living for the vast majority in this country that is comfortable; we do not need to hanker after more material wealth as was done in times gone by. It is difficult, but, as a society, we must shake off this primal urge for more things of our own. We can end the flashy advertisements of shops desperate to sell us more and more, beyond our needs, and instead set up a system of sharing, such that the country consumes no more than is necessary for the production of life's essentials – food, water, shelter – and ample devices for all to enjoy the more interesting flesh on the skeleton of life: the arts, the sciences and competition where competition belongs, in sport and games for fun. If such resources are shared and used where they are needed, there will be no necessity for everybody to have so much material wealth, no need for them to spend so much money on resources borrowed from our neighbours in both time and space. Such freedom from the ancient curse of materialism is what we must try to achieve, in a post-capitalist, spiritually fulfilling world, in which it is recognised that obtaining goods is not required for happiness.

3.3 Atheistic Consumerism

It is no coincidence that the rise of capitalism in the western world coincided with the decline of faith and theistic religious observance. This decline is not a direct result of the Enlightenment, the scientific revolution which is equally important to theists and atheists, bringing about a new wave of understanding about the material world that is, in the theistic mind, an important part of God's creation. But this enlightenment of the mind did precipitate the abandonment of the old hierarchical feudal system in favour of the more fluid – but no less enslaving – system of capitalism. It was this new system, releasing the population from one hierarchy into another, placing emphasis on the individual and consumption of resources rather than on the community and working as part of a broader mechanism, that placed into the minds of many the idea that the accumulation of money and material goods were more important than spiritual accomplishment. Certainly the masters of the feudal world had, quite in contrast to the message preached by the founders of the religions they claimed to follow, accumulated wealth for themselves at the expense of their subjects. But they at least had regarded themselves, however superior in material wealth, to be equal before God with their subjects, manipulatively claiming that it was their unique place to have wealth on Earth but nonetheless recognising that they would be judged alongside the lowliest peasant after death.

Not so with the new, capitalist, hierarchy. This is a hierarchy based solely on monetary wealth, with little remnant of hereditary influence, meaning that it is a more fluid one than its predecessor, with a person able to travel between the upper, middle and lower classes comparatively easily. But though a person's label in this system may not be permanent, persons are labelled nonetheless. It becomes such that this label – dependent on fame and fortune rather than position and title – is the only important factor in judging the success of a life. There is no longer a notion of equality before God: as feudalism is swept aside, only those aspects of it that are fitting to the creation of profit are retained, and spirituality is not one of them. Hence, religion is rejected by capitalism, since religion places value on spiritual and moral gains, whereas capitalism places it only on the artificial and utterly non-divine notion of money.

The Britain of the early twenty-first century is not the Britain that emerged, battered but not destroyed, ready to begin a new era – or so we thought – after the Second World War. Its people are different now, but not in the way that was envisioned then. Somehow, after those first strides towards socialism undertaken by the Attlee government (see 'Politics & Progress'), we went astray, tempted and tricked by the allure of capitalist consumerism, to worship new idols – the products of mankind's own creation – and allowed ourselves to be enslaved to their capitalist hold. It was the removal of God from the centre of most people's lives in the wake of the Enlightenment that precipitated this enslavement. This change came as a result of the erroneous belief that there exists a conflict between the science of the physical universe and God-inspired religions that are in fact concerned with a deeper, moral, truth about our place and function in the universe. Sometimes the religious became too 'religious' in insisting that their particular, literal interpretation of Biblical stories provided a source of historical and scientific 'fact' that those stories were never intended to convey, and by their fundamentalist religiosity defied the more fundamental, moral truth of those stories, which advise religious adherents to be guided by universal love, not intolerance, and to use our minds and senses to comprehend God's will. Some scientifically-minded thinkers, on the other hand, became too 'religious' for objective science, trying to cut away all apparent purpose and meaning in the universe to devise a cold, rationalist notion of 'truth' as measured using scientific apparatus, without acknowledging the limits of our human understanding and the inability of objective science to capture the truths that matter to us as living beings: truths of how to live and to what end.

Gradually, the latter mind-set has won out over the former, but also over the more measured, liberal and loving theism of non-fundamentalist believers. For, rightly disillusioned by the Victorian capitalist environment of imperialism; the twisted religion used to justify the 'Protestant work ethic' and unequal division between 'rich' and 'poor' or 'European' and 'native'; and even, at its culmination, industrial-scale murder in the World Wars; society sought a new set of values in which to place its trust. Had things transpired differently, perhaps the revolutionary fervour that swept the Conservatives from power in 1945 would have gone further than it did: perhaps the true values of traditional English Christianity, somewhat side-lined by the Victorian capitalist emphasis on money-making and exploitative business, might have been restored. Then, sharing, humility and equality, regardless of material wealth and social standing, might have been the guiding principles of the Britain we have inherited today.

But instead, the heartless, abusive and divisive ways of early (pre-Second World War) capitalism, with its enslavement of the working man to the factory, was surpassed by something almost as misguided and undesirable: the attachment of all aspects of society – both rich and poor – to money and material success. The 'ordinary' person of the present is not akin to the peasants of centuries past, taking their important but poorly rewarded place within the hierarchy of society whilst the rulers took their higher seats, each accepting their role and trying to do the best with what they had, trusting in God even if they were poor. Nor are we like the factory workers and lower classes of the nineteenth and early twentieth centuries, taught to accept and even to desire a wholly unbearable status of inferiority and terrible conditions by an abused and abusive form of religion that taught them they must suffer for their salvation and expect no Earthly reward (see 'The Capitalist Revolution', above). Now we all judge each other not on the basis of hierarchy or productive 'usefulness' to society, but on the basis of money. Jobs that are sometimes worthless are created simply to make money; the development of ever newer, money-making, technologies is worshiped as an ends in itself. The entire country is held hostage to the 'need' for economic growth, as part of a culture of consumerism, at the expense of our environment and legacy of shared services. Even when money is raised to help those in need, it is obtained through rituals of idol-worship in the form of celebrity endorsers who are cheered and exulted like gods because they have obtained material 'success'.

We are all told to work through the day – these days not even stopping for a proper lunch break to talk with colleagues – then go home and watch the television, as part of a new religion of wealthy celebrity worship, and spend as much money as we can in the shops on the way or at the weekends. Even Sundays have been stolen from families, turned into just another day of retail and business in which the workers can do more of their shopping and spend their hard-earned money. The jobs they are working so hard at are largely concerned with making or distributing material possessions and making money for big corporations – all this effort, to produce very little of real importance. Even children at school are taught to study not for the love of the ideas they are exploring but in order to do well and get one such 'good job', and through the means of examinations to become competitors against each other.

The real goal of a good life should be spiritual fulfilment – that is what the hearts of this depressed generation seek, not really jobs for their own sake, and not really money. Such fulfilment comes from sharing our resources, treating each other as equals and loving one another, whatever possessions we may or may not have. There is no need to stressfully slave over resource-hungry endeavours; the real needs of society are much less than we make them out to be in material terms, and much greater when it comes to human relationships and interactions with others. A combination of medieval-like piety with scientific enlightenment could free us from the worship of material wealth, competitive high-flying careers and the worship of celebrities who are truly of no lesser or greater worth than anybody else. The sooner we achieve this, the better it will be for all of us: we must cast down the new idols, and restore our faith in love.

3.4 Control by Innovation

One of the aspects of capitalism that make it so environmentally as well as socially damaging is its insistence on continued replacement of the old with a new and supposedly better technology. Other political systems are not necessarily obstacles to necessary innovation; indeed they are often in some respects more likely to encourage it sooner, rather than waiting for a logically superior method to become 'economically viable'. But capitalism is particularly encouraging of the change-for-the-sake-of-change idea, in that perfectly adequate goods and technologies are swept aside, sometimes temporarily, such that everyone is obliged to buy – and hence consume – more, to meet the latest fashion. If we are all to do the most logical and sustainable thing – to wear the same clothes year in, year out until they wear out, for example, and to repair those we have, clothing companies would be unable to sell nearly as many goods, and the precious 'growth' that the capitalist system is reliant upon would cease.

This cycle of repeated replacement, carried out unstoppably except in time of national crisis such as world war when the principles of capitalism and profit-making – even private property – are abandoned for the common good, is replicated across many aspects of society. In music, for example, once everybody had a record player, it became necessary to produce the cassette to make money, albeit with some added advantage in that it allowed greater portability. But the cassette was allowed to continue only long enough to yield sufficient profit, then replaced by the compact disc. Each was released after a sufficient interval to ensure maximum profit by the music 'industries' that produced the machinery and the records, tapes and CDs – called 'industries' because capitalism degrades all forms of art and science it is allowed to access to profit-based commercialisms – and support for the previous method was removed. Likewise, the likes of Microsoft remove support for their previous computer operating systems to encourage the purchase of the latest one, although the previous ones were perfectly adequate, which comes at great environmental cost if all the equipment used to support the old operating system has to be recycled – or worse, dumped – and replaced.

Computing and televisual equipment must be constantly replaced under the capitalist paradigm – standard definition is, the public is told, no longer good enough: they must buy HD, and as soon as that is sold sufficiently, 3D, television. The human imagination – grossly underrated by capitalist societies of course because it cannot be paid for – is perfectly capable of providing just as useful and enjoyable an experience in standard definition as in 3D, but the public is controlled through innovation towards changing unnecessarily, even before their existing hardware is broken. Or, such hardware is sometimes engineered to malfunction after a much shorter time than necessary to avoid any resistance to buying the newer version, again at the great environmental cost of producing new gadgets. This phenomenon is becoming more and more common as companies realise that they make more money from many sales of cheap, short-lived products than only slightly more expensive ones that will last a lifetime – the old-fashioned make-it-to-last idea has been swept away. This is all part of an unconscious but inevitable consequence of the competition-based system; to survive, companies – which in turn are necessary to the survival of their employees in a capitalist world – must out-compete each other through the innovation of new, pointless improvements and the persuasion of the public to buy into these improvements. It is for this reason that armies of poorly-paid workers slave in China to produce so many goods, that precious metals we lived perfectly well without fifty years ago are now in such high demand that we cannot supply them quickly enough, and that the environmental problems we face cannot be solved within capitalism, where profit and growth always come first.

It is not the case that new technologies are necessarily bad or that they have no legitimate use that can bring great joy to society. The CD player, for example, does have genuine benefits over the record player in certain cases. We should deliver new technologies to the places where they are needed, with the intention of enhancing lives by solving genuine problems or providing genuine enjoyment if this can be done at no disproportionate cost to the rest of the world. The problem with the capitalist system is that innovation exists within it simply for the purpose of making money, and of controlling the populace to ensure that they continue to consume more and more, often needlessly. Technology is not created for its own sake or for the sake of the good that it can do: though there may well be other motivating factors in its development including a genuine desire by technologists to somehow improve the world, technologies are only invested in by the companies with the wealth to make ideas a mainstream reality if it can be shown that there is money to be made. For, in the capitalist world, a business that does not make money is not sustainable. It is this overriding motivation for profit that leads to waste, excess and the mistreatment of new technologies.

It has been argued that were it not for capitalism and the inequalities it entails new technologies with the potential to do much good would be stifled. There needed to be rich and wealthy people, the argument goes, to buy the first televisions, CD players and mobile telephones to motivate the invention of these products. Would not a socialist world be one of stasis and banality, paralysed by a lack of incentive to invent? In truth, it would not, for the simple reason that human inventiveness is not something that has to be bought. We do not require money or the profit motive to come up with new ideas and solutions to our problems. The first mobile telephones could have been created without capitalism, because such ideas themselves are not the products of capitalism – where capitalism, money and the need for investment comes in is in the widespread adoption of certain profitable technologies and the rejection of others deemed not to be profitable.

Under a socialist system of equality, it is true that there would be no rich class to become early adopters of the mobile telephone. But would this be a bad thing? Surely the earliest adopters of a new technology should not be those who happen to have enough money to buy it, but rather those who are in need of it most. Under a socialist system, there would be no incentive to encourage everyone to have a mobile telephone, and many might not end up with one at all. But nor would that matter, because it would be those with a genuine need for each technology that would have it, and nobody else would be any the worse for not having it. With a technology such as the CD player, which nobody fundamentally needs but which can contribute to shared cultural experiences that many people can certainly gain enjoyment and purpose from and which are an important part of human life, everyone would have access to the technology but that would not – in contrast to the capitalist system – require everyone to have their own copy. Very few people need to have constant access to a CD player to gain enjoyment from it, so it is a waste for everyone to have their own device when instead there could be a smaller number of communally-owned devices within each community, which each person would be able to access according to need. Likewise, most people may only really need a mobile telephone to make contact with others when going on a journey that involves some danger or uncertainty; sharing a few such devices to be used in such circumstances would be much more efficient than everyone possessing their own.

This logical approach, which allows us to venerate our resources gratefully and use them only as we have genuine need, does not preclude invention, change or the enjoyment of all the benefits of culture. Furthermore, it frees the individual from the need to constantly 'keep up with the Joneses', replacing their own goods all the time and having to worry about the maintenance and security of those goods. It releases them from control by capitalist advertisements and the constant presence of unnatural and not always welcome gadgets about their person all the time – for who amongst mobile telephone users does not complain at having to be always at their device's beck and call? – and allows them to live in a less polluted, less materialistic world. In a socialist society, the old saying holds true: 'necessity is the mother of invention'. Under capitalism, invention is the mother of necessity: the manufacturer actively persuades the public to buy new products that they do not need. The long-term costs for society – in terms of the environment and mental well-being in particular – are not taken into account in this calculation. Hence the abuse of new technology, the over-exploitation of resources and the brainwashing of society to 'buy, buy, buy': all are symptoms of capitalist control by innovation.

3.5 Capitalist Terminology

We can see the spread of capitalism even in the language that is nowadays used in day-to-day life. Countries become 'economies' as though their very purpose is to produce; people become 'consumers'; and workers, in a most vulgar tone of indifferent exploitation, are even reportedly termed 'human capital' by some businesses. We do not hear of people performing good services for their own sakes, but rather of 'social enterprises', under the presumption that such services will provide some form of profit for the individuals concerned: charity becomes a business in today's world. And so the

3. A Troubled Society

chains grow tighter, as everything in the world around us becomes permanently associated with money and with profit-making through the very words we use to describe it. It is a form of thought-control, infusing into the very core of the mind the idea that all things in life exist to be bought or sold.

As human beings, we remember things only when we have the words to describe them, so essential is language to our function as a species. How powerful, then, will such capitalist terminology be in shaping the future viewpoint of the young? Of course, very few people are sufficiently gullible to be entirely entranced by capitalist thought simply through the words they are taught. But these words are, nevertheless, an influential factor. We none of us are immune; searching through this very document would most likely yield the discovery of words or phrases originally invented or twisted in under capitalist auspices in the search for profit, which only goes to illustrate the extent to which capitalism has reached into almost every corner of all our lives.

A language is not a stationary entity, and there can be no question of freezing out from our discourse all those terms related to capitalism, in the hope of freeing ourselves from its perverse influence on our decisions. But we should reject such impersonal terms as 'social capital' and 'human capital' outright, as these phrases imply a degree of expendability afforded only to slaves, which under capitalism we are, though we ought not to be. It will be a sign of progress towards the more caring, friendly and free society, if we find the rest of the terms, if not displaced (for, once in common usage, it is only natural that a particular word or phrase not totally abhorrent will remain for convenience rather than as a sign of political persuasion), become outnumbered by phrases borrowed from cooperative endeavours. 'Comrade' might perhaps outnumber 'consumer', and 'industry' and 'enterprise' lose out to 'cooperation' or 'service'.

3.6 Living to Consume

One of the most prominent hallmarks of twentieth-century capitalism has been the phenomenon of consumerism. Unlike materialism, consumerism does not result from an in-built desire to obtain goods, but is rather a novel device invented for the creation of profit, having as its most unwelcome outcome the treating of individuals solely as 'consumers'. Of course, humans always have and always will consume, but consumerism goes beyond the satisfaction of our natural needs to make the using of resources – in the form of goods endlessly churned out by millions of factories – the sole purpose of existence. Consumption becomes, under this system, an ends in itself, rather than the means by which we are able to live, as it was for our hunter-gatherer ancestors. All of this is encouraged by the constant employment, furthermore, of advertisements in all their guises, designed primarily to convince members of the public into buying items they would otherwise have no desire or need for.

Consumerism is based on the idea that every member of society, having earned or received money by some method or another, will cause that capitalistic society to function by spending that money in shops or directly paying businesses, hence passing on the money to the employees of other companies, who go on to do the same. If, for some reason, we were to stop purchasing goods and services, for all of which there is a charge, of course, under capitalism, but leave the money where it was, this form of society would collapse. Without continual trade, there would be no 'capital' to pass on to the workers, who would hence stop working, and the goods and services they provided would cease to be available.

Consumerism and capitalism, hence, go hand in hand, because every person is regarded not as somebody with their own traits and personality, but as a user of resources, a buyer of services, who has a particular propensity to part with their money more readily for some goods and services than for others, and can be specifically targeted and encouraged to do so. This is where we see the more individual-oriented idea of advertising, made increasingly possible by the internet, arise: if a 'consumer' is particularly gullible to a particular way of presenting a product, or towards a particular product that a given company sells, that company can profit by targeting the consumer and playing on their particular likes. The flashy signs, the catchy tunes: they do appeal, but we must remember that they are placed before our eyes and ears for perverse purposes. Surely there is nothing wrong with the particular art employed by companies wishing to obtain our custom; it is the way in which this art is abused to entice and provoke the public, like sheep, into supporting those companies, that is unnerving.

The problem with consumerism is two-fold. First, there is the environmental impact of treating everybody as a 'consumer', that must 'consume' as much as possible: we are encouraged to spend money on things we do not need, and, once we realise this, and that the goods have failed to fill the gaps of longing created by the endless capitalist propaganda in all the media, these items are sold on or thrown into landfill sites. These days, of course, recycling is more widespread, but most goods are not completely recyclable, a large quantity of resources must be wasted, even if they are, to produce and recycle them, and the end products of this recycling chain may not be of the same quality as those that were begun with. It is far better not to produce unnecessary goods at all, than to recycle them into even less useful ones.

For items that are truly useful - the garden tool or kitchen appliance - we are encouraged not to share but to each buy our own, so that more money is spent, more people kept employed in resource extraction and production - often in dire conditions on the other side of the world – and the rich companies get richer, than had we instead lived as a community and pooled our resources. The whole system keeps working to guzzle as many resources as possible. Worse, products are often designed not to last as long as they could, so that we are attracted by their lower prices in the first place, and have to endlessly replace them as they break again and again. 'Buy cheap, buy twice' is often true, but, alas, so can be 'buy expensive, buy twice', as more expensive items are more likely to look nicer than to last longer; it is not in the companies' interest for their customers never to have to replace the item. It is, though, in society's interest as a whole, which is why consumerism acts against our best interests.

This leads us on to the second ill: that consumerism purposefully manipulates and disadvantages the welfare of people in our society. We are each left cut off from others in a ruthless capitalist world, blindly buying for ourselves rather than sharing, caring about goods more than good actions and the sheer pleasure of existing for its own sake. We are encouraged never to be satisfied, ever to hanker after more and better, and this is simply not good for our health: look only to the obesity epidemic to find an example of this. It was caused by consumerism. Consumerism does not care about public health. Consumerism does not care about landfill sites full of spoiled and tossed-away goods. Consumerism does not care about the reckless burning of oil and coal. We could have lived, more happily, though not as monetarily wealthy, without all these ills of the twentieth century, if only we did not cast ourselves into its cold and careless hands.

3.7 Supply & Demand

Over the decades and centuries of capitalist domination in this and other parts of the 'western' world, aspects of life in which there is enjoyment – in one sense or another, this constitutes a 'demand' – have come to be controlled by larger and larger corporations, whose primary motive is to procure profit by supplying products to meet than demand. But it is not enough to satisfy the greed for ever more money, production and consumption inherent in these capitalist entities, for existing demands to be met. More and more, the fears of a minority group – fears relating to illness, appearance, reputation, nutrition, childcare and all sorts of other things – have been exported to become fears of the masses so that profit can be made in selling goods and services that allay these fears. Capitalism creates demand artificially, then its proponents and profiteers claim that it is essential to retain the capitalist system of innovation in order to supply what is needed to meet that demand.

Once, though there were great and terrible threats to our existence – threats from disease, famine and calamity that technological innovation has indeed helped to allay –

and least our leisure time and entertainment were communal and free. The stories we told each other, the music we made and the ancient works of art we produced were shared creations. They may have been simple, and may not have been easy to spread beyond our immediate neighbours, but once publically aired they were free to be used by all as they pleased, much like the 'traditional' music we still use with no known author. Meanwhile, goods such as foodstuffs were procured locally and sold by individual retailers, whose purpose was to fulfil a vital role of distribution in society that was both wanted and needed. This was done without any desire for 'growth' or expansion of their own small outlet into other regions or other lines of business. In short, the things that we did with our lives were our own, as a community. They were not controlled by big business.

This was the case before the capitalist revolution of the nineteenth century, and indeed, to some extent, survived in some sectors until the commercialisation of capitalism occurred during the mid-twentieth century, before which time the pursuit of profit by creating demand to supply was confined to a greater degree to the realms of heavy industry and the bastions of the financial heart of the City. But now, commercialisation of all aspects of ordinary people's lives has gathered pace considerably, such that in nearly every sphere of need-fulfilment and entertainment, competition has emerged between opposing brands eager to supply often invented demands. Our 'needs' today are greater than they were before – we 'need' electricity, 'need' mobile telephones, 'need' cars and toys and exotic foods – because we have been persuaded that they are necessary to the attainment of a healthy and happy existence.

It is fear that is at the heart of this manipulative practice. We are made, through advertisements and cultural shifts, to fear that we will fall ill if we do not spray our homes with marketed disinfectants, that we will die on the roads if we walk or drive smaller cars, that we will lose touch with everyone and get lost if we don't have a mobile telephone, that we will smell or look ugly if we don't use all the shower gels, deodorants, makeup and cosmetics that their manufacturers are eager to sell. Sometimes, we have real needs that are exaggerated by interested parties; and other times the fears are completely invented and the advertised products actually cause harm. For example, the use of anti-bacterial sprays on surfaces in the home destroys the microbes that we naturally need and damages our immune systems, making it more likely that we will become ill.

The result of all this can be an unhealthy excess of one commodity or another, to the detriment of our minds and bodies and the planet as a whole, because it is in the interests of certain players' profits to convince us to purchase things in excess of what we should otherwise desire. When it comes to food, the effect can be particularly disastrous. Rather than aiming for health and nutrition, as any responsible society should do, capitalism encourages us to buy more food than we need, wasting some of it outright and becoming obese, then tries to sell us diets and 'healthy' or 'natural' alternatives that are not necessarily either of these things but are usually more expensive. But the pervasiveness of the control of large corporations is incredible: we spend all our leisure-time eating the foods, watching the films, using the computers and 'smart' telephones and games consoles that they want to sell us, not creating our own entertainment, because it is in their interests that we do so. Our very mind-sets have been manipulated: we have been indoctrinated into the myth that making and spending as much money as possible is the measure of 'success' in life, and frightened into surrendering our lives to consumption.

This situation can only occur because these companies – be they supermarkets, clothes manufacturers or film studios – are so large in the first place. Through out-competition, mergers and take-overs, all of which are encouraged by the cruel and cold rules of capitalist 'development', smaller groups that might remain connected to the needs of their local environs tend to be stamped out by larger ones, until an increasingly small number of companies obtains an increasingly large control over all the things that we hold dear, because they, not our friends and neighbours, become our suppliers.

We may live under a democratic political system in the United Kingdom, but allowing small groups of companies to control and manipulate each aspect of our culture is not in any sense democratic. It is they – retailers and producers – that decide which books we ought to read or which films we ought to see, through what they advertise to us to read or watch. This amounts to a system of control somewhat akin to a dictatorship by which a few individuals dictate the flow of ideas and resources and control the implementation of new technologies within society to suit their own ends. It differs in one respect: the corporations themselves are not single individuals, but groups of employees who are the collective victims as much as the collective perpetrators of such perversions of their own freedom that companies such as their own employers create.

Often, the retail workers in large chain shops or restaurant groups find themselves working well below the 'living wage' and unable to progress to better-paid positions, which leaves them without the ability to pay for their needs, such as access to the same quality of food, shelter and amenities as anybody else. Under the capitalist state, these needs are not automatically provided by the state, and these workers are therefore forced to scrape by on menial jobs that they would often rather not have. It is only because capitalism has been tempered by a sprinkling of socialist sympathy that the Minimum Wage exists at all to partly counter this. Profit-hungry large companies appear to take the view that their lower-level employees comprise the likes of part-time student workers whose working conditions, being temporary, need little improvement, even when many of the workers are actually employed for a much longer period of time than this. With so much of our production of clothes and other goods exported to foreign lands, it is no wonder that there are few other, more meaningful, jobs available, and so these workers are forced to perpetuate the dominance of the large retailers and the shop-centric throw-away-and-replace culture we now live in by staffing their shop floors. At the same time, staff pay needs to remain low in order to compete with rival stores. A driving down of wages, prices and quality of goods and the creation of a cheap and nasty plasticised and unsatisfactory world is the result.

Of course, were small-scale local businesses, managed democratically by an arm of government under the direction of and accountable to society as a whole to replace the large competing corporations currently trusted with the provision of so many of our goods and services, such difficulties as the need for 'competitiveness' would disappear with the need to make a profit at all. All that good businesses really need to do is provide the goods and services to those who need them, in the most effective and environmentally caring way possible, taking advantage of any innovations that are conducive to these ends.

Were such a shift to occur, we should also do away with the ruthless advertising, branding and waste of the sort currently used by the larger producers and retailers. These, desperate to secure custom and preserve their own reputations ahead of their rivals both large and small, have invested considerable amounts of money (that small businesses cannot afford) in building up public images – brands – that cause potential customers to choose them over other, cheaper or better goods providers, simply because of the aura that surrounds their logo. This aura might be attached to a celebrity endorsement, a positive concept that has been associated to the company through advertising, or the sponsorship of some particular event or even television programme. Such sponsorship, itself the subject of competition between rivals, can result in the event becoming hijacked to better suit the purposes of the company: placards sporting the sponsor's logos are often attached to stadia in sporting events, for example, even though these benefit neither the players nor the spectators. These placards have existed for many decades, arising out of the company logos painted onto factories from the nineteenth century onwards, but now billboards and placards can come to dominate in some areas and at some events with which the company has no real connection, and plaster our streets and buildings that should be filled with the creations of our own imaginations, not exploitative jibberish designed to make us spend.

At the same time, most companies do not apparently believe in the oft-quoted maxim 'no publicity is bad publicity'. Although some major advertisers have sought to 'capitalise' on the anti-ad backlash that has arisen in recent times amongst sections of the public that are all too aware of the motives of the companies claiming to be providing only a positive influence but in reality seeking only profit, by producing adverts that parody themselves, they are always eager to avoid the non-controlled use of the very brands and logos that they have designed to lodge deep in the minds of the beholders. These corporations want to have things both ways. They want to become integral and controlling parts of people's lives, but at the same time they don't want their particular brand name to be used without the permission by those same people in public. When clips from popular songs are incorporated into websites – or even shared with other web users – or a company's name is explicitly mentioned in a critical piece of journalism (as in the famous 'McLibel' case lodged by McDonalds against critics of its fast food) they are quick to sue for copyright or trademark infringement or for libel, preventing the free discussion of what has become an integral part of society – that is, the dominance of big businesses over our lives. This is done in a thoroughly undemocratic manner, but these corporations have the money – and hence the power – to do it.

Many of these advertisements and branding schemes are designed to distract the 'consumer' from what they really want or need from the product and direct them towards what is most likely to sell it. Special offers in supermarkets often make out that the lowest price is the best, and that hence the best product the person can buy is the item on special offer, even if they would prefer at heart another product. Bags of satsumas are notoriously 'buy one get one free', so that the buyer sometimes ends up getting too many and having to waste half of them. The supermarket makes such offers because it does not care about food waste – it wants people to buy as much food as possible – but wants to build up an image of itself as a place where food is available cheaply: one gets twice as many satsumas for the same price. But food should cost as much as it costs to produce it, including the wages of all those involved and the running of the machinery required. It's as simple as that. There is no need to drive down the cost price and run farmers out of business: if nutritious food is too expensive for people to buy, they are evidently not being paid enough, because this is one of our most basic needs. The gimmick of the 'special offer' and driving down of prices should be relegated to the past.

The way in which supermarkets manipulate us to decide for us what we shall buy, and how much of it, is illustrative of the wider trend in our world for control, not by the will of the inhabitants of the planet, but by that of a small group of large corporations that have fewer and fewer actual employees. They do not provide proper jobs to the people of the countries in which they sell their products, but use all too often what amounts to slave labour to produce branded goods cheaply abroad, at great environmental and social costs. These costs they distance from themselves with tireless campaigns to brainwash us in the richer parts of the globe into thinking of them as gleaming, untarnished and attractive, hoping that we will fall in worship before their altars of consumption. Any catastrophe, slavery and destruction in the poorer countries that produce the goods that retailers in the rich world go on to sell are blamed on the local companies that the multinationals have contracted. It is true, indeed, that the western companies do not appear to directly condone any of these ills. But nor do they take proper steps to prevent them, hoping instead that the horrors of the sweatshops will remain hidden, and that it will not come to light that it is their custom and demand for ever lower prices that keep them open and operating under such poor conditions.

The goods themselves – from designer trainers to plastic toys to computers and mobile telephones – are often far from essential to the wellbeing of the importing nations' citizens, who have been persuaded of the need to purchase them only by relentless advertising campaigns and the fostering of a societal attitude that encourages spiralling consumption. By allowing such large companies to proliferate, be it in the realm of entertainment, food, clothing, transport or any other aspect of our collective experience, we therefore not only allow them to dominate and rule over our own lives through the slavery of consumerism: we also create huge damage to people and places far away from ourselves, for no good reason. This, surely, can only be a very great harm to us all.

3.8 A State of Inequality

Ensconced within their towers of wealth and lives of material luxury, and with minds fixed on markets rather than the well-being of mankind, it is quite possible for the powerful in society – those who are well-educated, well-fed, and (most importantly where capitalism reigns) making and spending lots of money – to forget that there are many thousands, indeed millions, even in a supposedly 'rich' country such as the UK who lack what they need to live healthy and happy lives. In the capitalist mind-set, those who suffer lack are considered blameworthy for their own position, as though they are homeless or hungry by choice or jobless through sheer laziness or lack of natural ability. That anybody has failed to 'get on in life' by misfortune is discounted; it is regarded as their own fault, and that the rich man has more than the poor is put to his credit. The rich may take some glee in showing off his wealth by giving some tiny proportion of it to charity from time to time, but he is not expected to abandon his position of superiority by redistributing his wealth so that all may be on a monetary par. Thus we find that whilst some dwell in abundance to the point of waste, others live in desperate want.

This ramp of material inequality is not wholly unintentional. It keeps the wheels of capitalism turning, and comes partly in consequence of the capitalist notion that life's purpose is ruthless competition for money, which can buy its slaves not only luxuries but also power with which to accrue still more money. To drive the capitalist economy, people must be motivated by the desire to outcompete others – to work harder, play harder, produce more and consume more – to become a more 'successful' person than others, and to be envious of those who have more material wealth. This inevitably leads to a hierarchy whereby the rich competitively invest to get richer and the poor lack the resources to prevent themselves falling further into poverty; and all the while wealth is sucked up as if by some giant, energy-hungry vacuum cleaner, from the many at the bottom towards the few at the top. The poorest sink into debt; the richest reap the harvest.

Hierarchies have existed since the dawn of civilisation, but never has inequality been rising so swiftly, cruelly and destructively as it is today. Only the charity of private individuals and what remains of the welfare state – each of these being counter-capitalist elements within a largely capitalist framework – prevent mass starvation and death. The irony is that, in spite of this material inequality, people on both ends of the scale are equally unlikely to possess what is truly important: a peaceful, loving and fulfilling life. Such a life is not dependent on material riches, but it does require both basic resources that the poor often lack, and an attitude to life rarely found amongst the rich. In a world enslaved to the god of money, the poor are prevented from obtaining contentment because they lack basic nutrition, health and shelter and are made to envy the rich; the rich, likewise, are not content because they are blinded by their wealth and possessions, obsessed with hoarding and multiplying their money and with the competition to appear successful in each other's eyes. It would be better for everyone if access to material things of importance was made equal and money was taken out of the picture altogether.

A concrete sign of the extreme inequality in our society is to be seen in the sheer numbers of homeless, unemployed and desperate people one can encounter on the streets of any city today. The amount of food waste we produce and the number of homes standing empty in some parts of the country (currently estimated at ten for every homeless family) are clear indications that we have the resources to give everyone the shelter and sustenance they need; why, then, should any be forced to go without through lack of money? It used to be the case that most homeless people cited relationship breakdown as the cause of their calamity: unable to live any longer with their partner, friend or family they have had to sleep on the streets. Now, however, the so-called 'financial crisis' that has entailed such unnecessary cut-backs of government support for the health and welfare of the people it represents has meant that most homeless people are homeless simply because they could no longer afford to pay the rent. Houses are being viewed as property assets instead of as homes, and are being denied to the people that really need them.

Whilst families with children are quickly identified when they become homeless and, mercifully, found a place to live, the suffering of single people and couples who cannot earn enough money to meet rising rents and mortgages is apparently ignored. Ridiculous policies such as the need to prove a 'connection' to the local area before the authority there will help you to find somewhere to live and cuts to homeless support groups prevent this problem from being addressed. Heartless measures such as 'public protection' orders that give police the power to arrest people for sleeping rough – as though they had any choice in the matter – further compound it. It should not matter where a person is from or what work they did or did not do yesterday. Every person has a right, today, to a place of privacy, security and shelter if such can possibly be provided. To leave anyone to sleep rough – unless it is their genuine and well-reasoned desire to do so – is a violation of this right on the part of the government, given that it has the resources to satisfy their needs. Authorities, as it stands, are all too ready to spend resources putting up fences and evicting rough sleepers from public ground or the private land of the rich, and yet they fail to provide the poor their basic needs, which must be a much more urgent priority.

An important cause of the persistence of inequality is the attitude that pervades in a capitalist society, that the rich are praiseworthy for their own 'success' and the poor blameworthy for their own 'failure', as though a person becomes poor through sheer laziness or stupidity and that it is their own fault if they do not have what they need to survive. This mantra may give the rich comfort in their own prestige, but it entirely ignores the fact that we are all as much the product of our environment as of our genes, and that we have no control over either of these – at least in the most formative years of our lives. Our 'success' in any endeavour is as much attributable to good fortune and the assistance of others who have taught or aided us as it is to our own ability to make the most of the opportunities that fortune provides.

If we take a 'good' life to be one in which we are able to take up a fulfilling role within society, to have all we need to live and to be able to fully engage in human cultural and natural pursuits that bring us joy, recent studies suggest that the likeliness that a person will have a 'good' life is almost entirely determined by their upbringing as a child before they go to school. Primary school teachers can tell with some confidence, even within a few weeks of a year-group's arrival, which of the four- or five-year-old children will go on to be the most 'successful' in terms of entering a well-respected profession, living in relative comfort and studying at university; and which are more likely to face years of unemployment or even turn to crime. The ability to focus and engage sufficiently to do well at school is something that is learned before the pupils' arrival, with the key components in their 'success' throughout life consisting of a close bond with their mother or a mother figure, a fun and engaging learning environment at home and the reception of genuine love and concern from parents and carers in the first few years of life. If these essential ingredients have been lacking – if they have been neglected because their parents were not loving or were so poor that they had to work long hours rather than spending time with their children – the person that has had such a disadvantaged start can hardly be held to blame.

To address inequality in our society, we therefore need to stop regarding the unemployed, homeless or otherwise downcast as somehow inferior or less worthy of the good things in life than anybody else, and must ensure that everybody – regardless of their capacity or opportunity to work – has all the basic things that they need to live in health and happiness. It is imperative that every parent be given sufficient time away from their usual work to do that very important task of bringing a child up in a loving and educative environment, and they must be helped to do so. Caring facilities need to be put in place to provide for children whose parents are simply not interested in caring for them properly, so that for at least some of the time they can have the love and support of a mother figure. In this way, everyone can be given the best possible start in life and be in the best possible position to take advantage of their natural abilities and the opportunities that life affords them. Everyone has something to give, and should be put in a position ripe for them to be able to use their talents well.

Of course, early upbringing isn't the whole of the story, and those attending a good school will tend to do better than those attending a poor one, although within both schools the hierarchy of achievement will be largely determined by the quality of pre-school upbringing. Hence, we should strive for excellent standards of schooling for all children. The very fact that parents who can afford to in many cases choose to send their children to private schools shows that many of us acknowledge that the quality of schooling will have a big influence on our children's prospects and, in a competitive capitalist world, that we try to put them at a competitive advantage by sending them to private schools instead of state schools that we consider inadequate. Surely, though, it would be better to strive for a good education for all people, not just for our own children, recognising that we are all dependent on one another and that a good education for everyone benefits everyone in a cooperative society.

Therefore, to remove the spectre of inequality school standards must be brought up to the highest level in state schools and a separate private system abolished altogether. Furthermore, our schools should enable those whose particular talents are for practical crafts to flourish just as well as those more suited to academia, and the present push for everyone 'successful' to go to university ought to be abandoned, in that it makes people falling into the former category, though they are just as valuable to society, feel somehow inferior because their work does not require a university degree. Once everybody has access to good education that enables them to be their best, and everyone is praised for those skills that they do have instead of being belittled for 'failing' academic examinations, and society values and rewards all professions that are useful equally, inequalities in adulthood may begin to dissolve.

A profound inequality of care is also prevalent between different age-groups in our society. It is the elderly through whose efforts we were all brought up and the infrastructure we take for granted was, largely, built or maintained. But, once they have become too frail in body or mind to look after themselves, they are sadly often not taken into the loving care of younger generations but in most instances swept away into 'care homes' to while away their twilight years. In this way, the burden of looking after our elders is offloaded from the busily producing and consuming younger generations and onto those few people who are paid specifically to 'care'. The elderly are put 'out of sight, out of mind' from most people for most of the time, cast into a lonely existence under the care of strangers because their children or younger friends do not have the time to look after them.

The ability of the elderly to live fulfilling lives in which their actions have purpose for others is thereby greatly diminished, and their capacity for independence inevitably declines further. Left with nothing to do but sit in a chair all day, soon that is all that a person will be able to do. Capitalism is cruel: these were the same people who, in their earlier years, were busily satisfying its demand for growth through production and consumption, with the false promise of an easy life in retirement based on the material wealth they had accrued. But the truth is that such material things as money in the bank and goods in the house are not sufficient to maintain a good life. It is relationships that are central to our well-being, and, isolated in care-homes and devoid of the loving care of family and friends, retirement becomes a banal nightmare. Once we are no longer able to work productively, capitalism takes no account of our former loyalties: we are cast into the same heap of irrelevance as the younger homeless, unemployed and handicapped who are likewise deemed unworthy of attention.

The solution to this age-related inequality is, of course, to keep elderly relatives and friends in the centre – not at the periphery – of younger people's lives. They should be cared for in the homes of relatives or by the communities of which they, before the onset of infirmity, formed a more active part. Surely, it should be with gratitude and thankfulness for all they gave in their lives that we treat our elders, and we too will gain from loving them as equals through receipt of their love in return, and, additionally, their wisdom born of long experience. The elderly have a lot to teach the young. Furthermore, by failing to create systems and customs of care for our elders, we only condemn ourselves to decades of disrespect when we become old. Capitalism tries to fool us into thinking that youthful productivity will never end, if only we compete hard enough to stay 'on top' and maintain our material comforts. But in truth we shall all, eventually, wither and perish: there is no 'elixir of life'.

Yet our last years should, in a just, rewarding and caring society, be made to be our best. It is not the fault of individual younger people that prevents this from being the case today: they are forced to move far afield from their families or to work long hours by the capitalist demand for productivity and a failure to properly, equally distribute useful work on the part of society as a whole. For society today doesn't recognise that caring for one's elderly parents, relatives and friends is, like child-care, one of the most important aspects of anybody's work. Herein lies the rub of inequality: while money reigns supreme, doing jobs that earn us money is at the heart of our waking lives. If, instead, care for the joy of other beings is placed at the centre of our lives, everyone will be treated with equal respect, we will recognise that time is best used in serving our neighbours, and inequality will vanish.

Myths of Equality

How is it that such a state of rampant inequality as we currently endure has been allowed to develop, beginning its most rapid rise in the 1980s and not just persisting but continuing to strengthen today? How can it be that the rich and fortunate are allowed to make more and more profit even as the poorest go entirely without? One reason is that we are fooled, collectively, into believing that inequality is not on the rise but is actually falling. Even as what we might call 'hard' inequality – that is, economic inequality that means that power and access to resources are not equally shared, causing some to suffer drudgery, unemployment, jobs that they despise, hunger or homelessness – rises, we are distracted from noticing this by a fall in what would then be termed 'soft' inequality.

The gap between the materialistically rich and poor – the 'haves' and 'have nots' of the capitalist world – is rising. But other, traditionally stronger, divisions between different 'sorts' of people is falling, so that we are made content and blinded from this travesty. Inequality of the latter kind, though we here refer to it as 'soft', is by no means to be downplayed. It is in itself an unjustifiable and undesirable travesty that is to the hurt of all mankind. But it is 'soft' in that its most debilitating effects are indirect: it is but one possible cause of 'hard' inequality, which is the sort that causes the more material harm. It is 'hard' inequality that is hardwired into the capitalist way of doing things – it is essential for the capitalist system to function – and is precipitated directly by capitalism itself. Getting rid of its 'soft' progenitors will not eradicate it.

Soft inequality entails prejudice based not on economic or meritocratic grounds, but rather upon arbitrary categorisations of humans that ought not to affect their abilities or opportunities at all. This sort of inequality was rampant in pre-capitalist times, but since it is not necessary for – and indeed runs counter to – the production of profit, capitalism has not stood in the way of its fall. So, over the past decades and centuries, we have witnessed a decline in gender inequality (women now have the vote and males and females are represented in all kinds of jobs, even if the latter are still under-represented in some areas), 'racial' inequality (explicit discrimination on the grounds of ethnicity is illegal and heavily frowned upon; racialist political movements are condemned by the general populace) and sexual inequality (in the UK at least people are free to express their sexual orientation and marriages between homosexuals are now legal). Such inequalities as these spring from long-held negative prejudices, often born of over-zealous religiosity or ignorance, that have declined with the spread of enlightened education and cultural mixing but have not been entirely eradicated.

Only occasionally was this decline in spite of capitalism and the pursuit of profit – abolishing the slave trade, for example, lost slavers a lot of money in the short-term – but more often it has been encouraged by it. If women are allowed to work and compete for high-paying jobs, they will be able to produce extra goods and services to sell, so the economy – and the wealth of the richest – will grow. If they are allowed to buy things of their own fancy and accord, there will be an increase in consumption and purchasing. At the same time, women are encouraged to adopt the 'masculine' trait of ruthless competitiveness when they rise to traditionally male-oriented positions of authority in business, and people from other cultures are encouraged to supress their traditional practices and enter into the profit-making capitalist mind-set when they are assimilated into the capitalist culture. Hence, even as different groups are put upon an equal footing, under capitalism the diversity between these groups is simultaneously diminished. Discrimination against women, homosexuals and ethnic or religious minorities is certainly immoral and its decline should be welcomed. But it is only because such discrimination is unprofitable that capitalism has encouraged its alleviation, and the means by which discrimination has declined has incurred negative side-effects such as homogenisation.

Meritocratic discrimination – that is, judging people on the basis of their previous monetary achievements and their perceived 'worth' to society according to a particular capitalistic means of measuring worth – is, on the other hand, profitable, and is therefore encouraged. Hence, the wealth of the rich is allowed to grow even as the poor languish in ever-increasing disability caused by their relative lack of power and material wealth in a materialistic world.

4. Respecting the Planet

If there remains any doubt in our minds about the need to act immediately so as to reorient society in a direction more conducive to human life, it is dispelled by the imminent environmental crises that threaten to engulf us if we continue as we are. Let us be under no illusion, however common it may appear to be, that environmental issues are somehow less important than social or even economic ones, in that they affect 'other species' – the polar bears that risk extinction, the beautiful forests that are cut down – more than ourselves. No myth could be further from the truth. We must always remember that we are part of the natural world, and our wellbeing – from the refreshing sight of a natural landscape to the very oxygen we must constantly breathe to live – is utterly dependent on the environment around us. Greenhouse gasses will disrupt the climate to which we are accustomed. A world devoid of forests and the great diversity of species it currently hosts will be one of mental depravity for ourselves. It is truly our own habitat that we destroy when we concrete over the plants and drive out the other animals.

Furthermore, the economy and society are intimately interlinked with the environment: neither could exist without it, and the problems endemic in each cannot be solved without considering the environmental resources on which they depend. Therefore, not only are environmental issues not niche ones, but they in fact should – uniquely perhaps – be of prime concern in every single decision we make. The environment itself is the most important consideration we have to make when attempting to improve the standard of living of Earth's inhabitants. Yet, under the yoke of capitalist exploitation, we continue to destroy and degrade this vital foundation of our own existence. In this chapter, we shall explore some of the ways in which the animals and plants around us are abused by humanity, and attempt to suggest a way to transcend current conventions and produce a more sustainable civilisation, a theme to be taken up in greater detail in later chapters.

4.1 The Industrial Abuse of Animals

They are and always have been around us: those fantastic feathered wonders gliding easily through the air. Long has mankind dreamt of soaring like the birds, which freely flock over all the Earth by virtue of that chance mutation that first empowered some hopping, fluttering creature to spread its wings and fly. Many, many ancient millennia has it taken for this marvellous group to spread and colonise, diversify and flourish in myriad beautiful forms. Yet in the sudden flash that is ten thousand years of human civilisation the happy freedom of the billions of birds has been eclipsed by a cruel, unnatural exploitation of truly astronomical numbers of individuals. Fifty billion – some seven times our own population – is the astounding number of such souls humanity condemns to captivity and death every year, most having suffered a cruel and protracted demise that stretches across their entire lives. And that is just the birds: even a cursory glance at our society will reveal that much of what is eaten, and many of the human-crafted products that are used involve the suffering of billions more animals: the pigs, cattle and sheep brought into existence only to be fattened and killed in their millions; the mice, rats and primates cruelly made to endure the painful side-effects of concoctions we invent with the hope of extending our own lives or sometimes deliberately afflicted with unbearable mutations or diseases as part of medical research. Curing diseases that cause pain is admirable, but not when the development of that cure creates yet more pain and suffering. In future chapters, we shall explore both of these forms of animal abuse and ways in which they can be avoided.

But how have we come to this state of unimpeded abuse of our fellow beings? It was not always thus: before the industrialisation of agriculture, animals that are used for food, though usually domesticated, were not kept indoors under cramped conditions nor forced to reproduce in numbers far exceeding a naturally sustainable population. Many people knew intimately and cared for the animals that they used and lived alongside, and these animals had an existence that went beyond simply fattening and dying; they could live amongst nature, at least for a while. There was no need to genetically modify pigs or chickens at any rate greater than that achievable through selective breeding, because the animals lived in healthy environs protected by their natural defences against disease. Only when man became greedy for constant access to meat – producing so much that some can even go to waste today, rendering the animals' suffering of no avail at all – did he devise more intensive techniques. It is not surprising that when we come to treat animals like crops in monoculture fields we find them suffering from pestilences not seen before. The solution is not to mess with their genes, but rather to care for them in a more ethical manner.

The reason for the unempathetic state of affairs that has arisen between man and beast lies, perhaps, in the distance that nowadays separates the majority of people from the many, many animate beings that have lived and died in order that their meat might be produced or their drugs and cosmetics developed. With the rise of consumerism, the flesh of living beings has become just another commodity to be bought and sold, as cheaply as possible as far as the buyer is concerned, and as profitably as possible from the point of view of the seller. Animals, in other words, have fallen victim to money. When, amidst the supermarket shelves, a customer sees the neatly packaged and processed pieces of meat, they do not see the animals that lie behind them, the lives that have been lived and cut short, the blood that has been spilled. No more is there a partnership between man and nature: now mankind exploits and abuses beasts, dismembering and pulverising what had been living, breathing creatures until, as the 'horse meat scandal' of 2013 so plainly illustrated, it is not possible even to tell the species of the animals whose lives were lost in making the end product. So it is that the continued suffering, and the constant cull, is lost amidst the day-to-day lives of a population for whom the flesh of thousands is just another harmless product on the shelf. These 'consumers' mean no harm, but they do not see what suffering the profit-making businesses they buy from are inflicting. They have been blinded by the capitalists, and made not to see the atrocity that lies behind their meat.

A dangerous mind-set seems thus to have arisen with regard to other species, putting the value of not only a human life but, indeed, of human comfort above that of the lives of other animals. Somehow, the fact that other species are less intelligent than ourselves has developed into the notion that we alone are 'conscious', and we alone can truly experience reality. But, truly, we are but part of the amazing panoply of life that is the magnificent creation we see all around us. We, like all the other living beings on this unique site of habitability in a wide and lifeless expanse of space, owe our existence to the amazing creative force that is evolution, all springing ultimately from the same primitive ancestor and representing but the latest branches to bud upon the tree of life. Were one of us to travel back across the eons a few hundred million years, they would see the ancient ancestors of the animals, worms and arthropods swimming through the seas. Somewhere amongst them would be the ancestor of humanity: the progenitor to all mammalian life, indeed, carrying out its daily activity unaware entirely of the future life-forms, in all their splendid variety, that it would father. Look upon your ancient forefather. He has no hands to build with, no lips to smile or frown. He has no mind of mastery beneath his ancient crown. He is dumb and deaf and stupid to our eyes, and yet the works of all mankind in his far future lie. If we possess intelligence and skill it arises only out of the less intelligent but no less important creatures of nature around us and before us. Yet the humans of today might well seek to hunt that lowly creature, and drive him to extinction, taking for their justification his apparent lack of conscious emotion – or, more accurately, his inability to lodge any complaint. Where would we be now, if some chancing alien had chosen to exploit that 'unintelligent' form of life that was our ancestor and drive it to near-extinction? We should be the billions of voices never given a chance to scream, just like the dumb species we drive to extinction today.

Such a mind-set of destruction is by no means entirely unique to the twenty-first century, though it has now led to a scale of industrial killing never seen before. The

'Rape of the World', a term coined by Clive Poynting in his book *A Green History of the World*, was begun by European civilisation when it emerged from the medieval era with an exulted notion of human superiority and the right of man to exploit nature regardless of the cost to other beings. Within Europe itself, inconsiderate hunting of thousands of squirrels, badgers and other animals for their furs had been underway for centuries, but in the seventeenth to nineteenth century hunters began to travel further and further afield to find sufficient stocks of animals to kill. Indeed, the search for furs was a major factor behind the expansion eastwards of Russia and the development of European colonies because traders who had exhausted populations of various species of animal were forced to travel to find new quarry.

Time and again, no thought was apparently given to the lives and experiences – each beautiful and unique – of the billions of individual animals killed in the colonialists' orgy of exploration. When the once abundant population of some particular animal – whale, beaver, seal perhaps – had been destroyed in a distinct area, rendering further hunting impossible, the unscrupulous traders of these centuries did not stop to regret the irreparable damage they had caused to ecosystems and unimaginable suffering they had inflicted on individuals, but simply moved greedily on to the next region to find new supplies of animals to destroy. The passenger pigeon of North America was the most shocking example of this ruthless mechanism of selfish destruction. A population of perhaps five billion – similar to the current human population of the globe – once existed in vast flocks that could fill the sky for hours at a time when European settlers first arrived on the continent. By the early twentieth century, the species was extinct, having been regarded less of a spectacular wonder of nature than an easy to catch, cheap source of food.

Alas, the same ignorance and heartlessness towards nature, the marvellous spectacle of creation upon which we all depend, still predominates to this day within the capitalist society. It was not until the 1980s that laws were at last introduced to ban whaling, by which time the numbers of whales had declined so dramatically that hunting had become uneconomical, so that the pressure to please the big whaling businesses, allowed to trump ethical concerns until that moment, was at last lessened. Concern for the whales was present in society, but the profits of big business were allowed to overrule it. Such is the nature of capitalism. For many other species, it was too late that hunting was banned, if at all: repeatedly, the hunting of dwindling species has continued in the industrial age even when it has become clear that their numbers have dramatically declined and the myth of infinite replaceability has been shattered, pushing them over the brink into extinction. This has been brought about by our inability as societies to regulate ourselves, through the arm of government, against elite individuals' interests.

Unremitting competition has been allowed between countries and between companies within those countries for access to resources, which has led all these to step up their exploitation of resources before they are claimed by others, heedless of the long-term consequences. Cooperation between individuals and between countries would have averted such disaster.

So we see that human greed and the sort of poorly thought-out economics that ignores the limitations and true values of the natural world and sees it as an infinite resource to be exploited at will is leading to a genocide comparable only to a few mass-extinctions of Earth's past. Countless animal lives have been and are being destroyed, the once flourishing gardens of paradise are plundered and despoiled and the human populations that enjoyed and benefited from them are left miserably bereft. This mass killing has been allowed to continue, right beneath our noses, throughout the industrial era and up until this day, when habitats are still degraded and animals still abused in industrial-scale slaughterhouses. This is not to say that the taking of any life, plant or animal, is necessarily in all circumstances wrong, or that we should never have cleared any land or exploited any resources. But the premature extinction of an entire species or destruction of an entire habitat, and the exposure of living, thinking beings to tortuous existences cannot and should not be tolerated by beings capable of empathy. We are allowing the very pinnacles of creation to be toppled and the ensuing suffering is unbearable.

The Death of Birds

It is of great disadvantage to the United Kingdom that the law retains its position of permitting the shooting of some birds, particularly pigeons, with no apparent restraint. The glorious birds, not to be judged less highly than any of their – bigger or smaller – avian counterparts that are regularly fed by so many of Britain's bird-lovers in their gardens, do not deserve the pest-like description that some in this country seem desperate to give them. For days or weeks at a time across our countryside, many times is heard the dreaded thump of a gun, as somebody who can only be described as a cowardly aggressor hides behind his camouflaged netting and jumps up to fire on his unsuspecting prey. The great dance, for that unfortunate victim, is over; their grand display through the air finished in a single second, with the cruel thud of a bullet of death. From far and wide they are attracted in, with cruel devices, consisting usually of a pair of model birds on sticks, made mechanically to circle as though there was much food to be had where they fly.

But no food is to be found there. The birds flocking in for nourishment find instead death where those morbid messengers of deception take their circling flight. The killing of certain animals, it is true, has been justified by their parasitic nature: insects that live on our bodies of course must be removed, for example, for they in truth imperil themselves by making such an invasion of their host. But birds make no such invasion; they are simply trying to live naturally, in a habitat that has been, over the years, greatly reduced by humans in its ability to support our wild cousins, without direct damage to man or his property. Perhaps it is argued that these pigeons somehow damage our crops, eating seeds that have been planted. But only those who follow the agricultural practices of Mao's China would make such a mistake. The truth is that birds are far more likely to eat the insects that damage the crops than the crops themselves. Perhaps the farmer chooses to use pesticides, to pollute yet more of our land and make life yet harder to live healthily for all the inhabitants of this island, and has no need for the natural methods of pest control. Perhaps he has no regard for nature's balance, which keeps all species in check with one another. If so, he is making indeed a grievous mistake.

The fact of the matter is that pigeons and other such birds pose no real threat to agricultural production; if they do appear to be a nuisance to the crops, the well tried-and-tested techniques of scarecrows and bird-scarers are perfectly adequate solutions and leave the birds still alive to keep other 'pests' that can really do damage under control, without the need for pesticides. The shooting of pigeons is not done out of agricultural necessity, but out of the desire for sheer fun that certain deranged individuals appear to have in inflicting death upon their neighbours. The hunting instinct, so essential to a human living in the wild and searching desperately for food, lives on within them, but rather than restrain this instinct with love and empathy, some of those who delight in shooting living beings decide to continue to kill, even when we have developed agricultural technology that has left this practice far from necessary. We have converted the land into fields so that hunting is no longer needed for food; it is wrong that this always regrettable but once unfortunately necessary practice should now become a thing of fun and sport. Such is an insult to the balance of nature and to all animal life on this Earth.

4.2 Pollution of Paradise

The result, inevitably, of the great capitalist urge for growth – the consequence of such a vast quantity of resources being consumed by such a system – is the equally vast quantity of waste produced. New technologies, not tried and tested over centuries but hurriedly rushed-out globally for the sake of profit, often have unforeseen drawbacks at the end of their 'lifecycles' or during their use. These are unforeseen but not unforeseeable: the problem under capitalism is that undesirable consequences that could easily be identified by an impartial onlooker will simply be ignored during the development and production of the product in question if they have no impact on the profit that can be made. Government regulations are an essential check on this, forcing companies to follow less profitable but safer paths that are better for society as a whole, but they do not go nearly far enough to ensure that the best possible outcome for society is obtained. A programme of public ownership, by contrast, would remove the drive for profit and enable the introduction of environmental sustainability and social good, both of which are required for a stable, happy, long-lived society, as the main aims of all production.

Through lack of such objectives, we are left with profit-making devices that provide attractive short-term solutions for individuals but which have dramatically negative impacts on the wider world of today and the future. Vehicles that pour out smog clog roads that criss-cross the country, their discarded tyres slowly forming mountains of unusable non-biodegradable rubbish[21]. Countless other plastics lie, failing to rot, in landfill sites and in a huge unintended artificial island in the middle of the once beautiful and life-giving Pacific, now choking the animals that try to exist there. Meanwhile, perfectly usable products and methods embraced in the past are discarded, with more fossil-fuels burned to produce their slightly 'improved' (usually in some superficial way) replacements, which themselves are not likely to be long-lasting. All of this leads to the poisoning of the very planet on which we depend, and has direct consequences for ourselves, for those who live alongside us in poorer parts of world and for the generations who will follow us in the future.

It is easy to forget, living in the modern world, just how far human civilisation has shaped and continues to alter the planet on which it is built. What was once vast forest has been converted into fields and buildings; where once the animate inhabitants of the land were free to move there now stand roads and people, and the people are ready to protect themselves from the wild creatures of the country, hence putting those other creatures in danger. We may assign 'conservation areas' and 'green belt' zones, but we are deluding ourselves if we think that by protecting these small, isolated regions from the air, water and land pollution that we allow to spill out across the rest of the paradise that once was, we shall be able to preserve all those myriad ecosystems that we, alongside all other dwellers on the Earth, depend upon to live. We must realise that we become indebted to all other creatures on the planet, living now and in the future, with every drop of unnatural pollution we produce, wherever it may be.

The truth of the matter is that we did not evolve to live in this modern, urbanised world. We evolved in the older, natural world, constantly changing but in a gradual, biological manner that allowed for steady adaptation and the increase in diversity of life (except when hampered by external factors such as asteroid collisions). This is far

104

removed from the fast-paced changes we inflict upon ourselves today, and their psychological as well as ecological repercussions. That the number of species present in this paradise for life is now decreasing as a result of our actions is a warning call, that we have gone too far in our futile quest to 'improve' upon the perfect conditions that this planet possesses for life with creations of our own. The sheer complexity of life on Earth has inspired countless individuals to believe in a divine, intelligent creator, so amazingly powerful is Natural Selection. How can we, mere humans, possibly hope to better in a few thousand years the work it has perfected over billions?

It is for this reason that the natural world should take centre stage, and the technologies that we have rightly invented for our convenience should always be secondary in importance: more land should be left forested than urbanised, for instance, and 'green' land should be built on with extreme care. Goods and services should be within walking distance, so that the new species we have created in the form of the car need not be encouraged to reproduce (see 'A New Species'). The most dangerous pollutants, in that they often spread far and wide, are those of the air and water; air pollution can in turn contribute to land pollution by flooding low-lying areas, through enhancement of the planet's natural greenhouse effect, and forcing the reconstruction of buildings further inland on formerly unused ground. We may underestimate the amounts of these pollutants produced, because they are soon 'out of sight, out of mind', but, as the growing plastic island of the pacific and rising global temperatures show, their levels continue to increase. Those industrial processes and products that give rise to such devastating pollutants are not beneficial to society, and so should be abandoned, replaced with technologies inspired by the harmless techniques we have used for centuries, and lived contentedly with. There were no plastic islands or belching smoke-stacks, after all, before the industrial revolution.

An intriguing idea propounded recently was to colour-code countries' waste so that the source of the rubbish washed into the seas and onto beaches could be identified, illustrating the extent to which our cast-off materials travel across the globe. The 'developed' world might think itself clean in many respects, but such a scheme might illustrate the extent to which it dirties the rest of the world. Drinks bottles and other such rubbish has been discovered even in remote regions of Antarctica, after all. Unfortunately, though, it is not possible to colour-code greenhouse gasses, the most potent of the 'western' lifestyle's pollutants, as their warming effects spread across the globe. When the industrialised world's methods are exported to less industrialised parts, often replacing traditional methods designed to increase efficiency when resources are sparse with wasteful and harmful post-industrialisation alternatives, the problem can only get worse. For this reason, it is vital that parts of the world considered backwards by the capitalist consumer culture prevalent over recent decades in Europe and North America think carefully before they accept advice from the so-called 'developed world' (see 'Developing Devastation'). For our part, we in Britain should try to set a better example and learn from some of their more primitive, but more sustainable, methods: we need to develop to increase the sustainability of our practices as much as other countries need to develop to meet their people's basic needs.

This co-development of all the countries of the world does not require a complete eschewing of all industry and technology. What it will mean is an abandonment of the throw-away philosophy that sees us ravage our planet for ever more resources and dump our waste into the land, sea and air without fully accounting for the cost to ourselves and other beings. The energy-intensive production of supposedly 'disposable' plastic to be used once before being thrown away to linger indefinitely in landfill sites or gradually decompose into ever smaller, ever more dangerous pseudo-plankton in the oceans is unacceptable in a society that values its own purpose to foster joy, the environment that sustains it and the prosperity of its future existence. Packaging should be avoided wherever possible, and the localisation of food and goods production (see 'Work & Pay') should help with this by reducing the need to transport items long distances and facilitating repair rather than replacement of goods. Where packaging of some sort is still required – for example, bottles in which to store milk – naturally biodegradable materials should always be favoured above oil-derived plastics which, even if they are supposedly biodegradable, pose a risk to other organisms' health. Simply recycling packaging such as this cannot be the answer, because each recycling cycle reduces the quality of the material, so that it cannot be used to store foodstuffs lest some of the plastic molecules leech into the food and into our bodies and after a few recycles the plastic becomes utterly useless. Glass does not have these problems and can be recycled indefinitely; paper and cardboard cannot, but are derived from renewable sources and will safely biodegrade so long as the inks used to print on them are non-toxic. Cardboard boxes and sleeves and glass bottles and containers can, of course, also be reused many times before they have to be recycled, saving the energy of producing them from new. Plastics, which start to degrade more rapidly than glass, do not have the same capacity for re-use.

Plastic Menace

The first synthetic plastic was Parkesine, first forged in a time and place right at the heart of the industrial age, Birmingham in 1856. But it was between the 1920s and 1950s, especially when cheap and versatile materials were needed in quantity to facilitate the

Second World War and the recovery from its devastation, that an explosion in the varieties of plastic available took place, mainly produced from oil. Since then, their use has increased worldwide year on year: in 2009, 230 million tonnes of plastic were produced worldwide, with an average annual increase of 9% since 1950. There was a slight decrease from 2008, but there is little hope, given the current attitude of societies towards plastics, that this will continue[22]. They have become an integral part of the fabric of both the industrialised world and the poorer regions wither the influence of industry has spread. Those who provide plastic products to these regions seldom provide the means to dispose of it, and it's not difficult to see how large quantities of plastic reach the oceans from the shores of Africa and Asia when even in the UK – where regulations and recycling are widespread – rivers and beaches are lined with litter, and a city as modern as Los Angeles can release as much as thirty tonnes of plastic into the Pacific per day[23].

Many of the effects of plastic pollution on ocean-dwelling animals are undeniably clear. Plastics cannot be digested, but are mistaken for food – especially when they break up to the size of plankton – by fish or birds, and remain in their stomachs, gradually poisoning them, rendering them infertile, blocking their intestinal tracts or even making them feel artificially full so that they fail to eat real food and starve to death. The deaths of at least two whales have been attributed to the huge quantities of plastic detritus found in their stomachs[24]. Other animals become entangled in the non-degrading plastic, and it can cause further damage by choking the sea floor of oxygen.

The majority of plastic in the oceans, however, is not so easily visible as are these large chunks. Indeed, the 'garbage islands' of plastic trapped by ocean gyres in the Atlantic, Pacific and Indian Oceans are not, as is often imagined, great mountains of debris visible for miles around. These islands' very extent is difficult to determine, because most of the plastics found there are below the surface and comprised of very small specimens ranging from millimetres to micrometres in diameter. Many of these are the remnants of larger plastic items that have been broken down by sunlight, biology and corrosion; others, such as cosmetic scrubbing granules, were manufactured to be such a size in the first place. Depending on what concentration of these plastics we define as constituting part of a plastic 'island', its extent will obviously vary. The plastic islands are certainly not visible from aircraft, let alone satellites, and are difficult to see even by boat: most of the plastic contained therein can only be detected by taking samples of the water. But it is estimated that a plastic concentration of around five kilograms per square kilometre – more plastic than plankton by mass[25] – within a few metres of the surface extends over an area somewhere between the size of Texas and that of the continental

United States (it may change from year to year with ocean currents) in the largest of the 'islands' in the North Pacific.

What is most worrying about plastic in our oceans is, somewhat paradoxically, that its volume does not appear to be increasing, despite the amount of plastic being produced by humans globally continuing to rise year on year. This is concerning because we do not know where the extra plastic is going: there must be at least one mechanism by which it is being drawn out of surface waters, and presumably accumulating elsewhere, and this mechanism could involve a great deal of harm to living beings. Indeed, were the plastic to remain where it was, this would imply that it had little impact on life. But its disappearance implies that fish and seabirds may be consuming vast quantities, and either carrying them down to the ocean depths when they die or breaking them down into smaller pieces that could do yet more harm if eaten by other fish and accumulated in their tissues. The role of bacteria that colonise the floating plastics is also unclear: they may well be breaking down some of this plastic faster than we would otherwise expect, so that it has become too small for researchers to detect, but these smaller particles could be still more harmful to wildlife. It's also possible that plastic could be accumulating in ice at the poles. Or it may be finding its way somehow into deep-sea sediments, perhaps dragged down by the weight of accumulated plankton or pushed there by down-welling ocean currents. One study has found that plastic concentrations are up to four times greater in sediments of the Atlantic and Indian Oceans and the Mediterranean Sea than in surface waters[26]. If the plastic indeed settles there, locked away from doing harm to life, its effects may not be so pernicious as they would otherwise be.

But where plastic does interact with ocean life, it is becoming increasingly apparent just how diverse and dangerous its less obvious effects can be. By providing platforms on which insects can lay eggs, plankton can congregate and bacteria and viruses can multiply, plastics may be changing the biosphere in unexpected ways, favouring the survival of certain species above others and thereby disrupting the natural evolution of ocean food webs. Not all of those microorganisms that delight in plastics are benign. Populations of *Vibrio* bacteria that cause infections are known to be increasing – they can be easily detected because of their characteristic bioluminescence – and the spread over surface waters of viruses harmful to humans presents a similarly concerning development for all those who live and work on the seas.

Polystyrene is perhaps the worst of all the plastic culprits. It never biodegrades, but is easily broken up into tiny pieces that can be ingested by animals. Once released into the environment, it is a nightmare to recover. As early as 1974, 21 per cent of flounders in the Bristol Channel were found to have ingested polystyrene spherules[27]. Yet the use of this terror material is by no stretch of the imagination essential for humans to meet our needs. Paper-based alternatives make perfectly sufficient portable coffee cups and protective layers in packaged goods.

Plastics cannot be easily converted back into the oil that they came from, so, given that it is not indefinitely recyclable, if plastic doesn't end up in the ocean it must be either burned, producing harmful fumes, or buried and broken down somewhere on land – usually in landfill sites. Because it's not natural, plastic doesn't fully biodegrade – at least not for many thousands of years, and even as it does so the oil-derived chemicals it leeches can pose great harm to wildlife and even poison our own water supplies. The effects of plastic waste on land-based wildlife and humans are less direct than those on ocean wildlife, where the plastics are more easily visible, and research has therefore focussed primarily on the latter concern. But surely the effects on land should not be dismissed just because they are uncertain, and we have a duty not to risk potential future suffering by being irresponsible with our use and disposal of plastics today. Just because the plastics in landfills are out of sight, that doesn't mean they can't be doing latent damage to the health of all those living above them as they lurk in the darkness. A very concerning threat, especially as extreme flooding becomes more common with climate change, is that chemicals may leech out of flooded landfill sites into rivers and other water supplies, poisoning them. This could even happen without the immediate signs of flooding on the surface: groundwater rising into landfill sites from beneath can just as easily become contaminated by the deadly filth as surface river water. That's why recycling is especially important for plastics, which only break down very slowly into dangerous constituent chemicals not generally found in the natural world.

In 2013, of the 21.6 million tonnes of waste from households collected in the UK, only 5.7 million tonnes was recycled, with the rest either incinerated or sent to landfill. Recycling rates are certainly increasing (by around 0.2% per year) and the amount of waste sent to landfill has dramatically decreased since the turn of the millennium. But only 7% of the recycled component was plastic in 2013, most being the much more easily recycled materials glass, paper and card[28], despite plastics making up around 10% of the total waste: some plastic must still be going to landfill, and after all it cannot be indefinitely recycled. Unfortunately, neither this limitation on plastic recycling nor the express need to prevent plastic in particular going to are reflected in the European Union's flat target of 50% of household waste (indiscriminate of type) to be recycled by 2020. What doesn't seem to be recognised at present is that plastics production simply must be dramatically reduced if we are to avoid harming ourselves and our planet through both the production and the disposal of these harmful materials, quite aside from the damage they may be doing to our health during their use. Ultimately, any plastic we make must end up in our soil, oceans or atmosphere, and is capable of doing great harm to the biosphere in all of these places. Targets should therefore not focus solely on overall recycling rates (though encouraging paper, glass, metal and organics recycling is of course vitally important in a sustainable society): we must also enforce a determined ramping down of plastic production, towards zero in the near-future.

Of course, it is possible that not all the effects of plastic pollution will be harmful. Future archaeologists may revel in the opportunity to study our society through the indestructible detritus it has left behind, and it is even possible that long-playing records could become fossilised, leaving permanent grooves in rock that could in millions of years' time provide a way for advanced civilisations to listen to the sounds of our own era – rock music in the real sense. It may also be possible to begin removing plastics from the places where it is thought to be doing the most harm – ocean surface waters – and the Ocean Clean-up Project is already exploring a plethora of technological mechanisms by which this could one day be achieved[29]. Nevertheless, this effort will be futile if we don't stop releasing plastics into the oceans in the first place, and the harms that this unnatural suite of materials can do to our natural environment surely outweigh the benefits to any hypothetical future historians that using plastics for many more decades to come would provide. Reducing the amount of plastic we use should therefore be our focus, a trend that would also help us to reduce our dependence on the oil from which it is derived and eliminate some of our emissions of greenhouse gasses if achieved through the adoption of more sustainable materials and practices of manufacture and use, and especially by ensuring the reuseability and repairability of everything we make.

The extent to which a throw-away consumer culture has taken hold in recent years, and the damage that this is doing to our environment, is illustrated well by the example of disposable crockery and cutlery. Of course, we all need to drink to live, and to have some sort of drink – hot or cold – when we are out and about is not a bad thing in and of itself. But we should not drink hot drinks excessively, and certainly not at the expense of others' well-being. Increasingly, it seems, these hot condiments are served at cafes, workplaces, parties and on public transport not in ordinary, re-useable cups but in 'disposable' paper ones coated with plastic. Contrary to popular belief, these cups are rarely recyclable. Although some are biodegradable, the rest of these cups will persist – or at least their plastic sleeves will – in landfill sites and as pollutants cluttering and endangering the natural world. The same is, of course, true of plastic plates, knives and forks. All of these things cause environmental damage when they are made and when they are disposed of. Re-useable crockery exerts similar damage when it is made, but can be used again and again because it is more resilient, often at the same time (at least in the case of metal utensils) as being recyclable.

Using disposable utensils is done out of sheer laziness (it saves washing them up), haste (they can be used on-the-go) or the desire for profit (it may be cheaper for coffee chains to issue these cheaply-produced cups), none of which is a valid excuse for the associated environmental damage, especially given that the drinks they contain are often far from essential. Despite what some might claim, nobody genuinely needs a cup of tea or coffee. People have been persuaded to 'need' them – indeed, have become addicted to them – so that coffee producers and sellers can profit from the continual purchases of those who claim not to be able to live without their regular stimulant drink. We could simply stop drinking such substances 'on the go', which would undoubtedly improve the country's health and save a considerable amount of the energy wasted in boiling water. Another solution would, of course, be to simply ban 'disposable' crockery and cutlery that is not completely biodegradable. But this still leaves the issue of wasted energy and resources producing the cups in the first place. Better still would be to do away with 'disposable' utensils entirely.

In general, it is very easily possible to completely eliminate the need for most of the plastics we use. Items regarded as 'disposable' despite containing non-biodegradable plastic components can be made genuinely harmless by removing superfluous packaging and replacing the rest with re-useable and recyclable glass or paper alternatives. We can also halt the use of plastic bags and eliminate use-once versions of coffee cups, shavers, nappies, printer cartridges and pens entirely, in favour of longer-lasting, well-made reusable ones. Why not provide printers and pens that can be refilled with ink (in re-usable glass bottles) instead of cartridges, or shavers whose blades can simply be sharpened when blunt? But much, much more care must also be taken with the goods we make intending them to last. Before manufacturing any product, we as a society need to think carefully about whether we really need it, and in what quantity, how it might be serviced and upgraded to prolong its life (indefinitely if possible), and what will be done with the product itself at the end of its life or any of its parts that may wear out and need to be replaced. The manufacturers who currently seek to make quick profits through the rapid replacement of their often cheaply-made or quickly surpassed machines, gadgets and clothing rarely take the environmental damage done by manufacture and disposal of their products properly. We all know where to look for an explanation of why Earth's paradise is being so rapidly polluted, of why the ecosystems we love and depend upon and countless animal lives are being destroyed. It's the throw-away culture of consumer capitalism. And it has to stop.

Permeating Chemicals

'Chemicals' have obtained a bad name in many parts of the world. Chemicals, of course, are all around us, all the time and everywhere: they are the substance from which the world, natural and man-made, is built. But when people worry about 'chemicals', what they tend to mean are synthetic chemicals, those that have been manufactured or extracted artificially and that we should not be exposed to in our natural habitat in any large quantity, if at all. These are the sorts 'chemicals' we familiar with when we talk about 'artificial additives' in foods and pesticides and fertilisers than can leech onto them and harm our health.

But it's not only directly through foods that synthetic chemicals can affect us and our health and environment. Where in the past furniture and packaging was made from wood or metal, clothing was made from natural fibres and bottles out of glass, nowadays all of these things are often crafted entirely from synthetic plastics or sprayed with flame-retardant or preservative chemicals that we would not encounter naturally. Perhaps some of these chemicals pose no threat, but the trouble is that they have, to date, been assumed innocent until proven guilty: capitalist manufacturers are permitted to begin using chemicals and sell the products that contain them on the assumption that they are safe, possibly following a few tests on animal subjects. But it would be much better for our overall well-being if these non-essential additives to our lives were assumed guilty of harmful effects until it could be absolutely proven that they are safe to use.

The reason that the safety and well-being of the populace is not placed paramount when it comes to designing new products and methods and choosing the materials to use is that it is often more profitable financially to use these newer materials, and if their harmful effects are only traced many decades later there can be no immediate repercussions for the business involved in manufacturing or using them. Plastics have revolutionised the physical make-up of our society. They can be crafted into attractive and versatile shapes and colours, providing convenience and aesthetic appeal to the 'consumers' that manufacturers of foodstuffs and household goods and gadgets want through their packaging to persuade to purchase their products. They are also, when oil is drilled for without restraint and the costs of its use and extraction are not accounted for in its cost at source, cheap to produce. This provides a double incentive for manufacturers to use them: they are cheaper and can be made more immediately attractive than more natural products.

Yet evidence is emerging that these plastics are far from safe. Molecules from plastic bottles and containers are prone to rubbing off into food and drink. As a result, they are found within nearly everybody living in industrialised societies, if studies of concentrations of plastics such as biphenol A (BPA) in the United States population are anything to go by[30]. We don't know what the effects of this ingestion are as studying the long-term effects of one particular chemical in isolation on the human body is extremely difficult, but it could potentially be linked to many of the 'modern diseases' from which we suffer. Certainly, phthalates added to increase plastics' flexibility have been linked to birth defects, and the plasticiser and 'synthetic oestrogen' BPA and similar compounds used to coat till receipts and tins of food interfere with hormonal systems in the body[31]. Surely it would be safer to revert to plainer, less versatile but more natural alternatives for our food and drink packaging such as paper, card and glass that are known by experience not to leech chemicals into the foodstuffs they contain. Aluminium from drinks cans can also be ingested, and high levels of this metal, which is not found naturally in the plants and animals humans have eaten in the past in high concentrations because it is so difficult to extract from its ore, are known to have harmful effects on the brain. The long-term consequences of surrounding ourselves with new materials that our bodies have not evolved to be accustomed to are not clear.

To eliminate the hidden danger from such chemicals, we will need to bring about a complete reversal of the way in which our material world is heading at the moment. Presently, plastics are employed in more and more applications and we are moving further and further away from natural materials. Furniture is now often coated or impregnated with fire-retardant substances called polybrominated diphenyl ethers (PBDEs) that are known to reduce fertility and hamper child development and are therefore not intended to escape from these products. But somehow, they do, and concentrations of the chemicals in Americans' bodies have doubled every five years over the past four decades. Only now that this has been realised are the EU and USA taking steps to ban some of the chemicals[32]. Computers, televisions and handheld electronic gadgets are all coated in plastics, some of which must undoubtedly also rub off onto their users, and the inner electronics of these devices contain a whole host of nasty precious metals and synthetic compounds that could do great harm if ingested somehow. Cosmetics and some toothbrushes are full of tiny beads of plastic that could very easily be imperceptibly swallowed. The present paradigm is to ignore all this and put ourselves into close contact with these numerous unknowns until we have already begun to suffer from their ill effects. Many of these chemicals can end up being ingested by other animals too; fish are especially susceptible to the plastic beads used in cosmetics and toothpastes, and if humans eat fish whose tissues have been impregnated, the quantities within our own bodies will rise still higher. This paradigm not only exists in the industrialised world, but is also being exported to poorer countries, where concentrations of plastic are rising, and from where, through unregulated rubbish disposal, much of the plastic in our oceans is probably derived.

The present paradigm is also in favour of globalisation itself, rather than local production of the items that we need, and towards goods that are cheaply made and short-lived, as we discussed above. Protecting our health by removing plastics from the environments in which we live will require counteracting this situation at the same time. It's also essential that we become less normalised towards artificial scents and glosses in the world around us and become again content with the sights and smells of the natural world. It has become normal to apply cosmetics to cover up bodily odours and wash ourselves clean of the 'dirt' around us. Whilst it is certainly advisable to wash off synthetic chemicals and excrement after contact, the dirt of the natural world poses little threat and it is actually against our own health that we wash this off with synthetic soaps rather than our natural cleanser, water. Covering ourselves with cosmetics and deodorants is not healthy, and should not really be necessary in a society that celebrates the reality of the beautiful world that we live in rather than trying to mask it with artificial flavours.

Air Pollution

On Friday 5th December 1952, thick smog descended on London. The city had been known for its smoke and fog for well over a century, and it was amidst the wisps of this airborne industrial and domestic effluent that the dark tales of poverty and crime written by the likes of Dickens and Conan-Doyle and real-life horrors such as the murders of Jack the Ripper had taken place. But as the size, population and industrial output increased, the problem had grown worse and worse. This time, the smog was more impenetrable than ever before. Trains, cars and busses ground to a halt and public events were cancelled; it was impossible to see beyond a few yards. Calm, anticyclonic weather conditions meant that there was no wind to disperse the fumes, and the poisonous soup was added to minute by minute, hour by hour by the gasses pouring out of homes and factories.

The 'great smog' event was enough to provoke the government into action to deal with London's air pollution. For a world-renowned city to be crippled in this way, it had been finally realised, was not acceptable. The smoke came largely from coal, the dirtiest, most unhealthy fuel source used by mankind, burnt by the many power stations in the vicinity and in people's homes and offices to keep warm through the cold winter weather. This was added to by vehicle exhausts (diesel busses having recently replaced electric trams), industrial refuse and pollution blown across the English Channel from cities on the Continent. The resulting concoction of carbon dioxide, sulphur dioxide, particulates, hydrochloric acid and fluorine compounds was highly toxic, and those who could afford them had resorted to walked around wearing gas masks. Clearly, most couldn't. Around four thousand people are estimated to have died from respiratory failure during this single smog event, a further eight thousand similarly succumbed in the following months, and many more must have suffered future health problems that led to premature deaths.

Accordingly, in 1956 the Clean Air Act, a bill sponsored by the backbench MP Gerald Nabarro, was passed by Parliament. It made mandatory the use of smokeless fuels in certain designated areas and clamped down on the harmful pollution caused by domestic coal burning. The density of power stations in urban areas was restricted, and provisions were put in place for the erection of taller chimneys. Although the Act was not entirely successful, and had to be replaced by still more stringent legislation in the 1960s following further, smaller smog events, the effect on London was transformative and it marked a fundamental turning point in the history of environmental legislation. By limiting its air pollution, the iconic city of London set a precedent that has been followed by industrialised countries across the world, and a shift in mind-set that sees clean air, rather than industrial smog, as the sign of a modern, prosperous metropolis. It was this new mind-set that drove China to clamp down on its own embarrassing air pollution in Beijing at the time of the 2008 Olympic Games, and is causing it to adopt measures to curb visible air pollution much more rapidly than the Western powers whose industrial development its government seeks to emulate were ever able to achieve.

However, it is becoming increasingly clear that the problem of air pollution has not gone away. The former paradise that we have urbanised may not be so thickly, visibly and chronically polluted by noxious gasses as it once was, but even in supposedly cleaner countries such as our own the air we breathe – that most essential and precious of all the gifts of nature – is not healthy. London's Oxford Road has the highest nitrogen dioxide levels in the world, largely because of diesel-burning busses and cars fitted with converters to remove visible soot from exhausts, which produce the more toxic invisible gas as a by-product[33]. It is one thing for a government to act to reduce pollution that is visibly lethal, as Britain did from the 1950s and China is doing today, but quite another to persuade capitalist legislators to curb the less obvious but no less damaging pollutants that continue to clog our city air. Even following an event as serious as the 1952 smog it took four years before regulations were put in place to clean up London. Part of the reason for this was the government's refusal to act for fear of hampering economic growth until a group of back-benchers forced a debate on the issue to take place.

Yet it is not economic growth but the well-being of the people from whose mandate it derives its power that should be the government's overriding priority in all its policy-making. Economic growth is only useful insofar as it can in some circumstances enhance this well-being. The government must act to ensure that nobody's rights are violated, and there can be no more fundamental right than the right to clean air to breathe, something that we would all possess in the wild and must have in order to live. The government must act to preserve the health of ourselves, our descendants and the other animals that we live alongside by protecting this right. Whether or not this will hamper the economic output – still less the Gross Domestic Product – of the country is irrelevant because clean air is essential to our well-being, and well-being is the primary aim that economic output is itself intended to satisfy. In any case, the economic activity of people performing useful roles – which is indeed valuable in that it can enhance the future well-being of others in society – will not be hampered by a policy that prevents their health and life-span from being artificially curtailed. The profits of individual corporations may foreseeably be reduced in the short-term. But even if this mattered – which it doesn't, so long as people continue to be usefully, happily and healthily employed – the effect is unlikely to be a long-term one because a healthier work-force will work longer and better as well as more happily.

There can be no doubt, then, that if the air that citizens breathe is in any way polluted to the extent of long-term health effects it is the duty of the government, which those citizens elect to govern society in a way that enhances the well-being of all without undermining the rights of any, to address the causes of that pollution without offloading it onto other peoples elsewhere. This applies whether or not the pollution is visible by eye, and whether or not its effects are immediate. That's where today's governments are failing, and action needs to be taken urgently to mitigate a growing health crisis.

Untreated coal is by far the dirtiest fossil fuel, in terms of emissions of both the greenhouse gas carbon dioxide and health-hazardous gasses such as sulphur dioxide and particulates, per kilogram burned. From a climate perspective, the use of coal in all circumstances is unjustifiable; from a human health perspective it is certainly unacceptable to burn coal in the vicinity of other people if there is any chance of their breathing the fumes, since there are many other fuels and means of keeping warm or travelling available that render the burning of coal entirely non-essential. 'Smokeless' coal is available and is of course another matter, and may be useful for applications such as the operation of vintage steam engines where no other alternative is available. But it is not morally justifiable for a good government to do anything but ban the burning of non-smokeless coal where the fumes can be breathed by people. The fact that coal-fired power plants and small-scale domestic coal burning continue (in the areas not restricted by the Clean Air Act and its successors) illustrates that public health has not been taken seriously, for these undoubtedly contribute towards thousands of cases of respiratory difficulties and, estimates suggest, around 1600 premature deaths every year. The

European Union imposes limits on the legal emissions of nitrous oxides from coal-fired power plants, but these are clearly not stringent enough, even when enforced; in March 2015 the UK was condemned for allowing Aberthaw coal plant in Wales to be at twice the legal emissions limit[34]. No morally justifiable electricity generation plant can operate if known to be associated with even a single death.

In 2014 the Committee on the Medical Effects of Air Pollutants estimated that air pollution was responsible for around sixty thousand deaths per year, or between ten and eighteen per cent of all premature deaths in the UK[35]. But it's not just coal burning that's responsible. Nitrous oxide and dioxide emissions, and particulates released by combustion of diesel, have been on the rise in recent years as the use of diesel engines has increased, promoted in part by the greater fuel-efficiency of diesel relative to petrol in road transport. These emissions are produced right at the heart of population centres – the cities – making them particularly dangerous. These gasses can aggravate asthma and other existing lung and heart conditions, and have been linked to mental health problems if exposure takes place in early childhood[36] (unfortunately, the research was done in mice by deliberately exposing them to the chemicals, but the accuracy of the scientific findings cannot be disputed on the basis of such unethical origins). The effects of long-term low-level exposure are not known. This pollution from cars, busses and trains isn't visible like soot, but by filling the air that we breathe it is, slowly or quickly, poisoning many of us, rendering our cities fundamentally unhealthy places to live. We have swapped the fresh, clean air of paradise for deadly fumes, all to increase the speed with which we can move about our cities, to heat homes with coal and oil that could be warmed more cleanly, and to produce industrial products that we could often make do without.

There are many steps that can be taken to clean up this pollution. Cities – indeed, all densely residential areas where smoke does not have space to rapidly clear – should be free of any vehicles that give out air pollution, especially diesel busses and cars that pump out particulates. Electric trains, trams and taxis and gas-powered busses could easily replace these polluting monsters. Factories that chug out toxic fumes should be made to refine their techniques of production so that whatever they are making can be replaced with an equivalent that does not require such dangerous techniques. The farming out of polluting production to poorer countries such as China needs to be ended, to prevent our air pollution from simply moving to choke Chinese lungs. Around power plants, inter-city roads and other places where pollutants still need to be emitted, walls of trees can be planted to absorb the particulates and prevent their circulation. Non-smokeless coal as a fuel should be ruled out entirely.

And yet the British government continues to ignore the problem of air pollution, failing to impose regulations that would protect health, well-being and the right to clean air for all of us who live in, work in or visit cities or areas close to power plants. In April 2015, the Supreme Court was asked to order the government to meet even the European air quality standards; a move to completely eliminate harmful gasses from the air that we breathe seems a long way off. But it is essential that this pressing public health issue is moved far higher up the political agenda if we are again to be able to appreciate the clean air that is owed to us all.

Transformed Landscapes

Our world is a paradise. Its lush woods, forests and savannahs, its majestic mountains and resplendent rivers, provide a perfect habitat for humanity that cannot be bettered. Were we to live amongst nature, bringing it into every street of our cities, allowing life of all kinds to flourish on our farms and planting or preserving forests and other natural environments, this paradise would be one protected for all of us to enjoy. Human habitation need not, fundamentally, subtract from the paradisal state of nature. It is only since the industrial revolution that the extent of deforestation, urbanisation and disconnection from nature that we as a species endure has become chronic. This tragedy has not been brought about out of necessity, but through thoughtless greed and ignorance, and has hampered rather than enhancing our overall well-being. Yet, fuelled on by the capitalist lust for consumption and profit, it continues.

Until very recently, it seemed as though efforts to preserve the Amazon rainforest were succeeding: between 2004 and 2011, deforestation rates fell by some seventy-seven per cent. But in 2013, the 'economic recovery' of the world, spurring a demand for beef and soybeans to feed livestock for the slaughter, began to encourage the destruction of that most beautiful of environments to accelerate. Between October of that year and October 2014, deforestation rates shot up by four hundred and sixty-seven per cent in the Amazon. For the sake of non-essential foodstuffs, one of our most precious, ancient assets is being perhaps irreversibly destroyed. Furthermore, plans are being drawn up to build more roads – including a superhighway – through the forest, something that would not only prevent migration of animals and cause direct damage through fragmentation but that would inevitably provide better access for loggers and slash-and-burn ranchers to devastate what remains.

The Brazilian government, which claims jurisdiction over most of the forest, is in danger of yielding to pressure by agricultural lobbyists to ease the restrictions on logging that have been put in place, apparently heedless of the long-term unsustainability of a policy that involves unchecked and indefinite forest shrinkage. All this serves to compound the stress that the unique environment of the forest is already under from climate change, which could cause a dramatic increase in temperature and decline in precipitation in the region, partly of course as a result of the tremendous carbon dioxide emissions associated with converting the forest to agricultural pasture. Such a rich and interconnected diversity of biological organisms is there in the forest itself that most of the nutrient cycle takes place above ground; the soil beneath the trees is both shallow and unfertile. Therefore, with no trees remaining as anchors for the soil, this pasture land rapidly degrades into desert, leaving an empty waste in place of a lush environment supporting the richest concentration of life on the planet. Some twenty per cent of the Amazon has already been lost, and capitalist consumption is driving further destruction minute by minute. Unless action is taken, a whole plethora of species will be lost forever, a great number of individual life-forms perishing in the process, and the humanity of the future will lose access to this inspirational landscape and the great benefits that it provides.

Forests are not just beautiful to look at and live in. They provide living environments in which still more life – human and non-human – can thrive, and, as the 'lungs of the world', provide the whole planet with oxygen. They exert local climatic controls that keep the surrounding lands habitable, and, if carefully managed, can be exploited renewably for numerous resources useful to humans, from precious woods to medicines. That management has been going on for millennia: the Amazon, like the rest of the world's forests, has a long history of interaction with humanity and serves as a good illustration of the fact that the distinction between 'natural' and 'man-made' is an artificial one. There is no 'natural' landscape that has not been influenced by humanity (except perhaps that of Antarctica, although global warming is changing this) as a result of our success in colonising the entire globe; likewise, there is no human creation that has not been infiltrated by the rest of nature in some way. The environment around us shapes our thoughts even as we conceive architectural structures, and we are never apart from other species: bacteria creep onto even the most heavily sterilised of surfaces. We have and always will be part of nature, and like every species we change the other species with which we interact, and help to maintain – through adaptation and biochemical reactions – an environment on Earth that is precipitous to life.

What is new, though, spreading right across the world over the last couple of centuries, is a switch from small-scale, renewable cultivation of forests and other precious landscapes to the industrial-scale raping of nature in order to fuel unsustainable rates of economic growth. Instead of gratefully taking what we need from nature in close communication with the other organisms we live alongside, we have separated ourselves into vast urban spaces and polluted the countryside with artificial products that work against life, diversity and the holistic prosperity of the planet so as to extract as much as we can for the sake of production as an ends in itself rather than a means to need-fulfilment. Tribesmen have lived in the world's forests since time immemorial, taking from them the resources that they need and partially shaping them to suit their own needs as one part of the natural ecosystem. All the evidence suggests that the best way to preserve a forest and its fauna is to allow tribespeople to continue to manage the landscape. We ought to learn from them, acting in harmony with the rest of the planet's life-forms and welcoming the rest of nature into all our living spaces. Instead, we either unappreciatively ravish our land at the expense of our co-inhabitants or, where we do recognise the need to conserve ecosystems, we attempt to close them off from humanity altogether, exiling the tribesmen from the landscapes their communities have inhabited for centuries and are in the best position to protect and benefit from. The biggest driver of our pollution of paradise is this very artificial separation of mankind from the rest of nature – one that is as artificial as Descartes' mistaken separation of the body and the mind – which leads to an under-appreciation of our dependence upon all the ecosystems with which we interact, an unhealthy aversion to the 'dirt' of the outdoors and a state of depressed isolation from the environment we have evolved to live in.

The clearest symptom of this separation is the rapid growth of urbanisation over recent decades. According to the UN, fifty-four per cent of the world's population lived in cities in 2014, up from just thirty per cent in 1950, and the proportion continues to rise[37]. Whilst the peak in global rural population expected to accompany this change may seem like good news from the perspective of the preservation of ecosystems because human populations will be concentrated in smaller areas, if urbanisation is done in a conventional, capitalistic manner this switch will in fact be harmful both to our own welfare and to the health of the ecosystems we have traditionally lived amongst. More people living in such cities will mean more intensive production of food as traditional, sustainable methods of farming that require large amounts of labour are replaced by low-labour 'western'-style models that foster sterile monocultures poisoned by pesticides and fertilisers in which life cannot thrive. If the new urban areas mimic the cities of today in becoming havens of fast, cheap and dirty foods constituted largely of meat and processed cereals, a vast amount more land per person will be required to feed everyone. The amount of land required increases still further if we consider the amount of food that is wasted in cities, where supermarkets transport too much food (to offer 'consumer choice' and fill the shelves) over large distances and throw it away when the 'sell-by date' expires, relative to countryside where people live on crops they produce themselves and the food has only to be 'used by' the time it becomes detectably off. These effects will combine to mean that the same amount or even more land has to be cultivated, and because the cultivation is intensive undesired species will be unable to survive and the ecological diversity will decline.

Meanwhile, the people in new urban areas created out of concrete, glass and steel will suffer through their lack of access to the natural world. Densely urban spaces are plagued by a whole host of 'Modern Diseases' (explored in the chapter on Health) affecting both mental and physical well-being, fumes choke lungs in the absence of greenery and the real spiritual nourishment provided by contact with other plants and animals is lacking. And if not working to produce food in the countryside, what will all these urbanites be doing all day? Doubtless, there is some very useful work to be found in the design, construction and upkeep of buildings, in the study of sciences and arts, in the distribution (presently always via monetary transactions, usually in shops) of foodstuffs, services and other goods, the cleaning of the streets and provision of public transport. But in the capitalistic system, useful work such as this is not shared equally between the inhabitants of the cities. Many of these jobs are poorly paid, and workers have to spend long hours doing them, leaving them little time to pursue other interests and studies in life and to enjoy the company of their family and friends and the rest of the natural world. Others do jobs in the financial or marketing sectors that, as explained elsewhere in this document, do not do any good at all – and indeed can cause great harm by helping to perpetuate the slavery of capitalism. But the remainder struggle to find any work at all, and with urbanisation often comes rampant unemployment and, in the absence of appropriate welfare provisions for all to enjoy, dire living conditions for the families of those who cannot find work.

If nature was allowed to enter into our cities, they could become living, breathing pedestrianized environments covered with trees, flowering plants and animals in place of dangerous and unhealthy roads and cars. If useful city work was shared so that everyone had a meaningful job and also enough time to enjoy the humans, flora and fauna around them every day they could become healthy places for the body and the soul. If the myth of a better life in the city was abolished, and instead life in the countryside improved by using the best of our technology to make manual agriculture easier but still capable of employing many people, and allowing local communities to flourish by providing local food, goods and services for themselves, the trend towards urbanisation would cease and rural dwellers could enjoy the fruits of their labours with time to spare to enjoy the beauty of the nature all around them. Instead, by imprisoning ourselves within cities of our own creation from which the rest of nature is banished, we are putting in place of the natural paradise of the countryside manufactured landscapes of hell. This is the most tragic instance of the pollution of paradise of them all.

4.3 Changing Climates

It is now accepted beyond any doubt that levels of carbon dioxide in the atmosphere are rising. Since 1958 they have been measured at Mauna Loa in Hawaii, where in 2014 the level exceeded 400 parts per million (ppm) for the first time. Though the value at this particular location has no special importance relative to anywhere else on Earth, the trends it displays are indicative of global change. The carbon dioxide concentration rises in the summer months and falls again in winter, but the summer high and winter low have each been rising year on year since these records began[38]. The records can be extended back less precisely but nevertheless quite accurately for up to eight hundred thousand years using ice cores that have trapped samples of the atmosphere for each year of snowfall. They show that during this time carbon dioxide levels fluctuated between 170 and 300 ppm until the dawn of human industry, at which point levels stood at 280 ppm[39]. Current levels are therefore unprecedented since well before the evolution of modern *homo sapiens*. Most observers would also agree that other greenhouse gasses, such as methane, are also on the rise.

It is beyond reasonable doubt that it is these greenhouse gasses that have been causing Earth to warm for at least the past half-century. Carbon dioxide levels and global temperatures have always been strongly correlated and the theory by which each can influence the other is well understood. Some critics of the scientifically verified theory of modern-day 'global warming' have pointed out that 400 ppm is far from unprecedented if we extend our records back, through various less precise and certainly more uncertain methods, beyond 800 000 years. Tens of millions of years ago, carbon dioxide stood at thousands of parts per million in the atmosphere. But there are two important reasons why current levels are nonetheless unprecedented and concerning. Firstly, the Earth millions of years ago was a very different place. The Ice Age (defined as an epoch in which Earth has at least some ice cover) we are currently in began only 2.6 million years ago. Humans evolved after this, and are adapted to living in temperatures consistent with it. Life as a whole would continue to thrive quite happily in much warmer conditions that Earth has experienced before, but humans and other contemporary species might not. Secondly, carbon dioxide levels have fallen over an even longer timescale, hundreds of millions of years, in response to a rise in solar output. Carbon dioxide acts as a long-term 'thermostat' via the carbon cycle. As the sun's intensity has increased, warming the Earth, increased rates of weathering reactions have locked more and more carbon dioxide into rocks, drawing it out of the atmosphere and counteracting, in the long-term, the warming that would otherwise be induced. Hence, the huge drop in carbon dioxide levels over hundreds of millions of years has been essential to the maintenance of a habitable world.

To reverse this trend would not be at all desirable for life, let alone Ice Age life such as humanity.

During the current Ice Age, it has been first variations in the sun's output and, second, three 'forcings' of Earth's orbit that have most strongly determined the climate on the planet. The second has had arguably the stronger effect. The theory behind orbital forcings was developed by Milutin Milankovitch in the 1930s and 40s. He predicted that three variations in the Earth's orbit around the sun would be significant for climate. First, the ellipticity of Earth's orbit changes between 0 and 0.06 on a 93000-year cycle. When the ellipticity is high, Earth is closer to the sun on some parts of the orbit and further away on other parts relative to the case where the ellipticity is low (the orbit is circular). Secondly, the angle by which the Earth's rotation axis is tilted relative to its orbital plane varies between 22.1° and 24.5° on a 41000-year cycle (it is currently 23.5°). It's this tilt that controls the seasons: for half its orbit the northern hemisphere leans towards the sun (northern summer), whilst for the other half the southern hemisphere does (northern winter, southern summer). Hence, a smaller tilt angle will move the tropic of Cancer southwards and the tropic of Capricorn northwards and weaken the contrast between summer and winter conditions. The third important factor is the precession of Earth's spin axis, which essentially moves the position in the elliptical orbit at which each hemisphere experiences its summer over time. At the moment, for instance, the Earth is at its closest point to the sun on its orbit in February, during the Southern Hemisphere's summer. This makes the southern summer slightly warmer and the northern summer slightly cooler than they would be if Earth was closest to the sun in, say, July. The period of the axial precession is 23000 years[40].

The cumulative effect of these orbital changes, each of which acts on different time-spans, on Earth's climate is complex. None of the changes involves the Earth actually moving, on average, closer to or further away from the sun. Rather, they conspire to vary the amount of light that a given hemisphere of Earth receives in summer and winter. As alluded to above, Earth has been in a perpetual Ice Age for the past 2.6 million years. But the temperature record we obtain from ice-cores stretching back over the last 800 000 years indicates that during this time Earth has switched between relatively warm 'interglacial' periods such as that we are experiencing now, and especially cold, 'glacial' periods in which the ice cover was much greater. These variations aren't simplistically periodic. But careful analyses reveal that within them lie hidden the three periods predicted by Milankovitch, overlapping with one another. Glacial periods are thought to be brought about when the three orbital factors conspire to make the Northern Hemisphere's summers cooler than average, which allows ice to persist in the

Arctic more easily and to grow in quantity over time. So, in the long-term, it's the Earth's orbit that determines its climate.

But in the shorter-term, it's the sun itself that's key. The sun is a variable star on many different scales. Most easily observed are its 11-year sunspot cycles; when these cycles dictate that there are more sunspots, the sun's total output is slightly stronger and there is a slight increase in the radiation incident on Earth. This has a small but non-negligible effect on sea temperatures and pressures, lagged by three to four years. More important for us are the slightly longer-term variations in the strength of these maxima from cycle to cycle. A weak solar maximum (few sunspots) has been associated with the 'Little Ice Age' in Europe for example, when the Thames regularly froze over. Meanwhile, most of the global warming that was observed in the earlier half of the twentieth century has been ascribed to a rise in sunspots[41]. In essence, the global temperature curve roughly followed that of solar activity until about 1960.

Before the 1960s, humans had been pumping increasingly large quantities of greenhouse gasses into the air year on year, but their effect on climate was largely balanced by other anthropogenic effects, such as the cooling influence of aerosol gasses, which reflect sunlight back into space. Were the climate to continue to follow the sun, however, from this point onwards we should expect a slight global cooling. That the world has continued to warm is an indication that anthropogenic greenhouse gasses have become, at least since the mid-twentieth century, the dominant control of climatic change in the short term: the net anthropogenic effect, in essence, has become positive[42]. This is because greenhouse gas emission has continued to increase dramatically, much faster than that of aerosols: the aerosols were the culprits behind London's 'pea soup' smog of the 1950s, and were removed from smoke to improve air quality, though they nowadays cause health problems in many Chinese cities where the laws are more lax.

In general, this all shows that it's the amount of radiation incident on Earth and where exactly it is concentrated on the surface that determines to a large part the global average temperature, but that atmospheric gasses play a far from negligible role. Indeed, the rapidity with which Earth has switched between glacial and interglacial periods in the past can only be explained by the additional effect of carbon dioxide on top of the orbital changes. When the arctic begins to grow during a spell of cold northern summers, it reflects more light into space (because ice is more reflective than water) and the whole Earth begins to cool. This in turn causes the oceans to absorb more carbon dioxide from the atmosphere, accelerating the cooling. As the amount of ocean decreases with the spread of the ice, this absorption peters out, leaving Earth in a glacial state. So carbon dioxide really is Earth's thermostat.

This comes as somewhat of a surprise, because carbon dioxide isn't especially potent as a controller of the climate, when compared to the effect of Earth's orbit and long-term variations in the sun. Furthermore, it is at extremely low concentration in the atmosphere, which is composed of 99.96% nitrogen, oxygen and argon in dry areas. Carbon dioxide makes up most of the remaining 0.04%, but much of the atmosphere also contains water vapour, which is also a greenhouse gas and is much more abundant than carbon dioxide overall. Nevertheless, the carbon dioxide molecule's particular rotational and vibrational energy levels are separated by amounts that correspond to the energy of infrared photons, exactly the type that are radiated by Earth's surface. Hence, although they are transparent to visible and ultraviolet light (we can see through carbon dioxide after all) and therefore allow the sun's energy to pass them unhindered to be absorbed by the ground, molecules of carbon dioxide absorb the infrared light re-emitted by the planet's surface in order to move to higher energy levels. After atoms and molecules absorb energy in the form of light, they become 'excited', and re-radiate that light in order to settle back to a calm state. When carbon dioxide molecules fall back to lower levels in this way they emit this light in random directions, and the net effect is that some proportion of infrared light that would otherwise escape into space is reflected back to Earth, warming the planet. Its particular sensitivity to infrared light is the reason for carbon dioxide's especially potent and rapid effect, and means that changing carbon dioxide's concentration in the atmosphere can alter the climate on the timescale of decades. Our lives are adapted to life on an interglacial but not ice-free world, and we're not prepared for such a rapid change to a different scenario. Therefore, we fiddle with the carbon thermostat at our own peril.

4.4 Environmental Activism

The work of the environmental activist is a refreshing reminder of the ability of humanity to escape the chains of monetary wealth even in this Age of Capital. James Pilkington, an activist featured in The Ecologist in April 2011, has spent hours a day for months of his life vigilantly watching the fjords of British Colombia, Canada, not to earn the notes of paper and numbers on a screen most of us are wedded to as a means of obtaining the goods and services we seek, but simply because of the passion he holds for his quest to prevent ecological disaster. The contrast between the powers in this particular fight could not be greater: on the one hand, a man devoting his time and effort, which he could so easily have commoditised and translated into the goods we are constantly persuaded to desire, to strive against the absurdity of destroying the very landscape that inspires and sustains us; on the other, Enbridge, which, as an oil company cannot help but do, fulfils its lust for profit by pumping the planet for all the oil it can get away with, without care.

What the environmentalists who stage such feats appreciate is that our existence on this planet, and that of the other beings we share it with, is about much more than the 'wealth' of goods and power that, over the last couple of centuries, we have been convinced to strive towards. This artificial wealth cannot bring us joy and true prosperity; a real sense of satisfaction in life can only be achieved by allowing oneself to be in harmony with nature. It was in the natural world that our species evolved, and in the natural world will we always be at home, at heart. A habitat, such as the Canadian fjords, is a place of existence for a whole range of individuals: animals that, unlike ourselves, are constantly in contact and mutuality with the environment around them. Human beings have the ability to shape our own habitats, but to ceaselessly destroy those of other species and to construct in their place alien landscapes so at odds with our – or their – natural inclinations is not a mechanism conducive to a prosperous society. If oil companies like Enbridge get their way, the beautiful planet on which we live will be hewn to pieces for the sake of extraction of resources, like oil, that will be used to produce more artificial habitats and power more construction of poorly-made, cheap goods to the detriment of our environment and our true wellbeing.

Environmental activists are not content to allow this to happen. They don't only alter their own behaviour to avoid commonplace actions that they perceive as harmful: they strive through petitions, persuasion, political pressure, protests and direct action to change the whole of society's relationship with the world and to prevent the ecological destruction that causes harm to humans and other species alike. But there are many different philosophical motivations for environmental activism, and many conceivable ways of protesting, and it is important to consider the ethical implications of such action. Different activists have different views on the extent to which illegal or even violent actions can be justified in the cause of environmentalism. These views stem from the variety of values and perspectives that each activist holds. Although they act as individuals, in order to understand the behaviour of activists they can be loosely grouped into a number of broad categories either by outside observers or by their own self-identification. Here, we shall discuss many of these major organisational or philosophical groupings and attempt to draw conclusions regarding the efficacy of their methods and validity of their claims and inspirations in light of the successes and failures each has encountered so far in their efforts to bring about changes in behaviour and mind-sets relating to environmental issues. Their motivations may be different, but many of these groups agree upon the best environmental outcome in many cases. We shall focus briefly upon the specific views of these activists and will not attempt to draw together a 'happy balance' between them or create a coherent ethical framework on which to base our behaviour in light of the insights they provide. Such a framework will be reserved for Chapter 5, but many of the ideas for a more caring and prosperous society discussed therein and in future chapters are inspired by some of the activist movements discussed here.

There are two key motivating ideologies behind protection of the environment: the 'conservationist' and the 'preservationist'. Both want to limit the extent to which we use finite resources and damage other ecosystems. But whilst preservationists do this for the ecosystems' own sakes, conservationists do so in order to protect our long-term ability to exploit those ecosystems. The difference is subtle, but it can result in different policy outcomes being advocated by the two groups. For example, take an endangered coral reef. Both conservationist and preservationist activists would take action against the wilful destruction of a beautiful, accessible coral reef through, for instance, the dumping of waste into that part of the ocean. Both would want to curb the acidification of the oceans caused by anthropogenic emissions of greenhouse gasses, which results in the phenomenon of coral bleaching, effectively killing the ecosystem. Preservationists would take this action because they believe that there is real value in the coral reef itself to the animals that use it and to humanity as part of the aesthetic and inspiring environment in which we want to live. They would argue that the reef is part of a wider system of life that has taken millions of years to evolve and should be preserved for its own sake. Any company, government or individual that destroys the reef not out of necessity but out of cost-cutting or convenience has clearly not taken the reef's true value into account.

Conservationists, on the other hand, argue that natural environments should be conserved as a resource for humans to continue to use. In this case, the reef provides tourist income for local people, and quantifiable aesthetic and recreational benefits. It may also provide fish for humans, either directly or indirectly by fostering the smaller plant and animal life that larger fish eat before we catch them. To destroy the reef is to undermine our ability to continue to have access to all these benefits. Therefore the reef should be conserved, as a finite resource. The difference between the policy advocated by two outlooks only becomes manifest when we talk not of destroying the reef but of changing it for human purposes. The preservationist would probably be opposed to damaging the reef in order to provide better tourist access, because this would be degrading the ecosystem's value unnecessarily. The conservationist, though, would welcome any change that maximised humanity's ability to make use of an environmental resource such as the reef in the long term, and better tourist access might well do this. Hence, conservationists and preservationists both look at our environment with a long-term perspective. But whilst the former tend to take an anthropocentric outlook on environmental policy, speaking of the need to conserve the viability of 'ecosystem services' for humans, the latter advocate a more holistic one, viewing humans as only part of a wider web of life that has immeasurable value of its own.

Another disagreement between activists reflects the debate between utilitarian and deontological ways of making decisions. We shall explore these two oppositional ideas in more detail and their optimal reconciliation in Chapter 5, but here it suffices us to define utilitarianism as a will to maximise overall well-being, summed across all individuals, whilst deontology prioritises the maintenance of individuals' rights through strict adherence to distinct laws. Which individuals have deontological rights or should be included in the calculations of maximal prosperity are a source of further disagreement. Adherents of an anthropocentric view would seek to prioritise humans, whilst other activists might afford other animals and plants rights or take them into the equation for maximum prosperity. Some would include future generations, others would not. But both types of activist would probably oppose the destruction of the coral reef. The utilitarian will oppose it because it maximises the short-term prosperity of the agent who finds it cheap or convenient to dump their waste in this particular place but will be harmful to humans (and other animals and future generations) overall. The deontologist will oppose it because it violates the rights of the people who enjoy the reef as tourists or live nearby to enjoy a natural environment or the rights of the animals and plants on the reef to live at all. But if the reef was destroyed in the process of, say, creating a bird sanctuary used by thousands of birds that could be placed nowhere else, a utilitarian trying to maximise animal prosperity might support the project, whilst a deontologist concerned about the rights of the smaller number of animals living on the reef would not.

The inherent worth of the natural world irrespective of its use for humans that preservationists tend to champion is at the core of the environmental activist viewpoint known as 'Deep Ecology'. All Deep Ecologists are holist preservationists, but their beliefs constitute a 'deeper' philosophical movement to which not all of those concerned with preserving the environment necessarily prescribe. Deep Ecologists believe that all human interference with natural systems should be avoided, and that we should live as simply as possible in order to preserve the natural ecosystems that are of much greater worth than any man-made fabrication. So not only does human civilisation have the capacity through over-consumption and careless pollution to endanger natural ecosystems of inherent worth of which human beings are only a part. More than this, civilisation will always be in direct opposition to the natural order unless the flourishing of all life on Earth becomes its overriding priority. For Deep Ecologists, then, it is essential that the human population be reduced, interference in nature avoided and the pursuit of higher standards of living abandoned. Only those actions that cause no harm beyond what it would be natural for a human to inflict were we still living in our natural habitat should be taken. The movement has a profoundly spiritual basis, rooted in the philosophy of Benedictus de Spinoza, a panentheist who believed that there are no true individuals and that everything is part of one, unifying God. Deep ecologists distinguish themselves from 'shallow' ecologists, who campaign only to preserve or conserve particular environments or to scale-down the extent of human destruction of ecosystems and other animals, in that their motivation is rooted in the will for a complete transformation of humanity's relationship with nature and view of ourselves that would profoundly change every aspect of how we live our lives.

Deep ecology is a more recent manifestation, born of twentieth century consumer-capitalist industrialisation, of a wider movement of 'Romanticism' that has its roots in the seventeenth century. Even at the very cusp of industrialisation, thinkers such as the German philosopher Novalis and the English writers and poets William Blake, Samuel Taylor Coleridge and William Wordsworth, knew that the scientific, rational truth becoming increasingly prevalent in their societies could only explain a limited part of a wider reality. They called for resistance to unimpeded industrialisation and for an appreciation of nature and natural art that runs beyond their scientific utility. They were often disgusted by the abuses carried out in the name of scientific understanding and industrial progress against a natural world that they saw as supremely beautiful. The Romantics and their modern-day sympathisers are not necessarily against science and reason, so long as the thinker does not lose a more emotional connection with the world that they are studying. There is only a certain amount that can be learned from logic and books; still more important truths are to be gained from appreciating the natural world first-hand and exercising the imagination to carry us beyond the material. Hence, says Wordsworth in his poem 'The Tables Turned',

> Up! Up! My Friend, and quit your books;
> Or surely you'll grow double:
> Up! Up! My Friend, and clear your looks;
> Why all this toil and trouble?...
>
> ...Books! 'tis a dull and endless strife:
> Come, hear the woodland linnet,
> How sweet his music! On my life,
> There's more of wisdom in it...
>
> ...One impulse from a vernal wood
> May teach you more of man,

Of moral evil and of good
Than all the Sages can.

Sweet is the Lore which Nature brings;
Our meddling intellect
Misshapes the beauteous forms of things:-
We murder to dissect.

Enough of Science and Art;
Close up those barren leaves;
Come forth, and bring with you a heart
That watches and receives.

The 'Art' that Wordsworth refers to here is presumably that of modern industries as opposed to the more natural, observant art of the kind exemplified by his own poetry. The loss of contact with the natural world and our growing inability to see the consequences for our environment of our actions that has multiplied in the industrial world was clearly foreseen by Romantics from industrial society's very beginnings. There is much of this Romanticism in modern-day Deep Ecology, which recognises that we have begun to wreak havoc upon all the creatures of nature, including ourselves, through a more profound loss of the spiritual connection we once held with the rest of the web of life than the first Romantics could have imagined.

A similarly holistic and philosophically transformative view of society and the environment is that of the Ecofeminists, which emerged out of the broader feminist movement in the 1970s. Feminists as a whole agree that women have been (and in many cases continue to be) unfairly represented in important societal roles in our own and former societies because they have been made subject to domineering patronisation and control by men. But feminists do not all agree on why this has been the case and how the situation can be rectified. They can be loosely grouped into three main camps. First are those who believe that the differences between males and females have been purposefully overplayed historically by men for the males' own benefit. Women have been falsely treated as if they were too emotional, irrational and physically weak to hold positions of responsibility, to exhibit leadership over men or to work unless they rank amongst the lowest classes (peasants and factory workers), so that men can exploit them for sexual pleasure and they can be made to perform menial domestic tasks. These feminists argue that there is in truth little fundamental biological difference between men and women: except for sexual organs and pregnancy, all differences between the sexes are culturally imposed. Differences in taste, professional preference and outlook between the sexes are the product of a man-made gender apartheid and should be abolished – indeed, some of this sort of feminist might welcome a medical advance that allowed men as well as women to share the task of pregnancy – and an equal gender-balance should be imposed on every role in society, from business leadership and politics to looking after the house and family. Women, in other words, should be empowered to be more like men, who have enjoyed all the best advantages of human civilisation thus far.

Some feminists, however, reject this view. Whilst they agree that men have traditionally often exploited women and denied them their fair share of responsibility in society, they point out that this in itself illustrates a difference between men and women that cannot necessarily be culturally explained. These feminists deny that it is the case that men currently act as humans ought to do, and that it is only women who have been culturally conditioned to feel inferior. They consider it a degradation to women to expect them to become more like men: rather, men and women should be recognised as possessing different general views, abilities and outlooks that are biologically engrained. But rather than using these stereotypical differences to dismiss women as emotional or irrational, as men have traditionally done, these very differences should make it all the more important that women and men are involved in every echelon of society. Yes, women may be more inclined to heed emotional arguments where men tend to see cut-and-dried empirical ones, but for this reason it is important for both men and women to be involved in decision-making. Women are no less intelligent than men, and no less capable of making good, rational decisions. But the best decisions come when neither men nor women are solely in control: we should celebrate the variety afforded by having a mixture of both genders in our world and grant them equal access and opportunities. In order to bring this about, men and women should again be equally represented in all professions, but this should be enforced by government so that women do not have to adopt the competitive nature that men tend towards in order to compete with men for the top positions.

This, too, has its drawbacks, and the first type of feminist might present the counter-argument that by acknowledging biological differences between men and women we shall be excusing the continued suppression of female autonomy and denying women the chance to show themselves to be men's equals by competing with them for the 'top jobs'. The third branch of feminism tries to reconcile these two opposing views, and it does so from an environmental standpoint. Ecofeminism recognises that there are biological differences between women and men, and that men tend to be more competitive and domineering, which has allowed them to unfairly disadvantage women, who are generally more emotional and approachable. These stereotypes are not universally adhered to, and there will of course be many exceptions. Ecofeminists again argue that women and men should be equally involved in all high-ranking jobs and decision-making. But they go further, claiming that the environmental crises we face are a consequence of women not being involved in policy-making, because the same domineering male attitude that has historically subjugated women has also subjugated nature. Men have used both women and the resources of the natural world to their own short-term advantage because they lack the more compassionate and emotionally responsive outlook that women more generally hold. If women were equally involved with men in policy-making, they say, the holistic nature of the world would be recognised in policy and the ecosystems that men have only valued from an anthropocentric viewpoint would be recognised for their true worth and better protected.

Ecofeminists would probably not argue for equal representation of men and women in all roles in society, because they recognise that there are certain roles that require a greater emotional involvement – such as primary school teaching and counselling – and others that require more muscular strength, such as building. But we should never discriminate between men and women when recruiting for any profession, excluding women because they are women or men because they are men. The best person should be chosen for each job, it's just that this may be expected to result naturally in unequal representation in some professions. Most professions, though, should not be expected to exhibit such an unequal distribution, and most importantly decision-making should not be primarily in the hands of one gender. Therefore, educating men and women to the same standard – but not into the same masculine way of thinking – and enforcing equal representation in politics of male and female values would be vital first steps in bringing about better political decisions. But this doesn't mean equal representation for men and women in modern business and industry, because these are designed along the very capitalist, destructive lines that Ecofeminists want to abolish, and simply introducing more women into them would turn those women into pseudo-men. Like Deep Ecologists, Ecofeminists recognise that the most important change we can make as a society is to become better connected to nature and to adopt an equal reverence for all life. But they regard this as a fundamental part of a societal shift from the competitive, exploitative and discriminatory values of a patriarchal hierarchy to the cooperative, nurturing way of life that an emphasis on feminine attitudes would bring about. Therefore, business, industry and politics should be completely reorganised along inclusive, cooperative lines for the benefit of humanity and the wider ecosystems of life on Earth. In rejecting a purely scientific worldview, which they argue has been imposed as the sole 'truth' by men, and encouraging a more holistic and spiritually-aware way of seeing the world, Ecofeminists share many of the principles of the Romantic movement.

Activists falling into any or none of these ideological camps also face practical decisions regarding how to act to bring about change. Should it be peaceful or violent? Should existing laws be obeyed even in the process of trying to change them? These are the sorts of questions that any of us advocating for change must seek to answer. We can define three loose methodologies through which activists can try to bring about change, which shall term 'complicity', 'cooperation' and 'confrontation'. The least radical activists choose to act not only within the law but also within the capitalist system – they are 'complicit' with it. They do not call for the abolition of big business or the de-emphasis of profit as the measure of success, but attempt to bring about greater care for the environment by forcing big businesses to change their practices through either consumer pressure or government regulations. These activists may set up small businesses to go into competition with the big monopolists such as energy companies and supermarkets, with the intention of demonstrating that there are alternative, less environmentally or socially damaging ways of delivering goods and services and of changing consumer preferences towards these. The key for these activists is education – particularly of the young – to encourage other people to make the most environmentally friendly choices within the capitalist system and to encourage further change.

The main advantage of this type of activism is that it can provide real results from the outset. Setting up businesses to supply solar panels competitively has, with the help of government subsidies, resulted in a great uptake of photovoltaic technology in the UK and elsewhere in the world in recent years. Sometimes, other businesses can provide useful 'consumer' advice, such as those that inform the public of the environmentally destructive practices of the 'big six' UK energy companies and encourage them to switch to greener suppliers. Such businesses' 'business model' is based on payments from those green suppliers whenever somebody is successfully persuaded to switch. This sort of activism has also powered the development of pioneering new technologies to present 'consumers' or governments with additional 'green' choices that big businesses don't provide, such as new, more efficient ways of harnessing solar and wind energy, or local-grown organic produce.

But the problem with capitalist activism is that the more immediate changes it brings about aren't actually very radical and will not be sufficient to deal with the biggest environmental problems, including climate change and resource extraction. The reason is that they do not combat the capitalist consumer attitude that is driving such destruction. New technologies and smarter 'consumer' choices alone aren't sufficient: people must no longer be treated as 'consumers' at all, and must no longer be encouraged to buy more and more products and use more and more energy if we are to live sustainably in the world. This undermines capitalist business models: dramatically reducing the consumption of electricity is not compatible with a growing solar power 'industry' if it still has to compete with other forms of fuel that get cheaper as the demand is reduced. More efficient gadgets such as mobile telephones won't save much energy in the long-run if they continue to be used more and more or are rapidly replaced, and curbing these trends will undermine the business models of the developers of 'smartphone' applications designed to help people to save energy in other ways, or businesses trying to produce greener gadgets. The vested interest, if profit-making and competition remains the basis for manufacture, sale and distribution, remains geared towards 'growth' and increasing consumption. Consumption may be reduced in one way – using less electricity to power a television, say – but it has to be made up for in another – regularly replacing an old television with the more efficient model, for example. That's why, for all their valiant efforts, the companies big and small that have pioneered more efficient technologies and education schemes have failed to provide meaningful societal change that would really begin to combat climate change and habitat destruction.

In their attempts to bring about more meaningful change many activists are more explicitly political. But some favour cooperation, others confrontation, to bring about political change that avoids and sometimes directly challenges the market-oriented mechanisms of capitalism. Cooperation involves peacefully trying to persuade the populace to change their behaviour or to support policies and parties that prioritise environmental conservation or preservation, and politicians to adopt policies that the activists believe to bring environmental or social benefits, always working within the existing legal code. It may involve the signing of petitions, the production of posters and the staging of protests, or funding or actively campaigning for radical political parties. The publication of a book such as this one could be regarded as 'cooperational' activism, aiming to persuade and suggest change that the author believes will benefit their intended audience amongst other beneficiaries – perhaps with some hope of inducing voluntary and democratically engineered change.

But there are times when, in the eyes of some activists, cooperation with existing legal frameworks and engines for change is not sufficient in scope or speed to deal with pressing environmental or social crises. For them, activism has to become more confrontational to succeed: going beyond pressure by peaceful protest, they actively prevent legal actions that they see as crimes from taking place, sometimes breaking the law of the land themselves in the process. In this category are all those who stand in front of bulldozers to prevent habitat destruction, tie themselves to trees to prevent them from being chopped down and raid animal testing centres to release the inmates. On a less dramatic scale, it also includes those who carry out outright boycotts of particular companies or products as opposed to setting up alternative businesses to compete with them.

Such action is born of desperation and a feeling that a change has to happen immediately for something precious to be preserved before it is too late. Where it is successful, it can have great advantages, in that actions that society genuinely believes to be harmful are prevented. The downside is, of course, that the disruption caused by confrontational activists is not explicitly endorsed by wider society or even necessarily by those whose rights they seek to protect. It may be that the activist is misguided, wrongly thinking that chopping down a particular tree, say, will cause harm to the local community or to animals that live in its environs when in actual fact all would benefit from an alternative arrangement because the tree is invasive or liable to collapse and poses a threat rather than a benefit to life. Confrontational activists therefore have a responsibility to be as informed as possible about the issues on which they campaign, taking into account the opinions of all the parties they deem to be affected by the decision or activity against which they are protesting. But even if the respect for rights and the greatest overall benefit demand, indeed, that the decision or action is halted, if the vast majority of society has not been persuaded of this the confrontational activist risks arrest by carrying out their disruptive protest.

A confrontational activist is not a rioter: whilst the former should act carefully and with a clear goal in mind, ceasing their protest once this has been achieved and avoiding damage to individuals or infrastructure against which they have no protest, the latter is prone to inconsiderate and opportunistic thuggery and delights in the violent means rather than the end goal. The two, however, can sometimes become implicated in the same events, the latter pouncing upon the opportunities for pillage or destruction created by the former. These connections run, unfortunately, back to the very roots of the confrontational activist movement: the great Peasants' Revolt in England in 1381 was an activist movement in opposition to abusive taxes and poor governance, but even when a deal had supposedly been struck between the rebels and the government, it proved impossible to prevent over-zealous rioters from proceeding to raid the Tower of London and beheading two officials.

The connection extends right up to the present. In August 2011, a peaceful protest staged in London against the police shooting of an unarmed innocent was seized upon by rioters and looters, and erupted into a six-day spate of opportunistic theft and destruction that extended to cities across England. On the other hand, environmental confrontations are less liable to provoke such side-effects because they do not instil the same level of anger amongst the general populace and tend to take place on the front line of environmental destruction rather than areas of social deprivation that could act as tinderboxes for more general expressions of rage against social inequality to break out.

One of the most famous confrontational environmental protests in Britain of recent times was that against the M3 motorway on Twyford Down. In March 1992, with public enquiries and an appeal to the high Court having failed to prevent plans to build the last stretch of road across two Sites of Scientific Interest, an Area of Outstanding Natural Beauty and two Scheduled Ancient Monuments, protesters wishing to protect what they saw as an irreplaceable and previous natural landscape set up camp on the proposed route. They feared that the true costs and realistic benefits of the project had not been taken into account, that precious species such as the Chalkhill Blue butterfly would be lost, and that little gain would be had for local traffic for all this destruction. This was a clear case where, cooperational protests having failed, impassioned environmentalists could conceive no option but to confront the bulldozers directly and forcibly prevent the destruction.

The protest ultimately failed. Though protesters had created a human shield for the Down by literally standing in the way of or chaining themselves to construction equipment, on Wednesday 9th December 1992 the police called in a private security company with the remit to physically remove them. After altercations so violent that some of the security guards reportedly resigned in protest at their own colleagues' behaviour, the most resistive objectors were finally dragged from their positions on the Saturday and some were arrested. The protesters returned, however, several times in 1993 when the work had already started, but the police responded each time with further arrests, running into tens of people over the course of the year. In July, the Department of Transport succeeded in obtaining an injunction to prevent certain named individuals from coming near the construction site, and when some of these formed part of a five-hundred-strong force that descended on the Down two days later they were arrested and each sentenced to twenty-eight days in jail. This was the last major confrontational protest, though cooperative legal demonstrations continued to be held, and the road was completed.

However, the action was not entirely without result. The public uproar surrounding the M3 construction forced the government to rethink its position on road-building in general. In an attempt to prevent further protests of the same kind the Department of Transport took seventy-six of the Twyford Down protestors to court to sue for damages, but the attempt came to little: the case was dropped in July 1995. Meanwhile, cases taken out by protestors against the police for unlawful arrests and by the construction company against the Department for costs incurred through their failure to recognise the public opposition to the project were more successful. New anti-roads protest groups were founded as a result of the protests, and the Labour government abandoned the largest planned road schemes of the previous government when it came to power in 1997, aiming at reducing car usage instead of building new roads as a means to ease congestion. In this at least, the confrontational action, though it did not preserve directly the environment that the instigators wanted it to and did result in arrests and imprisonment, may well have been considered worth the effort by the environmental activists involved.

Therefore both confrontational and cooperational activism can play a role in bringing about wider political change, by demonstrating to the government the passions of at least some of their people. The former, though, should clearly only be carried out under exceptional circumstances, when working within the current laws of the land does not seem a feasible way of bringing about change. The different classes of activist discussed above would have different opinions regarding what constitutes acceptable circumstances for confrontational action, and no doubt there would be disagreement even between members of these broad and diverse groupings. A deontologist would argue that confrontational action should be taken where the rights of some individual or individuals would otherwise be infringed upon, and should not be carried out in violation of others' fundamental rights. A utilitarian would weigh up the costs and benefits of the action and whether or not it would be in the 'greater good', regardless of whether or not it involved infringements of what others would perceive to be 'rights'.

So, what are we to make of all these different ideas and methodologies in environmental activism? What can they teach us about the way forwards towards a more environmentally sustainable society? Clearly, there is a lot to be said for taking a holistic approach, viewing ourselves as part of a wider ecological system that contains other individuals with rights, and appreciating the value intrinsic to each organism and feature of the landscape. But we should neither be wholly deontological nor wholly utilitarian in our approach to environmental issues: whilst fundamental rights of ourselves, other animate beings and future generations must be respected, there will be calculations to be made regarding the most beneficial action within these bounds. The activists that campaign from all the different viewpoints we've seen can each tech us something about how to engage with society and its governmental structure. In many cases, despite their differing motivations, all these activists will campaign for the same policies and societal behaviour that will benefit nature, whether they see this as a good in its own right or beneficial because of the 'services' it provides for mankind.

But what it is most important to learn from environmental activists is a passionate will to think about and seek to improve our collective relationship with the rest of Nature. All too often, decisions are made that are bad for the environment and bad for society because the value of the natural world – either in its own right or as a resource for ourselves – simply isn't taken into account. A very outdated view of the Earth as an infinite resource and waste repository is not seriously believed by anyone, and yet companies and individuals that won't bear the cost of its depletion or damage treat our planet as if it were such. It's very important, therefore, to increase activism of any kind amongst the general public – to have everybody involved in thinking about the gift of Nature and its practical limitations and to democratically decide, together, how we ought to behave towards it. On the assumption, then, that society can become engaged in environmental issues and agree upon a framework for what we want to achieve in our interactions with the rest of Nature, the rest of this chapter argues for a particular viewpoint that promises if adopted democratically to bring about great benefits to mankind and the species with which we share this world.

4.5 Living 'in' the Earth

Our solar system contains many worlds. Mercury is a bare, dry rock, scorching hot on the day side and biting cold on the night. Venus' surface bakes beneath the crushing pressure of a thick, acidic blanket of gas forged by a runaway greenhouse effect. Mars is frigid and barren, just about clinging on to its preciously sparse shroud of carbon dioxide. Jupiter and Saturn have no surface at all, though their gassy bulk of hydrogen and helium is crushed by its own weight into solidity at their cores. Their moons are mostly rocky and dead, except for fiery tectonic Io, Europa the frozen sea and Titan, with its heady mix of hydrocarbons. Out in the inky-black frigidity of the outer solar system, Uranus, Neptune and countless dwarf-planets shiver in the dark.

But which of these would we rather live in? None, for certain, were we given the choice of our own Earth. It might be possible to live 'on' one of them – in an enclosure perched on Mars, perhaps, or a submarine on Europa. Indeed, men have walked on our own Moon. But we can only live 'in' our own Earth, or more precisely in its atmosphere. Only here are we protected and nurtured by a safe, pleasant sphere of air that balances the input of radiation from the sun and output of radiation from Earth to provide a temperature and pressure suitable for water to be liquid over most of the surface, the essential requirement for our life. We tend to take the atmosphere for granted, more so even than the oceans and the land surface. When pollution is far away – the 'plastic island' in the Pacific Ocean for example – we tend to forget about it and its costs to ourselves and other life-forms. So we notice the pollution of cigarettes, car exhausts and factories in cities when we taste their foul air and suffer directly their ill effects. But we ignore the invisible pollution – invisible methane and carbon dioxide or water vapour contrails that blend in with the clouds. Yet, as the examples of the other planets demonstrate, our atmosphere is incredibly precious. It is what makes the Earth uniquely habitable, and links together all its other systems – land, sea and life. It is what we are living 'in' for every moment of our lives, and it should be treated with care, not despoiled by the smoke of unnatural and unnecessary industries, if we are to maintain a healthy and happy environment for ourselves, other species and future generations. We have an ethical duty to each of these, according to the principle of empathy discussed in Chapter 6, not to consume or pollute to excess.

Prince Charles, in his book *Harmony*, makes the shrewd observation that the Christian Lord's Prayer has been modified in some modern translations to read 'on Earth as it is in Heaven' from 'in Earth as it is in Heaven'. Regardless of the theology of the prayer itself, he points out that this change indicates a wider change in human culture, whereby we have forgotten that we are 'in' the Earth, linked in as an inseparable part of a world that surrounds us and which we influence and intricately depend upon. We view ourselves as living 'on' it instead, as if Earth is simply a platform of resources from which we can take whatever we like without consequence or limit. This is what has led our societies to pollute the water, land and skies of the planet since the Industrial Revolution without thought for the costs.

As we shall see in Chapter 5, first industrial capitalists trying to make a profit, then economists and policy-makers trying to justify environmental degradation, have weighed up the costs and benefits of their actions without taking into account the needs of the rest of the world – a world of which they form just a part. Future generations and other species have been neglected in their calculations of the costs of polluting actions, and the benefits of products that last only for a short while have been exaggerated. The values inherent in people and ecosystems cannot possibly be accurately represented by monetary 'costs' and 'prices'. Animate lives are surely invaluable: life itself is its own purpose, and is infinitely valuable to the one who holds it. Were some external, supremely intelligent and impartial being able to accurately numerically compute the values of ecosystems that life in all forms makes up and relies upon, however, we can be sure that they would be priced vastly higher than any man-made products that could be produced from them. After all, ecosystems support countless life-forms present and future, including human beings. Man-made goods by contrast last only for a short while and are used by a handful of people before being discarded. That doesn't mean that they should never be produced, only that they shouldn't be produced at the expense of entire ecosystems or animate lives. To realise this, and to appreciate the true value of life and of Nature, is to live 'in' rather than 'on' the planet again. Acting on this basis means moderating our behaviour to protect the interests of those far detached in space and time from ourselves, but who are all part of the same, interconnected, living Earth.

This has important consequences for how we deal with the environmental problems that we already face. They are often born of an over-enthusiastic use of perfectly good technologies which, in moderation, could provide great benefit to life as a whole. For example, the internal combustion engine can help people who are disabled or need to travel far a great deal, as it lets us move goods around the country to where they are needed. Its negative side-effects have sprung from its over-use, exemplified by the importation of goods that could just as easily be produced from materials and labour in the local area and the commuting of persons over long distances to jobs far away that could be done closer to home. The aeroplane is helpful for researchers, aid workers or international delegations that genuinely need to travel across the globe and should therefore be provided with plane tickets if society as a whole considers the benefits of the travel to exceed the damage doe to the planet. The problem comes when plane tickets are sold to everyone from holiday-makers to jet-set businessmen at prices that cannot hope to account for the environmental costs of the travel. This monetary price becomes the only consideration of the traveller when they decide whether their travel is worthwhile or not, and the environmental burden is simply ignored.

In light of this and countless other examples of human industry and technology growing too large in scale as a result of capitalist pressure for growth and profit, we can see that technological innovation alone cannot possibly solve our environmental problems. Climate change will not be prevented by low-energy light-bulbs or super-efficient laptops. The production of too many goods, of whatever kind, is embedded at the root of the problem just as staunchly as is the over-use of internal combustion engines. Biodegradable plastic isn't going to solve the problem of the Pacific plastic island. The abuse of technology has been the cause of all human-inflicted biodiversity loss and ecosystem degradation, and there is no reason to think that new technologies, if again over-used, will not produce similar unintended side-effects, deplete our resources and the planet's life-support systems and pollute our own habitat. New technologies are necessary as part of the clean-up of the planet and transition to a more sustainable way of life. But it would be a fundamental misunderstanding of the environmental crises we face to think that new technology can be the sole solution, and that a curb in the consumption of the rich world and wide-scale behavioural changes will not also be necessary.

But learning to live 'in' the Earth again is not only beneficial in that it allows us to do our duty to one another. Protecting and appreciating the planet is not a painful sacrifice: we, when our industrialised society turned away from an appreciation of our place in nature, lost an important emotional attachment to our surroundings that concrete, steel and technology cannot replace. Worshipping the gods of capitalism has painful mental and physical consequences. Endless production and consumption keep us busy in our work or leisure at all hours of the day; the pursuit of money leads us to focus on the trivial and material that can easily be priced and to lose hold of what we value most dearly but cannot set a price to. Greed for more possessions, more to eat and drink and less laborious ways of doing everyday tasks makes us isolated and physically unhealthy. We ignore community in pursuit of individual success. We ignore natural food and surroundings in favour of too many sweets and comforts. We ignore contemplation and appreciation of our surroundings in favour of computer screens and busy jobs that often produce nothing useful but simply advertise and sell more capitalist products with which everyone can distract themselves. It is a more natural and happy way of life, as well as one that is better for others, though they may be distant in space, time or species, to live 'in' the Earth again. It's high time that, as a society, we agreed to do so.

What will living 'in' the Earth again entail? Its most important facet will be to treat the world around us according to what we defined as an 'holistic' approach earlier in this chapter, bearing in mind that all species are part of a single system of life, what James Lovelock called 'Gaia', that maintains the world in a state of balance most suited to diverse life through chemical and climatic feedbacks. We have to see ourselves as part of larger ecosystems operating in each region of the planet, able to change the rest of the world physically and biologically and intrinsically dependent upon all the physical forces and biological entities that exist in an ever-evolving balance that has provided the hospitable environment in which we ourselves could evolve and flourish. Industrial civilisation has wreaked a lot of damage on the planet, taking resources that cannot be renewed and destroying habitats at alarming rates over the past century in particular. Living 'in' the Earth means avoiding harm to sentient life wherever possible, living simpler lives in which technology is just as advanced but not necessarily as prevalent so that we all use far fewer resources than the average person in the industrial world currently does. It means giving other organisms space to recover by preventing any further destruction of 'natural' habitat and restoring parts of areas that humanity has especially heavily depleted into nature's care.

This doesn't mean attempting to 'revert' landscapes back to their pre-human states. After all, humans have always altered the landscapes in which we live, just as every other species does to some extent. Even supposedly 'virgin' rainforests today are managed by hunter-gatherer people living within them or have been in the past. Climates and species distributions are always changing, so that what was the 'natural' make-up of a region before humans may not even be feasible to reconstruct: some of the species may have died out, or the climate may no longer be suitable for them to survive, especially as a result of recent climatic change. Furthermore, taking humans out of the equation altogether can only result in failure for any area that is given back to Nature. Humans are like all other species in that we attempt to exploit our surroundings for our own benefit. If we deny this fact, and attempt to create environments that, ironically, are supposed to be natural and closed to future human interference, humans will interfere anyway at some point in the future, possibly with very negative consequences. What we need to do, then, is recognise what interaction humans will have with any given region of land. They may change its climate through greenhouse gas emissions or geoengineering schemes; they may wish to enter the protected area and appreciate the nature that it is our aim to foster therein. They may wish to use some of the flora and fauna as food. The region has to be allowed to adapt to these changes, and humans have to be allowed to interact with it, so long as their actions do not violate the rights of the other life-forms therein (rights that we shall return to in Chapter 5) or lead to an overall loss of biodiversity, which is something that we, as creatures in the living Earth, should seek to increase. The natural world is always changing even without human interference, and we shouldn't expect to be able to recreate a static 'golden age' of 'natural' conditions anywhere on the planet. But living 'in' the Earth means leaving nature to take its own course except where we need to carefully and lovingly manage it to grow our own crops, build our own buildings and meet our own basic needs. It means having respect for each and every animal, not just for those humans that happen to live in the rich world.

If we're going to feed and house the world's human population, we have to hang on to most of the land we have already taken over for buildings and agriculture. But we must put back areas of refuge for trees and animals at the edges of fields and along streams, reforest places that we have recently desertified and avoid destroying any further habitat or purposefully killing any wild animals, as a matter of principle. Putting in place 'wildlife corridors' between pockets of habitat is a particularly effective way of helping species to survive. It won't be enough not to destroy any further habitat if we want to live in a world that is rich in biodiversity and protect the individual animals that are currently endangered: it has been shown that species do not tend to die out immediately following habitat destruction, but survive in pockets of remaining habitat, gradually dwindling in numbers, until they become extinct decades or centuries later[43]. Although it will be argued below that protecting particular 'species', which are difficult to define and distinguish, should not be our aim, but rather the preservation of all the animate individuals that we can, the loss of 'species' however defined clearly illustrates a reduction in biodiversity, a subversion of the very purposes of Nature and the suffering of individuals. To reverse this trend, it is necessary that we actively encourage the growth of habitat in which other animal species can live. This is all in line with their rights, with our own right to a natural environment and with a concept of living 'in' the Earth amidst other forms of life of all kinds.

If we endorse a new, more efficient agriculture and live simpler lives, this need not come into conflict with our presently expanding global population, so long as we work towards population stability within the next few decades through education and support for those living in regions of high population growth. New approaches will be necessary across all aspects of society, ideas for which will be outlined in later chapters. But fundamental to them all is a change of attitude: we are not living 'on' the Earth, but 'in' it.

Preserving Species – or Preserving Life?

Simply step into the countryside and look around, and you can have no doubt that we are blessed to live alongside a wondrous variety of plant and animal species on Earth. But amidst all this beautiful diversity, it can be difficult to define what exactly constitutes a 'species' in its own right, especially for animals. The traditional biological method is to designate those that are similar enough to interbreed and produce fertile offspring into a common species, and assume that other animals that look and behave similarly are members of the same. This works well enough at a single location, where the whole species population occupying a particular niche will interact with one another and it will remain clearly distinct from the rest of the ecosystem.

But problems arise when we compare animals across different locations that cannot interact and are only subtly different, having diverged from one another relatively recently. Some Amazonian bird populations were only centuries ago isolated in different regions by the barriers formed by rivers. Though they look very similar and were traditionally classed as parts of a single species, they in fact have very different songs and do not naturally interbreed. A closer inspection, therefore, leads us to define them as eight separate species. If we try to hone down demarcations between species using genetic profiles – studying and comparing the DNA of each individual specimen – often the number of apparently separate species skyrockets because of the huge extent of genetic variation even in a single, interacting population. Then there are other animals, such as the Hoatzin, which are extremely difficult to place within the web of life because their history and closest relatives are so difficult to determine.

So, it's becoming increasingly clear that the concept of a biological 'species' is a slippery one. From our own perspective as members of the human animal species it's not difficult to see why. Although we are similar in many basic ways, humans exhibit a huge variety of appearances, behaviours and living environments that reflect our true nature as individuals. The same applies to other animals: each individual is unique, both genetically and biologically, and it's through random variations in these unique characteristics that evolution acts. 'Speciation' occurs when two groups of individuals become separated by some barrier (such as a mountain or an ocean) and begin to adapt as separate communities to their separate environments, until they become so different they cannot interbreed, at which point they would be classed as distinct species. This process is only partially underway for the Amazonian birds. There, a transition is plainly occurring from a single ancestral bird species to multiple descendant ones.

But the truth is that all species are in transition, albeit often less visibly. We share a common progenitor, and are all evolving as part of a continuous global community of life to become better adapted to our planet, which through this process is becoming increasingly diverse. In light of this, perhaps it is misleading to talk of 'species' at all. Species classification is very relevant to conservationists whose aim is to preserve types of organism that are the most threatened and biologically unusual, which makes sense from a human-centric perspective that seeks to retain the unique 'ecosystem services' that species can provide for us.

Yet surely the true value of animals, human and non-human, lies in their individual capacity to experience the enjoyment of a living existence alongside all the other individuals that make up the ecosystem they form part of and benefit from. Which species each individual belongs to and whether this is rare or common is beside the point. If we truly want to preserve biodiversity and prosperity for animate life on this planet, we need to allow the amazing natural ecosystem communities it contains to continue to evolve and flourish by protecting natural habitat and avoiding harm to individual animals wherever we can. Only then will each of us satisfy our most basic need of all, to live as members of a prosperous biotic community.

4.6 Biomimicry: Learning from Nature

Biomimicry constitutes a curious turn of events. For all our designs, all our machinery and technological developments, we have, in adopting this practice, come to realise that the best designer of all when it comes to the prosperity of life is, in fact, Mother Nature herself. After all, the current makeup of the planet – its plants and animals, habitats and inhabitants – is balanced specifically to be conducive to nothing other than life. Through the process of evolution, this life is constantly changing, adapting to each change that has come before as new species develop and others fall into extinction. Those that currently flourish are the ones best able to survive in their own local environment, until that environment changes or another, even better adapted species evolves to push the evolution of life in a new direction. It is a magnificent phenomenon, the natural world, extremely complex when compared to all other systems we see around us in the universe and extremely efficient in its use of resources, which are constantly recycled and rebalanced. Individuals and individual species may rise and fall, but the entire system is utterly conducive to the production of life as a whole. Only alien processes – the industrial pollution of mankind or devastating collisions with objects from space – serve to decrease the variety and success of life in general; natural processes only add to it.

It is therefore fitting that we humans, the only species capable of self-reflective thought and therefore of carrying out truly 'unnatural' actions, ought to seek to minimise such actions in our technologies and cultures. The cold, ruthless 'efficiency' of the capitalist world focuses solely on short-term successes; by looking to the natural world we can appreciate longer-term efficiencies, since it is fine-tuned automatically by the processes of evolution to bring about the long-term success of species able to live in each of a myriad of different ecological niches, the very same environments into which we, having spread across the globe, wish to be able to survive sustainably. The nature surrounding us, upon which even we for all our technologies are dependent, is utterly sustainable, barring outside influence. But, with protecting life as its principle, it is more than happy to sacrifice individual species. If we cannot live within it without exceeding our means, it will cease to support us, and we shall ourselves run the risk of becoming extinct – or at least greatly diminished – through our own foolhardiness, alongside countless other species that have the misfortune of living on the planet at the same time as we have chosen to carry out such a dangerous experiment as our opposition to nature amounts to.

Nothing is wasted is nature; too often the 'efficient' mechanisms of the industrialised human world, though they appear to produce the desired outcome more quickly and with smaller human effort than the more old-fashioned, naturally-inspired practices that they displace, end up wasting a large proportion of the energy and resources that they use. Just as the computer requires a vastly greater amount of energy to make the same computations as the human brain, so most other human technologies appear clunky in comparison to nature's methods. The problem is that the infinite availability of energy and other resources is often erroneously assumed, just as it is assumed by classical economics that the atmosphere can hold an infinite amount of released greenhouse gasses without any impact on human activity. Such unfounded assumptions cannot be made within nature: the life-driving forces of evolution are bounded by physical laws that simply do not allow it.

Clearly, to support a population that is much larger and more widespread than would 'naturally' be the case (prior to 'unnatural' civilisation), humanity cannot simply abandon its technologies and allow nature to take its course. Rather, our aim should be to tame nature to our ends, mimicking its efficient processes to support our population without undermining the ecosystems upon which we depend and overexploiting our resources. By adapting the technologies we have devised over the past few centuries to function in the less wasteful, more organic manner that was seen before their deployment, we can construct a more efficient, 'natural' and ultimately viable society. This means using our machines to help nature, not to cut against it, by mimicking the ways it has found, through evolution, to achieve tasks that we wish ourselves to carry out. This would be a return to the mind-set of the more nature-conscious pre-industrial human, with the benefits of modern science, technology and awareness of our place in a world much larger than our immediate surroundings. In this way, we can avoid the perils they faced – pestilence, famine – as well as the crises of our own time – mass extinction, pollution and dangerous climactic change.

One of the most important ways in which our forebears mimicked nature but we do not is in the use of manual labour. In today's society, we shy away from hand-work such as weeding the fields and harvesting the crop in favour of more 'efficient' mechanised methods. But these methods require large amounts of fuel – usually oil – that past civilisations were able to do entirely without. We have a large unemployed population, and bodies that are adapted to carry out physical exertion. Why, then, should we choose the 'cheaper' option of farming all our fields with tractors and using more and more of a finite resource, when the natural limbs of the human body are able to achieve the same result much more efficiently (in terms of energy expended and energy gained from the crop produced) but with a much larger labour force required? Surely, as far as jobs go, the production of food is amongst the most important. We should be giving jobs on our farms wherever possible, then, to men and women, and not to polluting, energy-hungry artificial machines. That would be an obvious way of utilising the life-giving systems that nature has spent millennia working to achieve.

For, in trying to produce our own machines and techniques in place of those that nature can provide for us anyway if we only encourage the appropriate natural ecosystem or study a species that performs the job we wish to achieve, we are in essence putting a lot of effort into doing something that millions of years of evolution has already accomplished. How can we hope to rival millions of years of work in just a few years of our own time? It is not surprising, then, that the methods we have invented, when they ignore nature's blueprint, are so ineffectual. All our current technologies need to be rethought with methods of the past and methods gleaned from the natural world in the forefront of our minds. Sometimes, this might involve a return to techniques that were previously employed successfully – as with certain organic farming techniques or the use of sails on ships – whilst at other times it may mean creating entirely new technologies that mimic nature in a way we have not tried before. For example, research is being carried out into using layering effects to produce colours in clothing, rather than harmful dyes. The beautiful wings of butterflies are coloured in exactly this way.

The key advantage in mimicking the natural world is that we know that the side-effects of these techniques, new to us, cannot be great, because they have been subject to the gradually perfecting processes of evolution. Keeping warm, keeping cool, performing calculations, moving without traffic jams, travelling large distances without releasing correspondingly large levels of pollutants: all these problems have been solved by ourselves and other species through natural evolution countless times. The best way of surviving in a particular environment is to look at those particular ways of doing these things that are adopted by the local wildlife. In this way, methods that are efficient on paper but not in practice can be avoided, and techniques suited only to certain environments need not be forced upon others. For example, today air conditioning is increasingly employed everywhere that it is hot with grave environmental consequences when it would be better to use the other, location-specific cooling mechanisms that often exist. After all, our former selves survived in most of the same places that we do today, long before the capitalists came to sell them industrialised, polluting ways of doing so in greater short-term comfort but at the expense of the long-term prosperity of everyone involved.

In fact, the earliest human technologies – those that first allowed our population to expand sustainably both in number and in geographical range – mimicked nature in some way. How could they not, given that nature was all we knew and nature surrounded us at every moment, waking and sleeping, before we created the wilderness of urbanity? Before the rise of civilisation, which was characterised by decidedly unnatural innovations such as settled farming and permanent dwellings and roads, there existed technology for many hundreds of thousands of years. The first technology – that of fire used for cooking – has such an ancient pedigree that we have evolved since its invention, to the extent that it is difficult for a modern human to live healthily without cooking or processing food in some way. Large brains allowed our ancestors to harness fire, but in order for *homo sapiens* to develop the still larger brains that we all have today, it was necessary to divert energy to the brain from another part of the body, which must, in consequence, shrink. Because we were able to process food, our intestines were not required to work so hard to draw energy from what we ate, Therefore, the intestine has grown smaller even as the brain has expanded since the wielding of fire. This is a cultural feedback upon evolution that has effectively made us dependent upon culture and its associated technology to survive; without the technology to cook food, we should still need the technology to grow far more of it to feed ourselves than would naturally be available. But the technology of fire was given us directly by nature, probably first delivered into our ancestors' hands quite literally from the heavens during a lightning storm.

Other early technologies were similarly first delivered by then inspired by nature – from tools made from simple pieces of flint to spears with points resembling teeth. The clothing that was necessary for us to travel into the far north of the world was at first made of animal skins, directly utilising the method of natural protection against the cold used by other animals. When we invented sewn clothing, this was in mimicry of these early garments. It is of course impossible for humans to survive for very many months without any kind of clothing away from warm, tropical regions to this day. When we first invented paints and boats a few tens of thousands of years ago, we must have been using natural pigments to paint natural phenomena on our cave walls and mimicking natural rafts of wood that floated on the sea. Only as technology has become more advanced has it slowly migrated away from its original natural fabric and function.

Despite this, we must not become carried away with the idea that only those innovations that mimic nature are good, and that everything else must automatically be bad. Such an absolutist view can hardly help us to cope with a world that has already been altered by humanity to such a degree. In many ways, modern human society is dependent upon non-natural technologies that have allowed our population to expand and spread to an extent that could not have been achieved without it. But it is when we come to assess where to go next when we refresh and replace existing technologies, seeking to reinvigorate sustainability in a modernity that has become dangerously over-exploitative of Earth's resources and out of touch with nature, that biomimicry is the most useful guide. The danger with new unnatural innovations is that they may entail unforeseen consequences that do more harm to our planet's inhabitants than the benefits of these technologies prevent, whereas nature's solutions, having been fathomed out by biological agents over thousands of generations always under evolutionary pressure to be sustainable, pose a much smaller risk of inadvertent disaster. The plainest example is that of materials: natural and nature-inspired materials are indefinitely recyclable because they are formed from chemicals that are readily accessible to the biosphere and the species that create them have evolved alongside other species that have come to benefit by breaking them down, after which the constituent nutrients can be re-used. When our society was dependent largely on natural materials such as wood and metals, it didn't matter that worn-out items were thrown away, for they posed little threat to environment whence we took them in the first place. But when we began to delve deep into the Earth's crust to extract oil, and used it to produce versatile and cheap plastics, suddenly disposal of our waste – which simultaneously increased in volume as a result of the consumerist mind-set put in place by the very same capitalism that led to the introduction of plastic in the first place – became a huge problem, one that we are heavily burdened with today, as we explored earlier in this chapter. Looking to natural replacements for plastics is the most logical way out of this.

Already, the prospect of reinvigorating biomimicry is gaining ground in many fields. For example, the behaviour of ants is being studied to determine the best way of evacuating buildings[44], and a return to using human sewage (after processing) to fertilise fields has been mooted as a way of keeping key minerals within the food chain and preventing soil depletion[45], a mechanism certainly employed by nature and by ourselves until relatively recently. Such efforts must be rolled out more generally and more radically if we are to build a new, more sustainable society capable of living within the natural world long into the future.

Natural Capitalism?

Competition is cruel. To Base a society upon competition is to automatically condemn some segments of it to at least relative misery, for in any competition there must always be losers as well as winners. Therefore, proponents of inherently competitive capitalism – who tend to be those who have gained or are gaining from 'winning' the competition – must invent arguments to defend it against the inevitable moral criticisms. One of their arguments runs that competition is 'natural', in that it is the basis of the Natural Selection mechanism through which we and all other species have evolved. Therefore, competition within human society and the resulting inequality between the rich group and the poor group are supposed to be 'natural' and thus ethical. The 'best man wins' because he has more merit – is a better specimen – so deserves greater happiness. Furthermore, it is argued that a second form of competition, that between corporations that are also likened to 'species', is the natural way of producing innovation. This supposes that evolution by Natural Selection involves 'survival of the fittest' and death of the weak. But that famous phrase was not invented by Charles Darwin, the discoverer of Natural Selection; it was coined by Herbert Spencer, the first 'social Darwinist', and does not accurately reflect the true nature of Darwin's theory.

Groups within society are not the same as species within nature. The same 'Natural Selection' arguments put forward for allowing monetary competition to give rise to inequalities in standards of living and wellbeing were also invoked by the social Darwinists in an attempt to justify discrimination against particular ethnic groups in the nineteenth and twentieth centuries. The idea that mentally or physically handicapped people should be removed from the gene pool or that one 'race' of people are superior to others, who should be exterminated from the population, is now almost universally acknowledged as abhorrent: all human beings have an equal right to life and are equally valuable parts of the marvellous creation that is global humanity. Clearly, then, the ethically minded already accept that genetic competition within the human species and the attempt to 'purify' the human race by sterilisation or extermination of 'inferior' specimens are not desirable or permissible. How, then, can we justify competition for wealth and wellbeing, which are more detached from the way in which Natural Selection works than is competition for existence and the ability to reproduce, on the basis that this competition is 'natural'? How also can we justify making competition between companies the basis of innovation in our society?

Natural Selection is not cruel. It is true that it must involve the dying out of entire species, usually over the course of many generations, as a result of those species' failure to adapt to changes in their environment that are usually gradual. These changes favour other species in competition with those that die out, which are better able to reproduce and gradually become more dominant. But those other species may not be from an entirely separate gene pool; they needn't necessarily be aliens that have moved in from outside. They may, in fact, be variants descended from the very same species that goes extinct. Sometimes an entire evolutionary lineage can die out, but it is more likely that when a particular species becomes extinct it is because it has been forced – through competition with other species – to diversify and split off into new, better-adapted daughter species. In that sense, the competition between species is 'friendly competition' – they are cooperating to encourage each other to diversify, change and adapt to the environment. All species evolve and change: it's not that the fittest survive unchanged and the weakest die out entirely. There are not 'winners' and 'losers'. Likewise, within each species it's not necessarily only the 'fittest' members that survive. It's the fittest members that have the best chance of reproduction, but their weaker counterparts don't simply die, like a company crumbling as a result of capitalist competition with a bigger, stronger competitor. The members of the species that compete for mates are all working together to ensure that, through this friendly competition, the genes that will allow that species to flourish most in that particular environment will be passed on.

So competition between individuals in nature isn't like capitalist competition, which leaves some cursed by too many goods and too much comfort and others painfully devoid of both. Natural competition does not breed inequality; rather, it is part of a wider cooperative scheme in which all individuals play a part. Individuals within a species cooperate in an attempt to allow life to continue to flourish – they reproduce with one another to produce offspring that have the best possible adaptations to their environment. It may seem that one male 'loses out' when he fails to reproduce with a given female who chooses another. But in fact, because both males' objectives are that the species continues to survive and adapt, both can be happy in the knowledge (to anthropomorphise their feelings) that the female has chosen the male that will provide the best chance of this occurring. There is no depression amidst animals in the wild. It may seem that one deer 'loses out' when they are caught by the predator whilst the faster specimen escapes. But both deer, before either died, might be happy to know that the adaptation most suited to the survival of their species and its descendants – fast running – would be the one passed on to future generations when the surviving deer reproduced. Both deer will die eventually; neither is unhappy to know that it will die first. There is no true unhappiness in Nature, except that caused by human interference: in nature, animals suffer in body but not in mind. Individuals within a species thereby cooperate to produce the best possible outcome for their species and for nature as a whole, if nature's goal is to be as varied, widespread and adapted to life on Earth as possible.

Competition between individuals in capitalism is very different. If an individual 'loses out' in the capitalist game they cannot be happy in the knowledge that the survival of humanity and the goals of nature will thereby be furthered. If they are actively persecuted, sterilised or even murdered by other members of the human race intent upon Social Darwinist 'purification', they know only that evil and heartlessness have been furthered (notice that in nature no species 'purifies' itself by sterilising or killing its own members; there is a peculiarly human motivation for such actions, for most species rely upon predators of another species or the selection of mating partners to propagate good genes) whilst their own lives, which nature intended to be joyous, have been made miserable. If a person spends their life in relative poverty, lacking access to the goods and services that they need and which are enjoyed by the rich, they know only that the fortunate have floundered their wealth on selfish materialist desires and the unfortunate have lived in misery. Human beings do not live, today, as animals in the wild. Therefore human beings can be depressed. They can suffer in mind as well as body, and inequalities produced by capitalist competition that is dressed up as 'natural' produce just such suffering.

It has been said that competition between species drives change, and this is the primary reason why competition in a capitalist system is endeared by its proponents: that it will drive innovation in nature just as it does in society. But to suggest active 'competition' between species is misleading. In truth, the process is passive: random genetic variations occur inevitably within any species; those variations that give organisms the best chance of reproduction survive. Less beneficial variations worsen the reproductive chances of the individual that holds them and that individual is more likely to die before reproducing so that their genetic lineage dies out. There is no choice in the matter: one species does not purposefully innovate in order to compete with another; rather, changes in the habitat surrounding the species inevitably result in *random* adaptations to these changes becoming selected for over time. Innovation, then, comes about not because of active competition (though this is how it may appear to an onlooker) but because of a cooperative response to changes to the environment in which the species lives. In this way, the species eventually dies out and other species – whether descended from it or not – take its place in that particular geographic location under altered conditions. Because, over the long term, the conditions in every part of the planet are constantly changing, new life-forms are always being created and innovation is inevitable. Life of all kinds is always cooperating with the other life-forms that shape its environment and with the physical planet itself to produce novelty and variety. That is the ultimate purpose towards which life is evolving: to become more diverse, more widespread in all its forms and therefore more resilient against damaging episodes such as meteor impacts that would entirely wipe out less diverse life.

Friendly competition is part of this development: it is a tool, using which all the species in an ecosystem work together to keep each other's populations in check and to drive each other through coevolution towards better adaptation to their environment and the greater flourishing of life. The predator keeps down the numbers of the herbivorous prey, but this allows the plants that prey depends upon to survive and prevents a population crash, as well as protecting other species such as insects living on the grass that the prey eat. It's like a Hegelian argument. The eighteenth-century philosopher Hegel proposed society is in a state of progress brought about by disagreements that push us ever away from contentment with stasis. Each side counters the other when arguments arise, and the optimal balance is eventually settled upon so that all sides benefit and progress. This is not really true of our current society, but it could be true of a more ideal one that mimics nature, where it certainly is true in the form of cooperative, friendly competition between individuals of interlocking species. The trend over time is always for nature to produce a wider and wider variety of species by this means. Species don't 'outcompete' each other so much as they force one another to diversify and change, until the original species 'die out' because they have been so transformed that they have become a different species. There is no such thing as a 'victorious' species that 'takes over' another species, merges with it and grows into a bigger entity, occupying more and more environmental niches until it is the sole species left in the ecosystem.

This is not at all how capitalism works. Under capitalism, corporations choose to compete with one another to obtain the most profit rather than cooperating to provide the best possible delivery of goods and services. One company outcompetes the others, and grows bigger and bigger, attempting to become the 'victorious' company that dominates the marketplace in a most unnatural manner, so that diversity in the market *decreases* over time. Instead of innovating in response to changes in their environment – human culture and its changing needs and passions – these corporations innovate first and then persuade (through marketing, peer pressure and sometimes even falsity dressed up as science) human society to change to adopt those innovations. Corporations are not like species: species are part of a cooperative developing system that responds to its environment through innovation. Corporations compete with one another, and in order to distinguish themselves and gain 'competitive advantages' they introduce unnecessary changes then shape the cultural environment to suit these changes. In nature, it is not competition that produces innovation. In society, competition introduces innovation, but it is unnecessary innovation.

This innovation has profound environmental implications, of course. Innovation in itself is indeed 'natural' and is not wholly undesirable. The sort of innovation we need is the sort that adapts our society to the environmental challenges that face it: for example, we need to innovate to produce renewable energy to avert climatic change, and may need to innovate to geo-engineer the climate. In the past, we needed to innovate to produce revolutions in medicine, for example, through such actions as the development of vaccines, the sanitisation of our streets and the creation of the NHS. We still need medical innovations to cure diseases of the modern world through medicines and behavioural changes. These innovations, though, are innovations that society can see that it needs and that it must inevitably adopt if it is to survive, in response to the environment in which it finds itself and the changing desires of the populace.

The situation is not entirely akin to species adapting themselves through Natural Selection, because, as we have already seen, adaptation via Natural Selection is involuntary. But it does involve innovation for the good of all, which can be directed by society as a whole through the arm of a government that provides an overall, democratic and well-judged oversight of the various components of society that work together to bring about change. Publically controlled industries, far from being averse to innovation of all kinds, can provide exactly the sort of sensible and reactive innovation that we need. Innovations almost always have unforeseen consequences, but these will be easier to identify and rectify when society is cooperating to produce changes that are overseen and regulated by itself. There can still be competition within public industries, but friendly competition, mimicking nature and providing a Hegelian argument whereby each of a nationalised network of small businesses is free to innovate and share its ideas and findings with the others in the network, all the companies being publically owned and none of them able to take over any of the others or to grow to operate outside of the community they are tasked with serving. Friendly – not fierce – competition will provide innovation with society, not big businesses, firmly in control.

Private corporations that are in competition with one another do not provide this sort of innovation. They invent new products and ways of living, and in order to sell their goods and services they persuade society to change in response to this. They try, too, to persuade the environment itself to change, though in this they are not so successful. Take the example of the mobile telephone. There was no specific need for everyone in the country to have such a device before they were manufactured en masse by a plethora of competing companies. These companies, though, have persuaded the majority of people to purchase one and to become dependent on it, for all the services that it is supposedly able to deliver. Now perhaps some people really were in need of some of these features – travellers needing to contact someone in emergencies, say. In such a case, small companies under the direction of the government should have been asked to develop devices capable of doing this, and they should have been distributed to those that needed them to use for the period that they needed them for. Instead, we have a situation whereby almost everybody has come to 'need' mobile devices to stay in touch, to play games, to get directions and all sorts of other things on the go – all things they somehow didn't need to do before. They have been persuaded by the companies that developed the products and competed to make them more and more comprehensive. The environment, though, has not been persuaded to change to make the production of those devices any easier. The touch-screens that people have come to 'need' still rely upon precious metals extracted under horrible conditions in faraway places from dwindling mines. The energy required to power the 'phones still requires huge fossil-fuel-powered electricity generators to be run, and the climate will change as a result. A similar story applies to various other modern-day devices that we didn't really need. All of the environmental and social destruction they produce arises from innovation for the sake of innovation and competitive profit that is not, in fact, natural at all.

So much for the notion that competition between companies is the 'natural' way of producing innovation, and for Herbert Spencer's Social Darwinist notion that competition between individuals is 'natural' or conducive to the happiness of society. The former produces unnecessary innovation that traps people into ways of thinking that corporations – not they themselves – have chosen for them; the latter traps certain sections of society into disadvantageous positions, unable to take up the opportunities enjoyed by others. Both situations are conducive only to misery. Misery is not natural: nature exists to produce joy in the very fact of existence. In nature, individuals die, are rejected and are killed. But this does not make them unhappy. Within their natural environment, the changes in which the species they form gradually adapts to and eventually dies out when its offspring species replace it, no individual is miserable in their existence. It is only when we create artificial surroundings – a capitalist society in the case of humans, and a cage in the case of other animals or slaves – that we produce misery. We must therefore cast both of these off to obtain happiness for all of nature's creatures again. We must discard cages and allow ourselves and other animals to live amongst the rest of nature. We must discard capitalist competition in favour of the more truly natural cooperation that will bring us joy.

The Ecomodernist Approach

Much of what has been argued in this section rests on two key tenets: that living simpler lives, closer to nature, will make us happier and enable us to live more sustainably prosperous lives; and that we should emulate nature in our own technologies if we are to make them as resource-efficient and sustainable as possible. Neither of these tenets is accepted uncritically by environmentalists, and they stand in especially stark contrast to the relatively new philosophy of the 'Ecomodernists'. It is therefore necessary to present the arguments of the Ecomodernists, to explain why their approach will not lead to a more joyful and prosperous world, and to defend the merits of returning to nature against their contrary approach.

The *Ecomodernist Manifesto* states that the movement's central aim is to create a 'great Anthropocene' by using 'growing social, economic and technological powers to make life better for people, stabilise the climate and protect the natural world'. They accept, like most environmentalists, that humanity must 'shrink its impacts on the environment', but disagree with the notion that we can achieve this by harmonising more closely with the natural world. By contrast, Ecomodernists advocate distancing humanity further from nature, intensifying agriculture, urbanising the population and centralising energy supplies through new technologies in an attempt to decrease the amount of land taken up by human activities. They argue that this will constitute the next stage in a trajectory of increasing agricultural efficiency and decreasing land-use per person that has been taking place for millennia, leaving much more land for the rest of nature to flourish in at the same time as sustaining an increasing human population[46].

It is true that we should set aside as much land as we can for the rest of nature to enjoy if we value the wellbeing of other species as we do our own. However, this should be done alongside a sustainable agricultural and architectural system. The Ecomodernist manifesto does not make clear how intense industrial agriculture and centralised energy systems can be made sustainable, when at the moment these sorts of systems are exactly those most dependent upon finite, non-renewable resources such as fossil fuels. Very intense, small areas of agricultural production would require vast resources of chemical fertilisers, pesticides and energy to sustain them, which would have to be extracted from elsewhere, hence endangering wildlife indirectly. How such a system could be sustained for long, requiring human technologies to replace natural cycles of regeneration, is not clear. An agriculture that instead uses more land and embraces natural processes to regenerate and indefinitely sustain the viability of that land organically, as advocated in this book (see especially Chapter 10), would allow other species to live alongside us even on our farms and fields, as opposed to completely 'natural' uncultivated areas. Hence, a diversity of lifeforms would be maintained under both systems, but there would be less need for individual animals to suffer in the latter case, since pesticides, traps and unsustainable resources would all be avoided. Both systems are capable, perhaps, of feeding the world's population in the short-term, but in the longer-term only the more natural, organic method is feasible.

A second objection to the Ecomodernist approach relates to the emotional health of the people of our planet. We, as a species, have evolved to live amongst the other beautiful plants and animals that characterise our world. The movement of the world's human population into densely-packed cities represents a distancing of ourselves from nature in our everyday lives that is quite alien to our own natural predispositions. Today's capitalist culture, by emphasising the value of things we have produced ourselves - buildings of concrete, glass and steel, plastic goods and gadgets, cars and planes - and encouraging us to enclose ourselves in air-conditioned, central heated private boxes instead of spending our time contemplating and appreciating the natural world, is having a profound effect on our mental and physical health. It is no wonder that so many people have allergies and suffer from colds and other illnesses, when so few live amongst the muck of the farm, where the vast majority of our ancestors dwelt and built up their immune systems. It is no wonder that so many are obese when many do little exercise other than walking to the car and moving around their homes and offices while at the same time eating heavily processed, unnatural foodstuffs. City life exposes us to toxins belched out by our pollution-spewing machines that lead to cancers and other ailments.

But most importantly, the sheer lack of other animals and plants living natural lives around us that we experience in cities - a lack that cannot be made up for with house-plants and cultivated parks - exerts a painful psychological strain. We all need to feel the freedom of the countryside, to escape from one another and our own species' oppressive creations. Day trips to the countryside once in a while are not enough to satisfy this primeval urge. That is why depression is foremost amongst the 'modern diseases' that plague us today. Concentrating still more of the world's population into cities will only make this worse, at the same time as posing a whole host of environmental problems – how do we sustainably feed, water, shelter and employ so many people living in such a small area? – that the Ecomodernist manifesto fails to address. The authors claim to 'write this document out of deep love and emotional connection with the natural world'. But they do not say how this love and connection could be maintained and enjoyed by an entirely urbanised human population. The countryside is where we have evolved to be, and it is in dwelling amongst nature that true joy and prosperity lie. We should be greening our cities, not further urbanising them to squeeze in more people.

The secret to a joyful life lies not in more complexity and material distractions as the Ecomodernists, with their emphasis on modern technology and the 'progress' of industrialisation, make out. It lies in greater simplicity and humility, in recognising our utter dependence on the natural world. A prosperous, joyful humanity is not one that is 'decoupled' from nature, but one that is decoupled from material excess. Whilst human history has witnessed a progression towards increasingly efficient agriculture, it was only with the industrial revolution that we began to lose on mass our connection to the land. It is wrong, therefore, to suggest that moving the majority of the world's population into cities would be part of a positive natural progression that is already underway, or that doing so would be necessary to save us from environmental catastrophe. Modern technology can and should be embraced to make organic, localised farming as efficient as possible, but on an environmental and social level as well as an economic one: living close to the land and eschewing very intense methods of farming is better for our own quality of life and mental health – it is more socially efficient – is better for the animals we farm with and which live alongside our crops – it is more environmentally efficient – and it can still feed our population despite a lower yield per acre of farmland than that which the very intensive but ultimately unsustainable methods advocated by the Ecomodernists would provide.

The Ecomodernists apparently deny that there is a limit to the human population that can be sustainably fed and happily coexist. Whilst this limit may well not yet have been reached, it is obvious that there must ultimately be a maximum number of people that a finite planet can support, and furthermore that the more human beings there are, the fewer resources there will be for other species to enjoy. This does not mean, of course, that we should take Draconian measures to restrict population growth. But it does suggest that packing a limitlessly growing human population into very dense cities will not be ultimately feasible. Rather than continuing with this paradigm of growth and 'progress' that has dominated human development only since the dawn of the urbanising industrial age some two or more centuries ago, it may therefore be more logical to return to the pre-industrial norm of smaller, more scattered but steadily populated communities living off local resources.

This would be no Luddite return to the past: today we have electricity, transport, medical care and other modern technologies that our forebears did not have and which could continue to enrich our lives in comparison to theirs. It would instead involve a fusion of old and new so as to sustain a larger and more educated population than the pre-industrial one, but one that retains a profound connection to the natural world around us. Even if, in the short-term, fewer people could be sustained in this model than in the Ecomodernist urbanised world and global population growth would have to halt sooner, in the longer-term it would support many more generations of human beings living happier, simpler lives on the basis of renewable resources, as part of nature's web of life and not in opposition to it. Only by these means can humanity take its proper, humble place as one amongst many species living together in harmony in the Earth.

5. The Capitalist Approach to the Environment

Despite all the problems that the current financial system has created, socially and environmentally, there are those who advocate an attempt to resolve some or all of the issues we have explored over the last two chapters within the current capitalist system. This method, here dubbed 'The Capitalist Approach', is supported by all the mainstream political parties in Britain today, and presents a less politically risky 'silver bullet' solution than a more radical overhauling of our social structure might have, in that it rests upon capitalistic ideas with which many people are already familiar. This chapter lays out some of the basic tenets of this method of small change, and the potential good that it can do. But it also details the drawbacks, which, unfortunately, require a much more vigorous revolution in our thinking to overcome: these include the continued emphasis on short-term advantages (money and power in abundance for the monetarily rich, swathes of cheap goods with which to buy-off the monetarily poor), the aspiration for money rather than wellbeing and spiritual peace, and the extraction of more and more resources to fuel economic growth. Such stumbling-blocks as these mean that retaining capitalism cannot be compatible with the continued prosperity of our species.

5.1 Carbon Trading and Carbon Taxes: Capitalist Environmentalism

'Capitalist environmentalism' is an oxymoronic phrase. Whatever the best intentions of its users, the capitalist system is geared towards the fulfilment of one aim only: profit, and profit is certainly not on the agenda of the environmentalist. However, in their search for profit, capitalistic businesses are certainly keen to dominate all aspects of society's agenda, and, as environmental issues become more and more prominent on the stage of global politics, they have been, unavoidably, brought within the framework of the drivers of all change in a capitalist world: financial markets. In our diluted form of capitalism, these markets are unable to dominate entirely the political system, but, increasingly, they have been allowed to extend their grasp, helped along by an increase in privatisation. The notion of carbon trading simply extends this trend into the realm of what are surely a public, not a private, concern: environmental degradation and, especially, climate change.

Carbon Trading

The idea behind 'carbon trading' or 'cap and trade'[47] is that the costs of carbon dioxide emissions can be treated like the financial costs of goods. As such, they are subjected to the rigours of the financial markets which, just as they do for monetary costs, of their own accord settle down into a state of lowest possible 'carbon cost', and hence increased environmental profit. The system works by literally transforming carbon dioxide emissions into monetary expenditure, which is reduced by cutting those emissions, and, it is claimed, aids developing countries, which emit far less than developed nations, and hence have accrued some sort of 'credit' in comparison to their richer neighbours. Carbon dioxide has been commoditised, the only way in which its impact can be written into a capitalist system.

In the most basic form of carbon trading, every business has a 'cap' set on their carbon emissions, and is given an equivalent number of 'carbon credits' by a central authority such as the domestic government. Those businesses that pollute a lot and want to emit more carbon dioxide are permitted to do so only by buying more such credits from less-polluting businesses that have not used all theirs up. The idea is that carbon dioxide levels will be prevented from rising – because the total number of carbon credits will never be increased – and every business will be incentivised to reduce its emissions so that it can accrue spare credits and sell them for money. Governments could even buy back credits to reward businesses that slash emissions. A market in carbon emissions is, effectively, set up, and the price of the credits can fluctuate according to supply and demand. In more complicated schemes, polluters can buy more credits by offsetting their emissions, for example by planting trees to absorb excess carbon dioxide.

This system is a commendable effort by those working within the financial system to reconcile capitalism, which, by its very nature, diminishes resources and degrades the environment, with the planet-saving drive to cut greenhouse gas emissions. But financial systems, as the repeated 'crashes' of recent decades have shown, are inherently unstable, because they are inherently greedy for short-term wealth. Individuals within the capitalist empire may seek to use its great power over man to good effect, but the ends of any capitalist venture, by the same checks and balances that they try to exploit to pursue environmental motives, always lie in what makes the greatest profit.

The truth is that there are numerous problems with carbon trading, most of which are inherent within its capitalist roots. One lies with the valuation of the carbon credits in the first place. The price of these credits cannot possibly reflect the cost associated with the equivalent carbon dioxide. For one thing, it is a fallacy to believe that any monetary price can be ascribed to lives lost, ecosystems and cultures destroyed and homes and landscapes ruined, which makes it impossible to break down the true 'cost' of each gram of carbon. Economists may try to evaluate the cost of climate change by adding up the economic growth lost through human deaths; the cost of performing 'ecosystem services' for ourselves that other species used to provide – such as pollination of crops – but that climate change has disrupted; and the huge costs of adapting to rising seas, temperatures and cases of illness that will come with global warming. But all of these things are difficult to estimate and fail to capture the true cost, which is not monetary but physical and emotional. Furthermore, the calculations that have been done, fallible as they are, suggest that even the monetary costs of emissions evaluated in this way are so high that carbon credits should be far too expensive for any business to afford. Therefore, their prices in existing schemes have been set somewhat arbitrarily at much lower values to encourage companies to buy and trade them, making it far from clear that carbon trading places sufficient restrictions on businesses to produce emissions cuts that are anything like sufficient.

Once these carbon credits are allowed to fluctuate in price on the free market like any other capitalist commodity, further problems arise. Capitalist businesses always aim at making profit, not necessarily doing what is best for society. Therefore, the more businesses start to reduce emissions so as to be able to sell carbon credits, the less money other businesses will be willing to pay for those credits, and their price will fall, which will disincentivise any further emissions cuts. The price will only rise again if businesses begin to pollute more, so that there is a demand for more credits. Hence there is no impetus within the system for emissions reduction unless the regulatory authority begins to artificially inflate the price of carbon credits and decreases their total number. But that would be interfering with the market, rendering the whole notion of free-market capitalism being able to solve the carbon crisis through carbon trading a nonsense. Governments might as well simply place caps on emissions by law and do away with any kind of trading scheme at all.

What's more, the very concept of carbon trading inherently favours the richest companies – which tend to be the biggest polluters – because these can easily afford to buy more credits, usually by investing in large offsetting schemes. Smaller, more sustainable businesses may lose out to larger, richer ones. There is also a profit incentive for companies to collude in defrauding the system. One business can pretend to have cut emissions and sell its credits cheaply to another, with no monitoring system in place to detect the fraudulent practice. Both partners are motivated by profit because they are part of the capitalist system, and neither is likely to be especially concerned for the environmental costs of their actions.

Another problem lies in the notion of offsetting. Offsetting schemes assume that every gram of carbon dioxide emitted or absorbed from the atmosphere is equivalent, and that burning a certain amount of coal in one place is made up for by planting a certain number of trees somewhere else, for example. But the carbon dioxide released by burning coal will remain in the atmosphere essentially for ever – unless we invent some way of extracting the gas directly from the air – whereas, if not looked after in perpetuity, trees planted to compensate may not survive. The emissions will only really be offset if the trees would not have been planted anyway in the absence of the offsetting, and careful monitoring would have to be done to ensure that they really do absorb the same amount of carbon dioxide as was emitted. The same caveats apply to other offsetting schemes, such as investments in renewable energy technologies for the less-industrialised world to prevent the increased use of fossil fuels there. They must be very long-lasting and must not have been going to take place anyway, otherwise the business' emissions will not really have been offset. There is very little assurance that either of these conditions will be met. Companies do not last forever, and the business that plants trees to offset its emissions today may not be around in twenty years' time to fund their continued preservation. Furthermore, the offsetting schemes may have other negative social consequences that are not taken into account. A multinational corporation should not be allowed to assume that it has the right to buy up land for reforesting or impose new technologies on poorer populations simply to enable it to continue burning up the world's supply of fossil fuels.

These flaws in the logic of carbon trading may seem obvious, and indeed they are. It's not likely that those responsible for inventing the idea and setting up the first carbon trading schemes were ignorant of their inherent limitations. Why, then, was this method invented and why has it been adopted in so many places? If the concern of its originators was truly to reduce carbon emissions as quickly as possible, carbon trading would never have been put forward as a solution. But the true motivation of the businesses and governments that set up these schemes has never been cutting carbon emissions; rather, the aim is to satisfy the public that they are dealing with climate change without actually doing anything at all. Oil companies support carbon trading schemes because they allow oil to be extracted as quickly as ever, the resulting emissions being supposedly offset elsewhere by the businesses that use it. Governments like them because they allow them to pretend to meet emissions targets, again through supposed offsetting. Big businesses like them because business as usual can continue, with emissions continuing to soar, for the cost of a few cheap carbon credits. The alternative – direct government legislation to force businesses to cut emissions for the sake of the whole of humanity and the planet we live on – would be bad for business.

At present we are able to hold back the relentless search for wealth from steamrolling over environmental protection only by the inbuilt communal nature, too often oppressed in the search for money, of human beings. We still have in our hearts a connection to our planet that allows us to see past short-term capitalist requirements and towards long-term prosperity. But by converting environmentalism into an enterprise in capital, encouraging all to surrender the problem of protecting the planet into the hands of the financial markets and to get on with powering the supply-and-demand fuel that it requires, we risk losing this essential check. Like the financial bubbles we have seen so often grow and burst, the carbon trading idea will likely appear to be working; carbon dioxide emissions will be cut, for long enough for society to put its faith in capitalism's ability to save itself from destruction. But, like those bubbles, the change will undoubtedly be short-lived. The same drive for profit will persist and, before long, environmentalism, having been thrust out of the public consciousness, will cease to be a key driver in this profitability. The system will revert to unsustainable practices to drive down prices, and we shall return to the same problem, but, precious time having been wasted, will find ourselves deeper within the hole we've been digging and with less chance of rescue. This is the danger of surrendering carbon dioxide regulation to financial markets.

But there is another problem with this idea: just as a financial system based upon monetary profit assumes infinite resources and ignores the implications of pollution beyond any fines that happen to have been set by the local authority under which corporations act, so a carbon financial system would ignore the costs of any measures used to cut carbon dioxide emissions which are not, after all, the only environmental problem of concern. It may be that the 'cheapest' (least carbon-intensive) option would be to cut down this part of the forest, and plant that type of tree elsewhere. In allowing such actions to be taken, removing regulation and allowing the market to flow where it will, we may end up destroying habitats and allowing species to become extinct, or polluting the atmosphere or seas with geoengineering chemicals that, whilst they lower global temperatures, have other, numerous adverse effects such as ozone depletion, drought, acid rain, less effective solar panels and more. In short, whatever we, through ignorance or otherwise, fail to put into the equations and the financial systems when the regulations are lifted will not affect the course of its meanderings, like a river downhill towards the sea, supposedly down towards lower global temperatures. Not nearly enough research has been done to say that we can put in all the required parameters at this time.

The environmental problems we see today are caused by the greed – greed for non-essential comforts bound to money – that goes hand-in-hand with materialistic capitalism. Capitalist systems and markets are not the place we should turn to solve these issues, not least because, rather than a kink in the system, they represent an unavoidable and major consequence of the capitalist model. Capitalism is, inherently, unsustainable.

5. The Capitalist Approach

Carbon Taxes

Although allowing an unfettered free market to dictate the course of our society and, in the process, determine our carbon dioxide emissions is proving disastrous, and the 'trading' of carbon dioxide emissions as discussed above, like other commodities under capitalism, would be little better, there are ways in which genuine progress can be made towards environmental protection – most importantly, combatting climate change – without completely overhauling the capitalist system. These simply involve the government taking more regulatory power over the energy markets, and imposing taxes, in one form or another, that force businesses and individuals to pay monetarily for the damage that their emissions do. Capitalism is not dispensed with, but the market at least is regulated rather than being given free-reign.

Some scientists have argued that carbon taxes are the best way of delivering the cuts to greenhouse gas emissions necessary if we are to avoid 'dangerous' climate change. A solution such as this may not deal with the underlying cause of environmental problems – which is the over-production and over-consumption encouraged by capitalism itself – but it could indeed be the best way forward, given that action on climate change has to be rapid if it is to be at all effective. We may aim to abolish capitalism altogether, in the long term, for the good of all the world's people and other animals, but this may take years or decades to bring about peacefully, logically and without economic or social collapse. Therefore, there is something to be said for reigning in the worst excesses of capitalism in the short-term, without abolishing it straightway outright, through government regulation that might just save us from its most urgently deleterious effects.

Since it was first adopted by a 1996 conference of European environment ministers, a target of keeping global warming below two degrees Celsius has been increasingly espoused by the world's politicians. It became the official target of the United Nations in 2010, as agreed upon at the climate conference in Cancun that year. But any such target must satisfy three key criteria in order to be effective. It must be sufficient to avert 'dangerous' environmental consequences – though what constitutes 'dangerous' can be difficult to define – and it must also be achievable – that is, both scientifically feasible and politically realistic. Otherwise, the target becomes meaningless: either it fails to solve the problem we are facing or nobody will put any effort into meeting it. It is important to have such a target in the first place to provide a focal point for actions of both national governments and the international community in their efforts to cut emissions by a sufficient amount and sufficiently quickly to avert disaster. Therefore, the target thirdly has to be simple enough for the voting public and their politicians to relate to and understand. Two degrees was originally adopted on the basis of preliminary evidence that it could satisfy all three requirements; in 1996, the world had warmed only about 0.5 degrees relative to pre-industrial levels, and capping future warming to a further 1.5 degrees seemed feasible; preliminary research stretching back to the 1970s suggested that two degrees of warming would not be especially unprecedented in the recent history of our planet (that is, since humans evolved) and would probably be sufficiently small to avert the most dangerous potential effects of climate change; and it was a catchy number, easily seized upon by public and politicians alike.

But over the last twenty years, hopes of meeting this target have been diminishing. The world continued to emit more and more carbon dioxide year on year until 2014, and there has been no binding international agreement to stop this upward trend. The 2015 Paris Agreement, though it involved a commitment to keeping the rise in temperature to below 2 degrees and an aspiration to limit it to 1.5 degrees, allowed each country to design their own targets for emissions reductions, some of which are so far outrageously lax. Every year that emissions remain high, any specific target for global warming becomes more and more difficult to achieve, requiring more and more drastic emissions cuts. Perhaps, then, two degrees isn't politically feasible after all. Even worse, more recent studies have suggested that two degrees isn't sufficient to avert climate catastrophe, and that a still more stringent target – perhaps 1.5 degrees or 1 degree relative to pre-industrial levels – should be adopted for the eventual warming of the planet. In light of this, it's becoming clear that an urgent political fix is necessary to change the direction of polluting societies as quickly as possible. That is where, some argue, carbon taxes come in.

In 2013, James Hansen – a scientist at the Earth Institute of Colombia University in New York – and colleagues published a landmark paper assessing above what threshold global warming should be considered to be very likely to be 'dangerous', and what steps might be taken in the immediate future to ensure that this threshold is not crossed[48]. Of course, any amount of climatic change can be 'dangerous', as the increase in extreme weather such as heatwaves, floods and hurricanes and the destruction of coral ecosystems we are already seeing testify. But those authors made a compelling case that any rise in temperature that brought us beyond the previous maximum temperature experienced in the Holocene would be unprecedented for current forms of life and would therefore be more likely to take us beyond 'dangerous' tipping points than would any lesser degree of warming. The Holocene is the geological epoch humans and all other species have become accustomed to living in, which stretches back for the last 15000 years, during which Earth has experienced 'interglacial' conditions. Before this, it was considerably colder. On that basis, the total human-induced warming of the Earth relative to the pre-industrial average should not be allowed to exceed 0.7 degrees, to match the previous Holocene maximum as measured by records – such as ice cores – that tell us about past climate. In other words, the 0.8 degrees of warming that has already been induced is more than we can afford, and no further warming at all should be allowed. Two degrees of anthropogenic warming, the study warns, could set off feedback processes – including the dying off of the Amazon rainforest, the melting of permafrost to release more greenhouse gasses and warming from the ocean, which has taken up a lot of Earth's excess heat in recent years (producing the 'hiatus' in global warming during the first decade of the twenty-first century) and will release it slowly back into the atmosphere – that will cause the temperature to rise by three or four degrees Celsius overall. The international community, in adopting the two degree target, has already acknowledged that such degrees of warming would be devastating to the planet's inhabitants.

The conclusion Hansen and colleagues came to was hence that net emissions of carbon dioxide should be made to decrease at once, and that carbon taxes would be absolutely essential – a 'sine qua non' – to bring this rapid change about. A target of one degree Celsius maximum warming, much closer to the Holocene maximum, would be much safer and more sufficient for the protection of life than a two degree target, and, what's more, could also be politically realistic and scientifically feasible if carbon taxes were used to bring it about. In the absence of a political revolution that sees the overthrow of capitalism and the rise of a more logical and reverential and less destructive wasteful cooperative socialism, a lot may be riding on the success of carbon taxes.

Although the rate at which we emit long-lived greenhouse gasses such as carbon dioxide determines the rate at which the planet warms, and short-term warming can be reduced by slashing emissions of shorter-lived ones such as methane, the cumulative effect of global warming will depend on the total amount of the longer-lived greenhouse gasses emitted by humanity. A proportion of the carbon dioxide we emit is absorbed by the oceans, but at least half will remain in the atmosphere for many thousands of years unless we actively remove it. Therefore, it is possible to translate a target pertaining to a maximum amount of warming into one specifying the maximum amount of greenhouse gasses emitted and retained by the atmosphere. This is what enables us to translate policies that cut emissions of greenhouse gasses into actions that prevent global average temperature change, and its associated effects. According to Hansen's study, the two degrees of warming target widely endorsed by politicians and the one degree target put forward to avoid 'dangerous' consequences correspond to 1000 and 500 Gigatonnes (Gt) of carbon dioxide having been emitted since the start of the industrial revolution respectively. Staying below the 500 Gt limit is essentially what any carbon taxing scheme would have to achieve to avoid devastating consequences of climate change over the coming decades that would harm 'young people, future generations and nature' as the title of the paper puts it.

Carbon taxes are intended to achieve this by forcing businesses to pay a certain amount of money – a tax – on every gram of carbon dioxide or other greenhouse gasses that they emit, providing a monetary incentive to emit less. The money raised is then spent by the government enforcing the tax on technology that either prevents emissions elsewhere or draws down, by some means, greenhouse gasses that have already been emitted from the atmosphere. This is an important point because although decreasing our target cumulative emissions from 1000 to 500 Gt is, according to Hansen and colleagues at least, necessary for our actions against climate change to be sufficient, such a target also has to be feasible. Emissions of greenhouse gasses cannot be stopped overnight: they have to be brought down gradually, whether at a faster or a slower rate. It is not thought to be possible to reduce emissions rapidly enough for them to reach zero in time to meet the one degree target without a sudden disruption of the social structures people depend upon to live. That's why politicians tend to favour the two degree target: it gives them – or their successors – more time to change the way societies work to bring down our emissions in time to meet the target. We should not try to deny this, but nevertheless can recognise that whilst the rate at which we can decrease our actual emissions may be limited, the rate at which *net* emissions are decreased – which is what really matters for the climate – can be increased by taking actions that take carbon dioxide back out of the atmosphere.

This carbon draw-down, it is hoped, will give us enough time to develop the new technologies and implement the behavioural changes that will enable actual greenhouse gas emissions to fall to near-zero in the longer-term. A sustained effort in the 'research and development' of less polluting technologies and the creation of less wasteful social infrastructure to enable carbon-cutting behavioural changes must be funded at the same time as the carbon draw-down if carbon taxes are to work. Neither the technology to power the whole of our societies without fossil fuels nor that required to draw down large amounts of carbon dioxide from the atmosphere currently exists, but carbon taxes, alongside an end to the subsidies paid to fossil fuel companies, might provide the funding that, in a capitalist world, would be necessary to bring both into reality. Just like in the war, when all our efforts were concentrated on resisting fascism, so now our research resources need to be pooled into mitigating climate change and its effects.

Admittedly, the 'carbon draw-down' component of this may sound rather like the 'carbon offsetting' of the carbon trading schemes that we have seen do not work. But with carbon taxes, there is a crucial difference: it is the government, not the market, that sets the 'price' set on carbon (this time the amount of tax per gram, not the cost of permits to pollute). The scheme remains capitalistic – it's still for the love of money, not people and the planet, that businesses are made to change their behaviour and cut emissions – but the government, acting on behalf of all in society, can employ experts to decide upon the optimal carbon tax to reduce emissions and raise revenues for the carbon draw-down schemes. These schemes, unlike 'carbon offsetting' ones, are controlled by the government, which means that society as a whole is taking upon itself the responsibility to ensure that they actually work. The polluting businesses are still motivated by profit, pushed into change by the desire to avoid taxes. But society itself sets the tax and captures the carbon. It's society itself that would suffer if this was not done, and there is no incentive to cheat. Capitalistic money-making is restricted and directed for the good of society by socialistic regulation.

It's important that different governments work together when setting carbon taxes. If, for the time being, the ability for companies to operate across borders under globalised capitalism is not abolished, companies in a country where there is a heavy carbon tax might otherwise simply move abroad to avoid it. Manufacturers that pollute heavily or abuse workers have already moved to industrialising regions such as South East Asia to avoid American and European workers' rights and environmental protection legislation. They must not be allowed to do the same to avoid carbon-cutting taxation. Placing a carbon tax on specific polluters rather than on individuals (who often have no choice but to use products and services provided by companies that pollute) or countries as a whole also solves the problem of the apportioning of responsibility for climate change. If individual countries are forced to reduce emissions, arguments arise concerning which countries should be made to reduce their emissions the most, and whether any industrialising countries should be allowed to continue to increase emissions in light of the fact that their societies have been left in a poor state by previous colonial actions by richer ones. Taxing companies instead avoids this.

Furthermore, different countries have contributed differently to the amount of the 500 Gt emissions target that we have already used up. Most African countries have produced a negligible amount of emissions to date, since they are only just industrialising. China is currently the world's biggest emitter but, integrating emissions across the historical record, the USA has emitted more. Few would argue that every country should be allowed to have at least as many cumulative emissions as the USA, because their populations may be smaller. But some would argue that it isn't fair for more recently industrialised countries not to emit as much per capita as the country which has the largest cumulative emissions per capita – not the USA but, in fact, the UK, which was the earliest country to industrialise and has a relatively small population. Even if the UK cut its current emissions to zero, some other countries might still protest the right to continue to emit until their per capita historical emissions were at least as great as the UK's, under the capitalist illusion that industrialisation and economic growth based on fossil fuels necessarily lead to a more prosperous and happier society. On the other hand, some would argue that it isn't fair to punish present-day populations for the luxuries of their forebears, even though the material wealth (and, it might be argued, spiritual dearth) of the monetarily richer nations of the world today was built on the economic growth – and greenhouse gas emissions – of these previous generations.

Such arguments scupper attempts to bring down carbon emissions on a country-by-country basis. But the carbon tax need not be done country-by-country; a single tax ought instead to be applied to all businesses across the world. Countries may have a history of having emitted more or less than one another, but businesses tend not to last more than a couple of decades on average. Historical emissions cannot be pinned on them to the same degree. What's more, a very polluting business in a poor country has no more 'right' to emit than one in a rich country. The emissions of the company will be correlated to its size and its failure to make environmentally friendly decisions. So a company has to be both large – which implies that it is prosperous and wealthy – and dirty to incur a heavy carbon tax. Small businesses will not incur a heavy tax because they operate at such small scales that their emissions will probably be low or can easily be made to be low. For example, a small business burning coal to heat its offices might easily invest in solar panels instead; a small farming community in rural Africa will likely employ local labour rather than expensive machinery (which is good for local employment and prosperity as well as the local and global environment) and so will likely have quite small emissions. A large company that has embraced emissions reductions will not have a heavy carbon tax either. It is the biggest businesses – the multinationals, especially fossil fuel companies themselves – that will suffer the most. Indeed, companies that are too small to meet some minimum threshold on net income (remembering that we are still acting on the assumption that capitalism has not been abolished) would, in a fair scheme, not have to pay any carbon tax at all, regardless of their emissions. It would have to be *net* income, not profit, though, on which this exemption was made, to ensure that only companies that are genuinely very small and genuinely cannot afford to cut their emissions, rather than those that are simply unsuccessful, will benefit. It would be, for similar reasons, on the basis of net income that the tax would have to be raised. This all applies right across the world – it shouldn't matter whether a big business is based in Cape Town or California, Birmingham or Bangkok. If it is making money by emitting greenhouse gasses, it should be taxed heavily enough to encourage it to change.

Hansen and colleagues appear to subscribe to this global viewpoint, proposing a carbon duty be imposed on imports and exports from the 'bloc' of countries that have the carbon tax to discourage companies from migrating outside the bloc and encourage other countries to join it. They estimate that if such a scheme had been implemented in 1995 it would only have had to impose global emissions cuts of 2.1% per year to reach zero in time to meet the 500 Gt target. Since this did not happen, and cumulative emissions have continued to grow at an ever-increasing rate, 6% per year would need to be achieved today, and that includes drawing down 100 Gt carbon into the biosphere from the atmosphere. They are optimistic that carbon taxes would provide a strong enough incentive to businesses – the mainstay of the capitalist economy – to adopt renewable technologies and encourage 'consumers' to purchase more environmentally sustainable goods and services. After all, big businesses do have a huge amount of power over 'consumer' choices, manipulating the general public daily into buying the most profitable products through advertising, the dressing-up of products and carefully aimed special offers. If, because of a carbon tax, the lowest-emissions products also became the most profitable, this apparatus could be put to the task of manipulating individuals into taking those actions that minimise emissions and help to avert dangerous climate change. It isn't perfect, but at least it could protect our planet for long enough that, when capitalism is finally dispensed with, it is still sufficiently habitable for us to enjoy it.

The optimism of carbon tax proponents derives from smaller-scale taxation schemes that have already been implemented and have shown some degree, at least, of success. The 'Carbon Tax Center', an American organisation that aims to bring about carbon taxation in the USA, dubs the Canadian province British Columbia's taxation scheme as 'the most significant carbon tax in the Western hemisphere, by far'[49] and backs up this claim with impressive statistics. Carbon emissions are reported to have dropped by nine per cent per capita between the scheme's inauguration in 2008 and 2012, during which time the tax was steadily increased, whilst the rest of Canada's emissions have continued to rise. Capitalists in the province will have been pleased to discover that growth in Gross Domestic Product (GDP) has continued, and indeed outpaced that in other regions of Canada, meanwhile. However, the scheme's success may partly be explained by British Colombia's anomalously plentiful hydroelectric resources, which mean that its electricity is already nearly carbon neutral and unaffected by the tax. The same organisation also points out that immediately following Australia's repeal of its carbon tax in 2013, falling greenhouse gas emissions from the energy sector began to rise again steeply, indicating that electricity providers that had been discouraged from using dirty fuels by the tax were beginning to do so again.

Wherever carbon taxes have been implemented, the results have been promising. But the true value of a carbon tax can only be realised if it is issued on a worldwide scale, and at a level designed explicitly to enable the world to meet its overall greenhouse gas emissions targets. The handful of localised endeavours that currently exist – in British Colombia, Ireland and Sweden – can never hope to provide a test of the potential successes that a global scheme, which would amount to a fundamentally different sort of carbon tax through its ability to prevent emissions from escaping abroad, could bring. While we wait for the renovation of economies from capitalism to socialism, the (capitalist) international community should take steps immediately to implement such a global tax so that worldwide carbon dioxide emissions can be brought down immediately. Once the world abandons economic growth and profitability as measures for success and profit-making, competing private corporations are replaced by smaller, cooperating socialist businesses, there will be no need for a 'carbon tax' because monetary incentives will no longer be relevant. In the meantime, however, the world cannot afford not to embrace this potentially very rapid way of driving innovations in technologies and behaviour that could make a huge difference in the struggle to limit climatic change.

5.2 The Current Approach of the International Community

Many of the environmental problems we face today can only be dealt with on an international scale, so when we come to consider the approaches that capitalist governments have employed in their attempts to remedy these, it is useful to take an international perspective. No single country can be blamed for climate change, deforestation or biodiversity loss. Most of the rise in greenhouse gas emissions since the failed Kyoto protocol was signed in 1990 have come from the expansion of coal-burning in China, and recent deforestation has obviously been concentrated in areas with vast rich forests – South America and Indonesia chief amongst them. But China uses a lot of the electricity it generates with its coal to produce superfluous consumer goods for Europe and North America, and these same countries import soya animal feed now harvested where Brazilian rainforest once stood. Biodiversity loss is associated with a global programme of urbanisation, road building and agricultural expansion.

The International Community as a whole is therefore responsible for all of these environmental crimes, and more. The rich world cannot blame countries that it formerly held under the colonial yoke for industrialising, particularly since its own drive for low-'cost' (monetarily) consumption drives manufacturing abroad to where labour is cheaper. But nor can poorer nations blame the richer world for trying to prevent them from trying to emulate current 'western' levels of consumption, which would have disastrous effects for everybody, so long as the rich world commits to reducing its own consumption at the same time. All these countries need to work logically together to abolish 'rich' and 'poor' altogether in favour of a happy and sustainable state of intermediate resource requirements for all. Industrialised and non-industrialised societies should each share technology, techniques and traditions with one another in a collaborative rather than competitive or exploitative relationship, to produce the best outcome for everyone. The trouble is that under a global capitalist system every county feels compelled to compete for wealth, resources, and economic growth, rather than cooperating for prosperity.

Before proceeding, it is necessary to consider what the term 'international community' actually means. Generally, it means a cooperative conferencing of all (or nearly all) countries in the world or in a specific region, often manifested in the form of the United Nations or one of its subsidiary groups. This 'community' acts as a macrocosm of a real human community of people living and working together: it represents all the peoples of the world that must live and work together, each with their own ideas and judgements regarding what is good and bad for themselves and for the world as a whole, and each with their own access to some portion of the planet's human or material resources. Members of the community can refuse to cooperate with one another, in which case those resources are unlikely to be used for the maximum benefit of all. The most wealthy and powerful members will keep that wealth to themselves, leaving the poor to suffer, and a 'tragedy of the commons' may occur whereby common resources are depleted exponentially and the community becomes unsustainable and collapses – a sort of Malthusian catastrophe. Or, the community can work together to decide upon sustainable and equitable ways of using those resources, raising up the poor and constraining the whims of the rich, to the benefit of everyone. The degree to which the international community has to date resembled the latter rather than the former scenario can be assessed on a number of different fronts, some of which we shall now explore.

Climate Change

It was clear to any observer of the 'Conferences of the Parties' (COP) climate conferences that the UN's Framework Convention on Climate Change staged from the late 1990s up to 2014 that there was a pervasive opinion within the UN that the countries of the world could work together to draft binding laws to tackle once and for all the most pressing problem that mankind faces. But it was equally clear that this trust in international agreements is misplaced, and that the reality of global cooperation is very different. Climate change is interlinked with so many important interests – ranging from genuine humanitarian and environmental concerns to the profit-interests of capitalist governments and businesses – that it will never be possible to devise hard-and-fast rules and targets that are universally perceived as fair. The most important contributors to climate change – China and the USA being top of the list for net emissions – are also the most wary of conceding sovereignty, and few countries will allow themselves to be forced into enacting legislation or to be punished for missing targets. Certainly, governments could not be considered very 'democratic', assuming that the 'demos' in question is the electorate that voted them into power, if they conceded excessive legislative power to people living elsewhere. In light of all this, it is not surprising that the attitude of the international community – to stage meeting after meeting vainly struggling to come up with targets and legislation to regulate greenhouse gas emissions – was getting nowhere, and needed to be revised.

After the disastrous 2009 Copenhagen conference, at which countries failed to agree to anything meaningful at all and which failed to stop emissions continuing to rise apace, the UN seemed to realise that a new approach would be necessary. The conferences until then had continually failed because so-called 'developing' countries refused to commit to legislation that will force them to halt rises in their greenhouse gas emissions, believing that this would prevent them from obtaining standards of living as good as those of 'developed' countries, and at the same time blamed the latter group for the emissions it produced by going through exactly the same process of industrialisation. Meanwhile, the 'developed' countries refused to slash emissions for fear that, since the 'developing' ones will produce far more in the future anyway, it would make little difference to the climate and would cause them to lose their economic advantages. Neither side wanted to surrender political autonomy or agree to anything that might tarnish the golden calf of economic growth. Hence, attempting to get everyone to come to a single agreement at the same time was shown to be a vain effort.

Nonetheless, international cooperation is without doubt of paramount importance in the global effort to mitigate and adapt to global climate change, as the monumental agreement made in Paris in 2015 at, so to speak, the eleventh hour for action on climate change, conclusively showed. This agreement, which at last saw more than two hundred governments around the world – richest and poorest alike – commit to keeping global warming by 2100 'well below' two degrees Celsius for the sake of all humanity and other sentient life in Earth, was made possible by the realisation that different countries have different things to bring to the table – different commitments, sacrifices and developments that they can each make. In the run-up to the conference came a number of voluntary targets by individual countries and agreements between a smaller number of important players, such as that come to by the United States and China in November 2014 whereby the former pledged to cut emissions by 28% by 2025 and the latter to cap emissions by 2030 and both agreed to work together for better air quality and environmental protection. It was under the steam of such motions of good will for the planet as a whole, and in a spirit of individual, manageable commitments by individual countries, that the deal was finally reached.

No single country can act alone to prevent climate change in excess of the internationally agreed target of a rise in mean global atmospheric temperature of no more than 2°C since pre-industrial levels, but every country will be affected by climate change, and all must realise that it is in the interests of the whole world that its severity be minimised. Agreements like that between the USA and China showed that the big powers are beginning to realise that blaming each other and waiting for the other side to act first will get no-one anywhere. Instead, each country needs to take the initiative itself and announce targets and means for cutting their own emissions, so as to lead by example and show their commitment to combatting climate change, which will show other countries that efforts they make in this regard will not be futile lone endeavours. That is why the agreement in Paris is so important: by bringing their individual commitments into a larger picture of cooperative action and responsibility, it gives the governments of all countries permission to be proactive and ambitious about tackling climate change by making alterations within their own jurisdictions without fearing that their efforts – and all the associated time and energy – will be wasted because other countries continue to emit.

But Paris is not a magic bullet; although most of the signatories ratified the agreement in 2016 it still remains for the parties to stick to their agreed targets and to continue to cooperate until a 'zero-carbon' world really is achieved, something that the agreement stipulates should come about by 2050. After all, the agreement makes no stipulations about exactly how the target is to be achieved, so it is up to each signatory to do the hard work of changing their societies radically enough to slash emissions within the coming decades. Investing in new, renewable technologies, which may itself be profitable in the long-term, will need to be a big part of this. But we must not allow the world to be tied by the chains of money. As well as developing new fuels and energy sources, it will be equally important to resist the allure of falling coal and oil prices when demand for these fuels begins to decrease, which in a capitalist marketplace would prevent them from being given up, and reject these dirty fuels out of hand for the sake of our long-term prosperity. It will also be essential to reduce electricity and fuel use around the world, resisting the temptation to roll out mass electrification of areas currently free of dependency on electricity, and encouraging those in the more industrialised world to use their superfluous gadgets, lights and vehicles less, to raise their thermostats no higher than is necessary, to cut down on food waste and superfluous material goods and to abandon the aeroplane when going on holiday for more sensible means of transport. All of this will actually improve the true quality of life, which is often hindered more than it is helped by an over-abundance of material goods and technology, but it cuts against the capitalist rhetoric that growth is good and would require us to sacrifice short-term monetary profit.

The danger is that the International Community will remain, by contrast, entrenched in a capitalistic world-view whereby the only reason for cutting emissions in the first place is to protect that cherished idol, 'economic growth'. Although this growth would indeed be ultimately threatened in a world filled with catastrophe, flooding and starvation induced by climatic change, which encourages even capitalists to do something to avert it, a continued emphasis on growth as an ends in itself rather than a means for achieving prosperity distorts the effectiveness of pledges and international agreements and limits their scope, because it implies playing off climate-change mitigation against other economic concerns to prevent this mitigation from impinging on economic growth. So, China is happy to combat coal fires in cities that choke its citizens at the same time as contributing to global warming, because this will allow those citizens to live longer and more productive lives that will benefit the country's economy in the short term. This is a good thing to do because it will bring about genuine welfare improvements. But if China fails to not only halt the construction of new coal-fired power plants – which it now appears to be doing – but also to close down its existing ones, the goals negotiated at Paris in 2015 may not be achieved. To cut out coal would certainly be an action that would bring enormous benefit to its citizens – as well as those of the rest of the world – a decade or more into the future but which would slow down the pace of economic growth in the short-term as factories and townships would have to wait for renewable sources of energy to become exploitable before their electricity use could be expanded. Likewise, if the United States only increases its use of renewable technology on the economic basis of increasing the number of jobs in its energy sector, can it guarantee that it will not continue to prospect for more gas to frack on the same basis, or that renewables will continue to grow in prominence if gas remains cheaper?

Rather, as the arguments put forward elsewhere in this document show, the desire for economic growth should not be allowed to impinge upon climate change mitigation. The ultimate aim of the international community ought to be to maximise the well-being of their citizens and the quality of the environment that they and the other animals they live alongside experience. 'Development' should never come at the cost of increased greenhouse gas emissions per capita, because those emissions will cause people in those same industrialising countries to suffer more, and therefore cannot be construed as positive 'development' at all. In the industrialised world, widespread behavioural changes towards a less consumptive and less energy-intensive lifestyle may not bring about economic growth but should be recognised as conducive to the well-being of the populace and immediately encouraged. The Paris 2015 agreement shows the international community beginning to demonstrate its commitment to fighting for the long-term well-being of its people above all else. But only if it really does tackle climate change in these more radical ways will we have true cause for hope that such an impending catastrophe can indeed be averted.

One way in which this could be done much better would be to implement bans on certain types of electricity generation – for example, burning the dirtiest form of coal, lignite – as has been done for other harmful substances. If the 1987 Montreal Protocol could be used to ban CFCs that damage the ozone layer, surely a similar treaty banning coal whose ignition causes far greater problems both directly and indirectly for human and other animal health (through air pollution and climate change) can be brought into force today. This could be used to pressurise Germany, for instance, to return to renewables and nuclear power and switch off the coal-fired plants it has so recklessly been switching on of late. It could also be used to ban drilling for oil in the fragile Arctic, where Shell is already recklessly prospecting[50], and to prevent the Czech Republic from destroying swathes of countryside and, perhaps, the entire town of Eisenburg in the pursuit of lignite.

Surely we value trees, birds and other living beings, not to mention our own future prosperity as a species, far more highly than the extra, cheap electricity that burning this lignite, extracted at such a heavy cost to our environment that is not reflected in its monetary price, would produce. Big businesses may not, if there is money to be made by converting unprofitable untouched resources into 'exchange capital' by exploiting them. But ordinary human beings, if they have any human compassion, must do, and it is the voices of the people – not those of big business – that their governments need to heed. Yet our voices are all too often drowned out by promises of short-term economic gains made by profit-hungry corporations. The International Community, freed from the need to please big businesses in any particular area of the world, is capable of sending a powerful message to governments across the world that mining and burning dirty coal is not acceptable. This can be used by governments as a legitimate basis to turn down permission for extraction that would otherwise be seen as economically advantageous, and could be a powerful means of preventing fossil fuel corporations from distorting our supposedly democratic governments to their own ends.

Clearly, not nearly enough of this sort of guidance is being produced by the International Community today, because governments continue to fund fossil fuel companies to seek out and extract more of the very substances that are destroying our future prospects. In 2015, this funding amounted to a total of $5.3 trillion per year, which is 6.5 per cent of global gross domestic product. There is no reason why any of this money should be given to these irresponsible companies at all. The oil giant Shell, for example, though it, like other such companies, talks about the need to use more renewable fuels in public, is still putting pressure on governments to allow it to extract oil. Indeed, the Guardian newspaper reported in May 2015 that Shell believes that global warming will reach 4 degrees Celsius above pre-industrial levels by 2100, far above the 2 degree target that UN climate change negotiators are aiming for, which suggests that they expect governments to subsidise them to extract a lot more oil over the coming decades[51]. The short-term profitability of the likes of Shell should not be placed above the welfare of life on Earth, and the International Community should come together to abolish profit-making in the energy sector entirely.

Nor should all efforts be concentrated on electricity generation and electric cars, which seem to be the arenas in which fossil fuel is losing ground most rapidly, because it is now cheaper to use solar panels and wind turbines in some circumstances and it is profitable to sell people new electric cars to replace their old petrol ones. If cars can be switched from diesel demons to green machines in the public's mind, their manufacturers will be able to continue to grow and profit by reversing the blackening of their industry's reputation that climatic change and emissions tests scandals have engendered amidst the public, so it 'makes business sense' to invest in renewable technologies that at least make companies appear green in these areas. Yet thirty per cent of global emissions are associated with agriculture, a figure that will continue to expand unless the International Community comes together to discourage increased uptake of heavily-polluting meat diets and clamps down on the use of nitrate fertiliser, which is necessary only in order to feed such large herds of animals and which makes its own hefty contribution to climate change through the emission of nitrate gasses. A further three per cent of emissions are associated with ships[52] and another five per cent with aeroplanes[53], neither of which are covered by the Paris agreement for fear of limiting 'the demand created by the world economy'[54]. If the International Community is truly concerned about preventing dangerous climatic change, not just about growing the economy by investing in renewables and snazzy cars, it must include all of these vital sectors in its emissions reduction programme.

As well as the mitigation of climate change, there also needs to be international collaboration when it comes to dealing with its consequences. This would be more straightforward if the biggest polluters were also the greatest sufferers, as is sometimes the case with localised air and water pollution, but the effects of climate change will not be uniform, and are actually biased against less-industrialised peoples. Though extremes in weather will become more likely across the globe, it is predicted that the sea-level will rise with climate change to a greater degree in some areas - especially the western North

Atlantic and western Pacific – than others, and low-lying countries will obviously be worse affected. Island nations, along with Vietnam and Bangladesh, will suffer most from this. More extreme droughts and floods will have their worst effects where these phenomena are already common and causing damage to homes, habitats and agriculture – Africa and Southern Asia in particular. Therefore, as has so often been pointed out, it is the less industrialised world, which is also less equipped to defend itself against extreme weather and sea-level rise, that has contributed the least towards but will suffer the most from climate change.

Internationally organised schemes to help people and animals of other species in the most affected regions of the planet will likely be essential to prevent extreme suffering, and industrialised countries that have been responsible for the bulk of the past emissions that have caused this problem in the first place do have at least some degree of duty to protect those whose rights to life and a healthy environment they will otherwise have indirectly violated through the effects of their over-consumptive and over-polluting lifestyles. This means that all countries around the world need to work together and listen to one another: who is suffering as a result of climate change, and who has the power to alleviate this suffering by changing their lifestyles and policies or actively providing expertise, technology and resources to undo or prevent climate change-induced damage? How and where can those who are displaced by rising sea-levels or the destruction of their own local environment through climate change be happily and safely relocated? These are questions that will require the engagement of multiple peoples and their governments to answer. Again, the Paris agreement has set an encouraging precedent, with richer countries pledging funds and resources to help poorer ones develop more sustainably. But it remains to be seen how effective this will be, given that 'economic growth' and developing western consumerist lifestyles are still amongst the aims of many of those bringing about change on the ground in the less-industrialised world. Bringing in fully-fledged capitalism in the name of 'development' will preclude sustainability.

One might conceive of a global framework for 'climate rights' associated with climate change, whereby the rights of each individual to pollute in the pursuit of free, independent lives were set against the rights of others not to have their lives ruined or ended by the consequences of this pollution, and the duties owed by each polluter because of their small personal contribution to suffering elsewhere were defined. But any such framework is unlikely to be universally accepted, and again agreements between individual countries and good-will offerings from the industrialised to the less industrialised world of lifestyle concessions and helpful resources are more likely to bear fruit. That's why no country should idly sit and wait for international agreements before acting on climate change: we all need to start acting now, inspiring one another through the progress we are able to make in the direction of sustainability and preparing the social and physical infrastructure needed to withstand the climatic changes that will come with minimal suffering. A country like the UK doesn't need to wait to be ordered by international agreement to provide expertise in new, sustainable technologies, help on the basis of prior experience to resist the growth of capitalist consumerism where it is on the ascendency and aid for adaptation to the less-industrialised world: it should act now, taking responsibility for the emissions it has already produced, so as to maximise the overall well-being of the planet's population.

The historic agreement in Paris in 2015 was only made possible because of the international community's much longer-running success when it comes to collaboration over the actual science of climate change itself. The Intergovernmental Panel on Climate Change (IPCC) was formed in 1990 and has seen produced regular assessments of the current and possible future risks associated with climate change and the extent to which it is anthropogenic rather than natural in origin. There have now been five such assessments, published in 1990, 1995, 2001, 2007 and 2014, employing the collaborative effort of hundreds of scientists to reach as accurate and reliable conclusions as it is possible to make. These are presented in great detail for the use of scientists and also in summary form to help policymakers to make decisions. Every sentence of each policymakers' summary is carefully analysed and debated over by scientists and delegates representing nearly every government in the world, and although they cannot be expected to be perfect the reports provide an internationally renowned and scientifically rigorous agreement that can be trusted. Each successive report has documented greater and greater visibility of climatic change in the world, become more and more certain that humans are to blame for much of this change and come up with better constrained estimates of how greenhouse gas emissions and climatic change are likely to proceed in the future. The level of international cooperation and sharing of knowledge and expertise witnessed in climate science is unprecedented, as is, of course, the importance of the issue in hand. This is exactly the sort of collaboration that should be encouraged between countries, putting us in the best possible place for mitigating and adapting to climatic change, even if that scientific consensus with regard to the facts cannot be translated into a global consensus on how to respond. It is, after all, the IPCC's Representative Carbon pathways (RCPs) used to predict future warming under different greenhouse gas emissions scenarios that provide the most useful indication to policymakers – and ultimately, therefore, to the public to which they are responsible, of what our future world would be like if various combinations of policies were to be followed.

We have already seen how imperative it is that the International Community cooperates to bring about a global carbon tax that would see polluting businesses penalised for their carbon emissions. This is, perhaps, our best opportunity to reduce greenhouse gasses rapidly, in that it works within the existing capitalist framework and will not have to wait for this framework to be dismantled. But few signs of such a global scheme are yet apparent. Instead, extremely dangerous economic theories have been invented to justify continued growth of greenhouse gas emissions. For example, many so-called 'developing' countries continue to invest in schemes to build western-style cities and roads and encourage the use of cars and coal-fired electricity on the basis of the preposterous claim that this will make life better for their people in the long run. In fact, of course, the 'western' lifestyle is an incredibly polluting one, with the average American emitting 4.54 tonnes of carbon dioxide in 2011, compared to just 0.01 for the average citizen of the DRC, Chad and Burundi and 11.97 for a citizen of industrialised Qatar[55]. Attempting to 'westernise' the lifestyles of the world's poorest would lead to catastrophic climate change that would make their lives much worse; indeed, it is the 'western' world that should change its polluting behaviour, and help poorer nations to establish prosperity without ramping up pollution. Building more roads and coal-fired power plants is certainly not the way to go about this. It is only the profit interests of the corporations that build them that have persuaded the International Community to go down its current, destructive developmental path and to allow or encourage such 'westernisation'.

A yet more dangerous fallacy is the notion that carbon dioxide emissions should be increased as rapidly as possible in the short term to minimise the effects of global warming in the long term, one which seems counter-intuitive and is, behind the mask, propounded by capitalist interests that have little concern for long-term prosperity and are seeking to maximise short-term profits. The argument, which we shall refer to as the 'maximum growth, maximum emissions' strategy, runs as follows. Maximum emissions of greenhouse gasses are a by-product of maximum global economic growth. The more growth there is, the more money there will be to invest in new technologies. At the same time, the worse climate change becomes as a result of the growth-driven emissions, the more costly will it become to deal with its harmful effects and the more it will hamper this growth. Strategies for extracting carbon dioxide from the atmosphere that are presently 'uneconomical' because it is too expensive to develop and utilise them will become increasingly attractive, and eventually profitable when the cost of the climate change they are designed to avoid becomes equal to the cost of these strategies. Therefore, market forces will suddenly drive the invention of new technologies that will enable us to extract all the carbon dioxide we have previously emitted and the climate will return to normal.

This argument is flawed on at least three counts. First and most obviously, it relies upon the assumption that strategies to extract all the carbon dioxide from the atmosphere that has been emitted up to some future date actually exist. It could be that, despite all the efforts of all the investors and inventors in the world, when it becomes profitable to search for these strategies we will fail to find any. Then, the world will be faced with a situation whereby all our economic activity is based on high-emissions technology, the concentration of carbon dioxide in the atmosphere is already much higher than even the 'business of usual' predictions of the early twenty-first century would have placed it, and there is no way of reducing it or even stopping it from growing further. The planet will be catapulted into unthinkably catastrophic climatic change. This makes the maximum-growth policy an extremely risky one.

Even without this huge long-term risk, the policy is undesirable in that it will maximise the short-term effects of climatic change, causing Arctic warming, coral bleaching, extreme weather and species extinctions to accelerate at their maximum possible rate. Many of these changes will be irreversible – we cannot bring extinct species or families killed by floods, storms and droughts back from the dead. If the point of profitability of the mythical technological 'fix' to climate change turns out to be a long time into the future (we cannot know what the 'cost' of this fix will be), there will be a great deal of suffering in the interim, and even once it is implemented it is unlikely that this 'fix' could return things to normal overnight. Drawing down carbon dioxide from the atmosphere, whatever the method invented to do it, would surely take a long time, given that the gas is present in such low concentrations (measured in parts per million). Earth would then take time to adjust to the new concentrations and might exhibit some degree of hysteresis rather than returning to its previous state.

The real repulsiveness of the 'maximum growth, maximum emissions' strategy can be best seen if its implications are spelt out explicitly. The policy amounts, essentially, to polluting our planet so badly from here on in that we will suffer so much we'll have no choice but to invent a remedy. It is akin to somebody trying to lose weight by eating as much and exercising as little as they can so that they become so fat that they'll be given liposuction. If liposuction is suddenly found to be dangerous in some way and is banned, or the person makes his or herself so ill that they die before they can have it, the weight-loss strategy can hardly be said to have worked. If left alive, the person will be in much worse a state than they were before they began it. And if they weren't willing to diet and exercise to start with, they are hardly likely to do so when it becomes apparent that the quick fix they had been banking on doesn't work. The idea of following such a procedure seems preposterous to us, even when we know that liposuction does exist.

Who could ever contemplate taking this strategy if it didn't, in the hope that it would somehow be invented at just the right moment?

The same is true when it comes to the 'maximum growth, maximum emissions' strategy. By following it, our economies will become even more dependent on fossil fuel emissions in the short-term. Then if the hoped-for technological fix doesn't appear, we'll find it even more difficult to 'lose weight the hard way' so to speak, by cutting our emissions through behavioural and infrastructure changes. The strategy is supposed to push us into changing the way we do things by force, by making the situation so bad that we have no other choice. But why should we make ourselves ill in order to force ourselves to invent a magic remedy to the illness? If we can see the illness coming on the road ahead, why not simply avoid it by changing paths now? It is much better for the smoker to quit before they develop cancer than to smoke as much as they can until they're so ill they have no choice but to stop. If we start cutting emissions now, and re-invest the resources currently spent on finding fossil fuels into developing low-carbon technologies, encouraging behavioural change and, indeed, searching for ways of extracting carbon dioxide from the atmosphere, we can start improving the prospects for our world and its people today. There's no need to wait until these strategies become profitable. The third great flaw with the 'maximum growth, maximum emissions' strategy, then, is that there already exists a much more reasonable, more logical and less painful alternative.

Of course, the proponents of the strategy don't seriously see it as a fix to the problem of climatic change. Instead, they see it as a fix to the international community's efforts to deal with climatic change, which they see as a problem. Eying up potential initiatives such as the implementation of carbon taxes and the encouragement of behavioural changes that might undermine consumerism, capitalist corporations are becoming worried that these efforts might hamper economic growth and put dents into their own profits. The strategy has been cooked up, therefore, as a way of legitimising the continuation of 'business as usual', so that companies can continue to profit as much as possible from providing goods and services in ways and volumes that cause pollution. The focus is still on short-term profit, not long-term prosperity. It is the responsibility of the international community to resist the pressure of these corporations and vested interests, and to reject the 'maximum growth, maximum emissions' strategy outright. Fortunately, heeding the cries of those already suffering from climate change and recognising that this is no time for taking huge gambles with the future, it seems to be doing just that.

The final question in the climate change arena on which international guidance is desperately needed is that of geoengineering, the purposeful alteration of the climate in an attempt to reverse the recent anthropogenic changes. Through the large-scale injection of sulphate particles into the atmosphere, the dumping of vast quantities of iron into the oceans and numerous other ways it is in theory possible for any one country in the world to bring about transformative change to climates across the whole planet in this way. This is a very dangerous situation because all forms of geoengineering carry with them risks and negative side-effects that might be acceptable to one country but not to others. Most of the ideas that scientists have proposed as viable means of engineering Earth's climate have not been tested, and one country taking it upon itself to implement them without further experimentation could prove disastrous. We have already seen the painful unexpected consequences of our greenhouse gas emissions for the climate; further meddling could have yet more dangerous implications that are equally far-reaching and unforeseeable. Therefore, it is important for the International Community as a whole to be satisfied that geoengineering attempts are necessary, adequate and safe before they are put into practice.

Furthermore, because geoengineering may one day prove essential to the maintenance of habitable conditions on Earth, research into this important topic of study should be internationally coordinated to make sure that the scientific resources available are distributed as efficiently as possible. Research should not be focussed upon schemes whose negative implications for local ecosystems or climates would render them ultimately unacceptable even if they proved successful in lowering global average temperatures. Nor should multiple, independent groups all be working in parallel on the same ideas unbeknown to one another: instead the International Community should act as a bridge whereby research can be shared and directed. In this way, the options and consequences relating to geoengineering can be assessed in the most cohesive possible manner to the maximal possible benefit. International cooperation is, in this perhaps above all other arenas, essential for success. Yet, few agreements on geoengineering have yet been negotiated, and no scheme for international collaboration has yet been put in place.

Fortunately, this is not an illustration of the state of international agreement over climate change as a whole. In these early decades of the twenty-first century, we have our only chance to limit our emissions sufficiently to avoid devastating climate change. That the International Community has, at least, agreed that every country needs to do what it can to limit global warming to much less than two degrees Celsius - and hopefully 1.5 degrees Celsius - by 2100 is extremely encouraging. This level of warming relative to pre-industrial levels is not unprecedented in the history of Earth's current state with ice at both poles, to which all animal life is currently adapted. Such an agreement could not have been made in, say, 2025 after another decade's unchecked emissions: 1.5 degrees would by then have become a fact of life.

The decisions we make here and now have, to a greater extent than at any other time in our history, the potential to have a profound impact on life in Earth fifty, one hundred and even one thousand years hence. To constrain our emissions so that global average temperatures do not stray to levels unprecedented for the last million years would enable us to protect the well-being of countless future inhabitants of our planet. It will be a monumental effort, but a monumental agreement has been made to start us down the path to achieving it. We can only hope that, like the butterfly flapping its wings that changes the whole state of Earth's weather a month later, this agreement – thrashed out over the course of a mild fortnight in Paris – will change (or rather, prevent us from disastrously changing) the future of Earth's climate in the decades to come.

One spanner in the works in all this is, of course, the election of President Trump in the United States, a man who has vocatively denied the very existence of climate change. Americans remain the biggest emitters of greenhouse gasses per person, and the ripping up of environmental protection measures – including climate change mitigation policies – by Trump's government could be disastrous for the whole planet. We do not have much time to reorient the world's economies away from fossil fuels and overconsumption, something that will require behaviour changes and technological transformations that are very difficult to bring about. The four years of a presidency, if they see one of the world's largest emitters travel in entirely the opposite direction, could set efforts to do so back by many more years than this, and, ultimately, doom our species to a climatic Armageddon. On the other hand, it is no longer by any means certain that if America refuses to act the rest of the world will sit on its laurels. It may be that China, already well on its way to transitioning to a sustainable future, with emissions already falling year on year, will become the global leader on tackling climatic change. If this happens, the United States may eventually find itself forced to follow suit. Nobody in the International Community should wait, though, for the big players to act: they must encourage one another, no matter how small their relative contribution to the problem, to cut emissions as soon and smoothly as possible. After all, any country that does this is placing itself at the frontier of a new, sustainable future, and this may place it at considerable advantage when the rest of the world starts trying to catch up.

Competition and Cooperation over Resources

In a finite world with a growing population, it is inevitable that conflicts sometimes emerge across countries' borders regarding access to resources. Rivers are an especially potent source of division because they deliver the most essential ingredient for life – water – but often either form or cut across borders. Whatever is put into or done to a river upstream will have effects downstream that may be detrimental or even catastrophic to those that rely upon it to drink, grow crops, wash, power industry and nourish vibrant ecosystems. If each country along the river's course only takes into account the effects that a given policy – building a dam, say, or injecting industrial effluent – will have on their own people and environment, many of these potential problems will not be taken into account when evaluating what is the right decision to make.

Water resources, unlike specific measures for tackling climatic change, should be an issue on which the International Community as a whole can and must agree, precisely because river pollution and disruption poses localised rather than global problems, so that the results of specific actions and policies can be explicitly identified. It is possible to carry out neutral and scientific analyses of the humans and ecosystems dependent upon river resources, and to make projections of the effects that the likes of dams and pollutants will have. Dams, for instance, make such a great difference to the flow of a river that any reduced water or sediment delivery downstream of a new dam will be obvious and its cause will be clearly identifiable. By contrast, the association between, say, a particular bout of extreme weather and global warming is often much more difficult to prove. River pollutants pose no bigger problem for accountability, because although no specific case of illness or poisoning can necessarily be ascribed to one particular source of pollutants in a river, a general degradation of health or the environment downstream can be traced to particular chemical pollutants known to be released by particular sources upstream. Therefore, violations of the rights of the inhabitants of downstream countries can be directly associated with specific actions carried out by a given country or a private company that is abusing the river upstream, and it should be possible to formulate laws stipulating penalties such as sanctions that should be imposed in response to those violations. In other words, with rivers it is clear who has done the damage, which populations they have harmed and in what way.

The International Community is currently failing to provide adequate protection of cross-border rivers, putting at risk all their animal dependents, including humans who rely on rivers for their very existence. Rivers that cross borders should be treated as internationally protected waters, with damming and the injection of industrial pollutants strictly prohibited unless globally agreed strict guidelines are met that ensure that no rights will be violated, that the river's dependents will be able to continue to live in a healthy environment and that net good will be done by the change.

The lack of such an agreement is what has led to political conflicts such as that regarding the Brahmaputra river, which has been the life-force of countless people and other animals in the region that is now Tibet, China, India and Bangladesh for millennia. In 2014, China announced that it had built a large dam on the river to generate hydroelectricity, much bigger than it had previously indicated would be constructed. Chinese assurances that the flow of the river will not be disrupted are hardly sufficient to reassure the people of India and Bangladesh, who fear that it and future dams that China plans for the same river will cause flash floods, landslides and water shortages. China has already dammed the Mekong river, Asia's seventh largest, to such an extent that Myanmar, Laos, Thailand, Cambodia and Vietnam have suffered devastating water shortages that have damaged the regions' once so habitable and beautiful environments[56]. Without an international agreement on the protection of rivers, the inhabitants of such lands are left to suffer with no hope of the recovery of their lands or help to adapt to the altered conditions. It is they, not the Chinese, who suffer the most from the dams, but currently China is under no obligation to take this into account.

The Chinese dams on the Tibetan plateau provide just one instance of where the International Community's failure to regulate rivers is causing crises; the same sorts of difficulties could arise anywhere in the world. The assurances of individual countries that the effects of their river-tapping will be negligible are not necessarily trustworthy: official scientific investigations carried out from the neutral standpoint of the United Nations are the only way of providing honest guarantees that lives will not be destroyed. A similar approach might be applied to the seas, where, in the absence of forceful regulations binding all countries, the dumping of waste chemicals and plastics continues to cause horrific problems for sea-life and for humans that eat fish contaminated by high concentrations of heavy metals and synthetic chemicals. Nobody is takes responsibility for their waste, the oceans are treated as free-for-all dumps, and everyone suffers.

The International Community has exhibited somewhat greater strength when it comes to fishing: official recommendations have been made regarding the largest catches of certain types of fish that should be permitted, and whale hunting has been largely banned across the globe. But there remains much to be desired in this arena, too, as these regulations are not based on a desire to protect the rights of animals in the sea, and profit motives are allowed to impinge too strongly upon the setting of quotas. So, for instance, whaling is still permitted for 'scientific purposes', which leaves room for the Japanese to continue it under that guise. A 2014 ruling by the International Court of Justice rejected Japan's claims that its whale-hunting expeditions provided useful science, but this may only encourage the Japanese government to seek out new ways of making the hunts 'scientific' so that they can continue in spite of international condemnation and a lack of public demand for whale meat in Japan. The interests of those involved in whale hunting are allowed to trump the rights of the whales; were these rights to be

186

upheld, whaling would be banned in all circumstances, whatever its potential to provide scientific gains. The reality is that little more can be gained from killing whales than from studying living populations, and in any case there is no 'right' to do science, so it should never be carried out in violation of any intelligent creature's rights to life and a healthy environment. The International Community is failing whales if it does not ban whale hunting outright.

Fishing quotas ought to be set on the basis of the rights of fish and humans present and future. Fishing as a whole might not necessarily be banned, because although it involves a violation of the right to life of fish, in some parts of the world fish are an essential part of the human diet, so that it is necessary to fish in order to uphold the right to a healthy life of the humans consuming the fish. Clearly, though, this implies that fishing should only be permitted out of necessity, and over-catches of fish, with some of the caught animals being wasted or consumed in excess of what is necessary for health and well-being, must not be permitted. Certainly, even if one disagrees with the notion that individual fish have a right to life, fishing using indiscriminate trawlers that devastate life on the sea-floor cannot be ethically justified. Nor can fishing in such high quantities that populations of fish cannot be sustained, as this undermines not only the fishes' own right to live and flourish but also the rights of other animals forming part of their ecosystem that depend upon these fish – including future human populations. Presently, though, the long-term sustainability of fish stocks is not the main consideration of quota-setters. For example, the EU fishing quota for 2015 allowed cod catches to increase by five per cent relative to 2014, even though this fish was only recently struggling on the verge of population collapse through decades of over-fishing and scientists recommended a twenty per cent cut in the catch in order for the species to recover. Even in specific parts of the sea where the quota for cod and haddock has been cut, the reduction is so small that fish populations are unlikely to recover. All of this has been done, in a continent across most of which fish consumption is not essential to the well-being of the human population, on the basis of the commercial interests of fishermen rather than scientifically-informed care for the sea ecosystem and its inhabitants.

The International Community cannot hope to regulate countries' use of resources within their own borders. But where the exploitation by one particular country of resources falling under the jurisdiction of multiple governments threatens to impinge – whether through depletion or contamination of the resource – upon the rights of people and other animals living outside that country's jurisdiction, the International Community has the duty to intervene. Therefore, though international laws on resource extraction may not be applicable to many mining, farming and energy generation activities that take place within the borders of individual governments' jurisdictions, this should be no reason to forbear regulating the likes of ocean and water resources which are shared by many different peoples. Currently, not enough international effort has been exerted to put such regulations – and appropriate sanctions should they be violated – in place.

Regulation of Chemicals and Drugs

International cooperation over the use of dangerous chemicals has seen mixed success. Whilst the Montreal Protocol saw tens of countries agree to phase out ozone-layer-damaging chemicals such as chloro-fluoro-carbons (CFCs) in September 1987, an agreement that UN Secretary General (from 1987 to 2006) Kofi Annan described as the 'most successful international agreement to date', many other substances that could have far-reaching effects on health via air and water transport are still used without international restraint. As was pointed out in Chapter 4, synthetic chemicals have been allowed to permeate quite literally into almost all aspects of our lives without due consideration of the harmful effects that exposure to these unnatural substances might have upon the health of their users and those around them. If those chemicals can spread elsewhere, every country should have a duty not to use them unless they are officially certified by international agreement not to pose any greater risk to the health of people or the quality of the environment than substances with which we are normally naturally in contact.

This is another area, then, in which there should be more, binding international agreements. If, on the other hand, international trade agreements such as the recently rejected TTIP deal (see below) were implemented, it would become easier, rather than harder, for businesses that care more about profit than human health to put chemicals that are regulated in, for example, the European Union but not the United States into more peoples' food, clothes and household items. Any such an agreement that diminishes control over potentially very dangerous and certainly unnatural substances should not be made without the public being made fully aware of its implications and of the fact that the safety of their food and furniture is going to become less certain.

Substances that are, when used in the right way, beneficial to human health are also in much better need of international regulation. Antibiotics, which are such a magical life-saving gift if applied where they are needed, have been rendered increasingly impotent through over-use and carelessness. Since their widespread synthesis in the 1950s, antibiotics have been prescribed all too liberally by doctors around the world, and the standard practice has been to take them for granted as a 'wonder-drug' quick-fix tool for all kinds of microbial infections that will always be available to us. In reality, antibiotics are much less dependable than this. To work their healing power, these drugs don't combat specific chemicals or injuries in the body, after all, but living beings – bacteria. As is well-known, life has developed its amazing complexity on Earth by diversifying through evolution to overcome every obstacle that is placed in its way. When antibiotics are applied anywhere, they wipe out most but not quite all of the bacteria present. The most vulnerable bacteria are, naturally, the most likely to be killed. Therefore, the small remaining population will consist of those bacteria best adapted to resist the antibiotic attack. These will then spread and multiply, propagating the traits that enabled them to survive, and in this way, the very use of antibiotics encourages bacterial resistance by diversification. With antibiotics, the more we use them, the less powerful they become.

This is a lesson that our industrialised, profit-driven culture has failed to learn. Instead of working with nature and recognising the adaptability and variety of life in all its forms, we have sought too often to try to obliterate everything that we perceive as an obstacle to the progress of modernity. Buoyed by the pride of our inventions, we have imagined ourselves capable of controlling the world and bending all life to our own ends. It is for this reason that a growing number of 'superbugs' resistant to antibiotics are plaguing the world, especially our hospitals. Antibiotics have been used with such abandon to treat even infections that are very unlikely to cause long-term harm – such as sore throats – or even as a precautionary measure when their efficacy is uncertain, that populations of resistant bacteria have begun to proliferate in place of their more vulnerable predecessors. The problem has been greatly compounded where antibiotics have been allowed to leak into the environment. Over-prescribed drugs are flushed out into rivers; packets and packets are handed out in unregulated countries such as India for every malady; farmers even use them to fatten up livestock in some intensive farms. In cases where the bacteria do serious harm and there is genuinely no cure other than antibiotics, the fact that these drugs are no longer potent could prove fatal. A quarter of streptococcus infections – which include pneumonia and meningitis – are already untreatable with penicillin worldwide, for example[57]. The wonder drugs of the 50s are, in this way, becoming useless, their power having been thoughtlessly squandered.

Antibiotic misuse on a local scale can have global consequences as resistant strains begin to spread. But there are clear steps that the International Community can take when it comes to antibiotics: guidelines must be laid down and enforced regarding when it is appropriate for antibiotics to be prescribed, and their sale without prescription should be outlawed, as should their use in farm animals except to prevent fatality. Antibiotics should only ever be used where they are really needed, especially given that they can have unwanted side-effects such as the destruction of healthy gut bacteria that can cause digestive and other problems. It may already be too late to save some of our existing types of antibiotics from eventual impotency, but it is essential that measures are taken before any new such drugs are developed to ensure that they, too, do not lose their ability to cure.

Meanwhile, developing these new drugs has to be a priority for the International Community, and it is a task that cannot be left in the hands of profit-making corporations. There is little profit to be made from antibiotics because their value diminishes the more they are used in a way that is not true of other drugs. Hence, private drugs companies are refusing to put very much effort into developing them, in a brilliant illustration of the failure of the capitalist market to serve the interests of the world's people. The solution, surely, is to reject this model of drug development entirely and for governments instead to collaboratively provide the resources and training necessary. In that way, the drugs that we really need can be developed and there will no longer be any need to encourage the over-use of drugs already developed to increase profits. When it comes to drug development, nationalisation is not enough: this is one rare realm where globalisation can provide a genuine benefit: after all, similar drugs are needed to treat similar infections around the world, and medication can help to save many lives in less-industrialised countries that cannot develop new drugs themselves. The International Community should fund scientists and provide adequate resources for drug development, which should be kept entirely out of the hands of profit-making private enterprises. For big businesses at present to profit from others' illnesses and to refuse to find a cure where there is no money to be made from it is a depraved perversion.

It is equally clear that more needs to be done on an international scale to ease the burden of drugs that cause harm rather than benefit and that blight the lives of so many people around the world. The illegal use of heroin and other opiates is a particular cause for concern. Eighty per cent of the world's opium originates in Afghanistan, and most of this is produced for illegal export, alongside a considerable crop of cannabis. Although many countries – such as the USA – that suffer as a result of heroin use have declared a so-called 'war on drugs', ironically it is warfare that prevents such illicit trades from being curtailed. Opium production rocketed after the 1979-80 invasion of Afghanistan by the Soviet Union, as the country fell into the rule of warlords seeking to make profit from the drugs with which they could buy weapons. Since then, the instability of the country has helped to prevent any effective action against drugs production, and although it initially declared poppy farming to be contrary to its strict Sharia Law, the Taliban now supports the industry as a means of making money to fund insurgency. American forces in Afghanistan rely upon local warlords for intelligence and military assistance, which prevents them from shutting down the opium trade these same warlords control. In a country blighted by war, up to fifty-two per cent of Gross Domestic Product may be associated with the drugs trade according to the United Nations Office on Drugs and Crime.

The case of Afghanistan highlights two steps that the International Community could, if truly committed to a better world, take to decrease the dominance of harmful drugs worldwide: halt wars, including US-led invasions such as those staged on Afghanistan and Iraq this century; and encourage socialism in place of capitalism. This would end the demand for weapons and the desire for profit from narcotics, and help to stem production of illegal drugs. In a socialist society, there would be no incentive to grow such drugs – since making money through their sale would be purposeless in a world where money means very little – except for personal use. Such drugs would likely be of a higher quality (and therefore less dangerous) since they would be grown for personal consumption, and the grower would only be risking their own health in growing them.

But there is, of course, another side to the coin: there would be no profitability in drugs in the first place if the demand for narcotics wasn't high. More international efforts therefore need to be made to discourage the uptake of drugs across the world and to help those who require rehabilitation to cure their addictions, including in parts of the world where governments are weak and existing medical help is deficient. If the deliverers of harmful drugs are operating at an international level, it will require international efforts to counter the harm that they are doing to drug users and their friends and families around the world. To this end, there needs to be international agreement relating to the classification of drugs, and which substances should be illegal to provide to the general public.

Again, it is the welfare of the people of the world, not the profits of the drugs providers, that should be put first. Therefore, there should be no question that cigarettes, a legal but nonetheless extremely dangerous source of an addictive drug, be not only labelled as unhealthy – a message that has still not been put across to many people in the less-industrialised world where smoking is on the rise – but also actively discouraged. The International Community should support governments against tobacco companies, and prevent authorities from being sued for taking actions that diminish these corporations' profits in the interests of the public. There is little evidence that such support is forthcoming, given the prospective power given to companies by deals resembling TTIP and the numerous court cases that have been brought against governments by tobacco companies in recent years (see *TTIP and TPP*, below). Misused drugs, including the nicotine in cigarettes, do a great deal of unnecessary harm to individuals, societies and the environment. Their long-term benefits are non-existent. A clear way of improving the welfare of the world's inhabitants is therefore to bring the production of all drugs under strict international regulation, to ensure that they are only used for genuinely beneficial purposes where their benefits outweigh their harms. The International Community should surely be making more effort to do this if it seeks to bring about a more prosperous world.

Animal Trade

The level of destruction of the world's wildlife over the past few decades has been unprecedented, an appalling catastrophe of nature perpetrated by human hands. The sheer degree to which we have failed to protect or respect the creatures we live alongside was demonstrated by the World Wildlife Foundation's 2014 *Living Planet Report*, which found that the global vertebrate population decreased by fifty-two per cent in just forty years, between 1970 and 2010. Further declines are likely to be caused by climatic change and the habitat destruction it causes either directly or indirectly in the future, but thirty-seven per cent of the damage done over the studied period was attributed to direct exploitation by humans. This means that we have fished and hunted our way into such a dire state: the largest contributor to the demise of our own, Animal Kingdom's population involved our actively killing other animals. 'Habitat destruction' was the second largest contributor, associated with thirty-one per cent of the decline, whilst only seven per cent was put down to 'climate change'. Many animal species therefore lie on the edge of extinction not because we have used their habitats to grow food or build buildings or accidently changed the climates they were adapted to with our greenhouse gas emissions. Their destruction, if it comes, will not be inadvertent. It will have taken place because humans have chosen to kill them.

The two factors of destruction that lie at the heart of this issue are overfishing and poaching. Neither of these can be regarded as local problems. The main reason why the population of elephants and rhinos in parts of Africa continues to decline despite huge efforts having been put in to protect what are iconic and well-appreciated species, which even in a capitalist world one would expect to be protected for the sake of the foreign dollars brought in by gaping tourists, is that whilst local poachers have been targeted and apprehended the driving force behind their existence – the global market in ivory and quack medicine– that pays their bounties has not been eradicated by the International Community. It is all very well to regulate against killing African wildlife and to put out anti-poaching patrols – these efforts have been running since the days of Edward VIII, who recognised the need to protect Africa from the big game European hunters of the interwar period. Indeed, great success was made in transforming these travellers from hunters to tourists, shooting with cameras rather than guns at the animals. But National

Parks large enough to allow wild animals to live naturally are by their very nature too big to police. It's the demand for ivory and other animal parts that has to be stemmed, and this can only happen if the countries where that demand exists – mainly Asia – agree to educate and regulate their citizens not to buy such cruelly garnered items, and the whole International Community agrees to properly regulate the movement of animal parts between countries.

Deforestation

Out of the need to protect the biological splendour of our planet, as much as out of a need to curb climatic change, it is essential that the heinous deforestation that continues to occur across our planet is halted immediately. The 467 per cent rise in Amazonian deforestation between October 2013 and the same month in 2014 illustrates that the International Community is failing to appreciate the urgency with which it needs to act. It may be local people under the jurisdiction of local governments that physically assault the rainforests, but the pressure to do so often comes largely from abroad. In the Amazon, most of the deforestation over recent years has been carried out to supply other countries (especially Europe) with beef and soybeans to rear livestock. An international effort is therefore the best way of putting a stop to it.

Changing diets could play a big part in protecting the rainforests. The International Community could do a lot more to prevent the 'westernisation' of diets and lifestyles, begun in the colonial era under the auspices that the Europeans had the right to teach the rest of the world how to live, in currently less-industrialised regions. Traditional diets across the globe tend to be low in meat and high in vegetables, grains and sometimes locally-sourced fish, with occasional locally-reared meat. Such diets can be supported sustainably. If a reduction, rather than an increase, in meat consumption were to be encouraged and bans placed on the transport of meat (which is, after all, always non-essential), livestock and soya livestock feed between continents, much of the drive for Amazon deforestation at least would dry up. We also need to look closely at the diet-based drivers of deforestation in other parts of the world. Oil, banana, coffee and chocolate plantations have replaced much of the Indonesian rainforest; the volumes of such plantation-based foodstuffs that can be exported should be capped to prevent expansion into the remaining rainforest without intensifying production. Meanwhile, a clamping down on the wastage of food including these items would help to curb demand. International trade in foodstuffs should be discouraged wherever that food can be grown locally (even if only for a season) in order to improve sustainability and protect the rainforests from the pressure for more land (see 'A New Agriculture'). The International

Community has the power to impose trade restrictions and to inform international development agencies of the ways in which sustainable, local, traditional and low-meat food production can be fostered in industrialised and non-industrialised countries alike in place of a globally homogenised western-style food system based around unhealthy processed meats and cereals grown using life-destroying pesticides and non-renewable fertilisers and with high levels of waste.

Deforestation and forest degradation are also caused by the extraction of minerals. Mining, and building roads with which to access mines, directly destroys forest, disrupts migration routes across large areas of forest and also enables illegal loggers to enter deep into previously inaccessible regions. It is not enough simply to invent standards and regulations stipulating how much forest can be cut down, how road impacts can be decreased and how damage to the local ecosystems can be minimised during mining. Experience shows that illegal logging and malpractice are extremely difficult to prevent in the midst of the jungle, and anyway any form of mineral extraction that disturbs the surface forest ought to be avoided if we are to prevent the degradation of these most precious parts of the biosphere. We do not need gold, silver or diamonds. We do not really need to precious metals used in computers, gadgets and other machinery that is periphery rather than essential to our happy existence as humans and certainly not worth more than the rainforests that and countless other species all rely upon as part of a heavily interconnected biosphere. The International Community should ban the export of precious metals and other minerals extracted from within rainforests, and instead encourage the recycling of those minerals that we have already removed. This would remove the impetus for harmful forays into the forest altogether.

All of this should be of paramount importance to the International Community because of the key role forests play in maintaining the global conditions suited to life – including human life – that we have enjoyed up until now. By drawing down carbon dioxide from the atmosphere and emitting the oxygen upon which we depend, forests really do act as the 'lungs of the world', alongside phytoplankton on the oceans, and we simply cannot live without them.

The Infection of Capitalism

In a diverse world of many different peoples, cultures and preferences, it should be the duty of the International Community to help each country to celebrate its own customs and values and to develop in its own way. This can only be achieved by drawing a careful distinction between providing much-needed advice, expertise, technology and aid for peoples that suffer or lack in some way to draw upon and allowing multinational capitalist enterprises to draw profit from exploiting the productive or consumptive capacity of vulnerable populations. The former allows maximal benefit for the world to be achieved from the learning and resources that our species has accrued and developed in the past by opening them up for every country to make use of, and indeed the sharing of expertise should be a two-way process between the more-industrialised and less-industrialised worlds in order for each country to obtain for itself an optimal level of sustainable industrialisation suited to its own traditions and environment. But all too often the International Community has allowed the latter phenomenon to take place, causing capitalist consumerist culture to impregnate itself across the globe to the detriment of those who were not previously cursed by its presence, as we shall explore in the chapter on 'Developing Devastation'.

The International Community could easily take steps to prevent this, most importantly by forbidding the very existence of 'multinational' companies that operate in more than one country. If an organisation is providing infrastructure, technology or aid to a country, it should be based in that country, and at least partly (though not necessarily entirely) run by the inhabitants of that country, to ensure that local needs and ideals and a local vision for the future are upheld. Each community, after all, must be empowered to be responsible for its own development, because it is that community that will benefit or suffer from the effects of that development. This applies equally across the world, be it in industrialised communities developing ways of becoming more sustainable and cooperative, or in traditional communities attempting to rid themselves of starvation and epidemics of disease. Such developments are not always all-encompassing: there are always some practices and technologies that do not need to change at all, in spite of what the consumer capitalists might tell us. So, whilst experts should travel between countries to share their knowledge of how to use or install certain technologies and material or spiritual aid should be dispatched out of good will or duty (in the light of climatic change and colonial legacies) from one country to another, the long-term implementation of the technologies and techniques that local people choose to adopt rather than reject and the distribution of this aid should be carried out by people employed and inspired locally to do so, not by multinational companies and charities which become easily distanced from the communities they are affecting and are often corrupted by the need to make money through their actions.

In recent years, however, we have seen the construction of American-style sky-scrapers in cities across the globe, the worldwide proliferation of fast-food chains and supermarkets based in Europe or North America and often well-intentioned and partially successful but ultimately unsustainable efforts by multinational charities to help countries to 'develop' in a one-size-fits-all culturally an environmentally insensitive way. All of this has been done because the International Community has not provided a unified, neutral, not-for-profit mechanism by which aid and expertise can be shared between countries on behalf of their governments and peoples, but has relied upon private corporate interests instead. This has given rise to a problematic form of globalisation that has made the world more homogeneous but no more harmonious.

Private corporations that introduce technological developments consider only the cash, not the consequences. Sweat-shops and factories have been set up in Eastern Asia with the sponsorship of these corporations, eager to profit by producing consumer goods cheaply where regulations are lax to sell all across the growing consumerist world. Many people have therefore not really been 'lifted out of poverty', as the much-vaunted phrase of the capitalistic narrative has it, but instead have been shifted into a different sort of poverty: out of the fields of the countryside, where food was not guaranteed and working hours were long but at least local customs and the vitality of the natural environment were there to refresh them, and into the cities: wildernesses of a far baser sort, constructed according to models drawn up far away on the basis of what other people in other societies have identified as good (or more accurately, profitable), where the working hours are even longer if employment is to be had at all, and the crowded housing may be more plentiful but is hardly safe or comfortable. The factories and sweat-shops belch out a smog of greenhouse gasses and particulates that choke nearby residents' lungs and a slurry of toxic chemicals that destroys the local environment. At the same time as using them to fuel the consumer culture of the consumers in the 'west', these companies seek to turn the people of the 'east' into consumers themselves, leading to disgusting quantities of discarded plastic waste clogging up the cities and rivers, through which filth desperate slum-dwellers pick in the search for recyclable gems they can sell.

This can hardly be called a 'lifting out of poverty', for it offers little satisfaction of the material needs of the poor, and can only remove access to the spiritual inspiration that they need to live a happy life. It has all resulted from a lack of constraints upon profit-driven companies seeking to move into the 'expanding market' of the less-industrialised world. Were the international community instead to have sent official delegations offering aid and expertise to post-colonial and other struggling regions, genuinely positive developments could have been achieved, learning from the experiences that the currently industrialised world went through centuries ago to prevent the same sorts of squalor and urban suffering from arising again. Through its failure to regulate and organise global sharing of resources, the International Community has allowed capitalist greed to triumph over forces of reason and compassion, and instead of a redistribution of power equally to peoples of all countries, we are left with a world less equal than it ever has been before.

TTIP, CETA and TPP

It has been one of the contentions of this document that capitalism is a threat to democracy, in that causes power to pass into the hands of the 'successful' few. In unfettered capitalism, it is not the will of the democratically-elected government but that of the biggest corporations that is obeyed. What is done is what is most profitable, and the needs, health and well-being of subjugated individuals not fortunate enough to share in the 'success' of the profit-makers are ignored. Fortunately, even in today's nominally capitalist world, governmental regulations do to some extent constrict the power of big businesses by preventing the exploitation of workers (through, for example, the imposition of a minimum wage) and protecting health and the environment (by, for instance, banning the use of chemicals that are not proven to be safe). We have argued here that these regulations do not go nearly far enough, and that there is a lot more that the International Community can do to protect the planet and its people from profit-motivated destruction, empowered by a democratic mandate to act on behalf of all people in the countries that comprise it.

By far the biggest threat to this democratic freedom are 'free-trade' deals along the lines of the so-called *Transatlantic Trade and Investment Partnership* (TTIP) that was proposed in 2014 to bind the European Union and the United States into a capitalistic trade agreement; its sister treaty between the United States and countries in the East Pacific, the *Trans-Pacific Partnership* (TPP); and a similar deal between Canada and the EU (CETA). These agreements, if enacted, would have increased the power of large corporations to dominate their 'markets' on a multinational scale and strip away the power of democratically elected governments to impose new or existing laws that in any way harm or have the potential to harm the profits of such businesses. For instance, a government could be sued by tobacco companies for enacting a law that bans colourful cigarette packaging, discourages smoking and therefore potentially harms the profits of these companies, for the amount of money they are expected to lose. Under TTIP, a European country could even be sued for existing laws if these are more stringent than those applying to the much less regulated market of the United States. There could be no surer way than such deals as these of maintaining the dominance and power of multinational corporations, eroding the environmental, health and workers rights' regulations of the EU, or of perpetuating the inequality in society that such a change would cause.

Fortunately, under public pressure and following the uncertainty surrounding anti-establishment votes in the USA and the UK that saw the former elect a volatile and inexperienced businessman as President and the latter preparing to leave the European

Union, TTIP and TTP have been put on hold. But CETA is dangerously close to becoming reality, potentially holding the UK bound to its stipulations for twenty years even after the country leaves the EU. Lest similar deals to these are proposed in the near-future, which is likely in the UK at least given the apparent eagerness of its government to seek new trading partners when it leaves the EU, it is worth dwelling upon their potential implications here. That would be a definitive contradiction of the British public's desire to have its own control over its own country's policies, which the EU exit vote – whatever its other motivations – clearly articulated. Lest this takes place, or similar deals are proposed in the near-future, which is likely in the UK at least given the apparent eagerness of its government to seek new trading partners when it leaves the EU, it is worth dwelling upon the potential implications here.

Negotiations concerning all these deals have been carried out largely in secret, initiated by pro-business officials in Europe, Canada and the United States alike in an attempt to circumvent the edifice of environmental and workers' rights regulations that have been introduced in the European Union in order to maximise profits. The deals were not intended to increase trade per se: trade barriers between the two regions are already minimal. The debate over TTIP and CETA is not therefore a question of free-market libertarianism versus isolationism or self-sustainability. Rather, the deals were specifically intended to increase the ability of multinational corporations to grow in global dominance at the expense of smaller-scale companies, and were proposed in their interests. This would be achieved in three ways: firstly, by removing regulatory barriers to using cheaper and more profitable methods of production and supply of goods and services provided by these corporations that are currently banned on ethical or environmental grounds. Secondly, by introducing private competition into sectors currently in public hands and thereby encouraging privatisation and opening up new markets to squeeze profit from. And thirdly, by allowing foreign investors to sue governments that refuse to remove regulations or privatise their industries for enforcing any laws that harm their profit-margins. Such a treaty represents an out-and-out strengthening of capitalistic and weakening of socialistic values within society.

It also represents a shift from democracy – rule by the people – to oligarchy – rule by a powerful clique, in this case the large multinational corporations that it most benefits and their top-ranking employees and shareholders. Because they are able to sue governments for lost profits, they have more effective power than people, who can only change their governments during elections and must join together in large numbers to do so. In a socialist, money-less society, suing the government for lost 'profits' would be an empty threat. Given that we do not yet live in such a society, however – and that any transition to such a society would have to be gradual to be effective rather than harmful –

these corporations would be able to exert a great deal of pressure on any future government, whatever its political persuasion, by financial means to introduce changes that will do a great deal of harm to ordinary people. For example, laws enforcing workers' rights, the prohibition of toxic chemicals, protection of individuals' data from misuse by 'tech giants' and food safety standards all dent the profits of multinationals. Governments would be forced to allow such laws to be circumvented or else risk very expensive law suits. Parliamentary sovereignty would be in tatters. This can hardly accord well with a UK public that rejected by referendum control by the EU of its country's policies, let alone control by North American businesses.

Europe currently prides itself in having much higher standards on chemicals such as pesticides, animal rights and food safety than the United States. Those standards, at the very least, would have to be thrown out under the deal, regardless of the consent or lack of consent of European citizens. One of the key aims of TTIP proponents was to allow American food and goods that falls below European standards of ethics or quality to be imported into the EU. The European populace, unlike the American one, has chosen to reject Genetically Modified (GM) food. Whether or not we agree with this decision, we must agree that this should be the European peoples' choice. With TTIP, however, regulations banning GM food or even requiring it to be labelled as such would have to be removed, allowing imports of such food to take place from the USA. In the USA, synthetic chemicals can generally be used in food and other goods until they have been proven to be harmful. Europe prefers to err on the side of caution and has banned many chemicals until they are proven to be safe. This position would no longer be tenable under TTIP: the onus would be placed on governments to prove that chemicals are harmful before trade in goods that use them could be stopped, overriding the European preference for health and safety. After all, it is very difficult to prove absolutely that any particular substance is to blame for an illness with which it is associated, and it may require many chronic cases of illness to be endured over years or decades that would otherwise have been avoided to prove this association. The EU currently bans around 1200 chemicals in cosmetics, only six of which cannot be used in the USA.

Because TTIP was an inherently capitalist deal, it is not surprising that production, consumption of resources, waste and the pollution associated with these was projected to increase if it were to be implemented. Not only would environmental regulations that restrict resource depletion and waste have been removed, but the cheapening of products produced by the multinational corporations would encourage more production and consumption of goods. There would be more waste as more of these goods were replaced in favour of a rapid succession of cheap substitutes in accordance with the capitalist model of consumerist growth. On top of this, of course, come increased greenhouse gas emissions, undermining efforts to deal with climate change, which would be worsened all the more by any deal that allows carbon-heavy Canadian tar sands fuel to be imported into Europe.

A deal like TTIP would cause further damage to society through job losses. The domination of one large company acting across many different countries rather than multiple small ones inevitably leads to job losses. Jobs, of course, are only good when they are purposeful and useful to society. The proponents of TTIP might therefore argue that it is a waste of resources – an 'economic inefficiency' – to allow the same job to be done in multiple companies by multiple people when one person in a single company will suffice. But with the elimination of these jobs comes the homogenisation of practice, which means that differences between different country-specific companies designed to reflect the needs of the particular people and cultures with which they interact are ironed out. It may well be that the people doing the same job in multiple smaller companies are each doing it slightly differently and introducing useful and valued specificities that would be removed if one company was allowed to displace them all. Therefore, the jobs that would be lost would probably not be those undesirable tasks of drudgery that we should indeed aspire to eliminate, but would rather be very useful jobs that are valuable to those who hold them.

The parties that were behind TTIP are well aware that the populaces of European countries will not stand for such an extensive corrosion of their democracies, loss of jobs and severe threat to their quality of life that would accompany the deal. That is why the negotiations were kept so secret, and why the exact extent of deregulation that will be involved in the deal was being kept strictly classified. It was only through great efforts by campaigning organisations and concerned political figures that the public was made aware of what was going on. Even government ministers of the partnership countries – even those who are to be involved in the negotiations – were only allowed to see the clauses relating to the deregulation in a special reading room and were not allowed to make copies. This put them at a severe disadvantage when it came to negotiating changes or provisos to the treaty, but was intended to mean that the general public heard as little as possible about it before it was too late to push for any such changes or to reject the deal outright.

Nevertheless, vocal opposition began to rise against TTIP in many parts of the EU, even before it was scuppered by political regime change. Especially of concern, it seems, to the public are threats to nationalised European health services such as the UK's National Health Service (NHS). Under TTIP demands, more competition would have to be introduced into these public services, undermining their purpose to heal the sick by introducing the profit motive into healthcare in mimicry of the United States, the land of inequality where healthcare provision for the poor is inadequate. US companies, for example, could be given the right to bid for contracts to run hospitals under an uninhibited TTIP deal. Fortunately, leaks of this atrocious proposition have led to such a public outcry that even right-wing politicians are beginning to make pledges to protect the NHS and similar health services in other European countries, and a clause to this effect would very likely have to be introduced into any similar future deal. But if such a clause allowed such politicians to gain acceptance for the rest of the deal, with all the social and environmental threats that it entails, it could prove disastrous for the rest of our public services, health and well-being and democracy as a whole.

TTIP would have prevented the gradual creation of a caring, socialist state by making it virtually impossible to nationalise industries once privatised, and the rebuilding of a fair future for Britain as endorsed by the rest of this document would therefore be harder to bring about. It would also directly restrict the freedom of individuals, as well as governments, in favour of that of big businesses. Copyright, patent and trademark laws would be made more stringent so that the dominance of the companies 'owning' these appalling inventions would be strengthened, and the sharing of scientific, technological and artistic creations on which our cultures are based would be fundamentally undermined. Internet Service Providers would be mandated to spy on their customers to ensure that copyright was not being infringed during browsing, in a move designed to protect the big players in the film and music industries in particular from having their profits undermined through sharing and cooperation between friends and loved ones. Again, any attempt by governments to prevent 'big bully' corporations from carrying out profit-preserving measures against relatively poor and helpless individuals would be regarded as an infringement on the 'right' to profit enshrined within the TTIP deal and lead to those governments being sued. Once entered into by any given country, therefore, a deal akin to TTIP would be very difficult to undermine or reverse.

Similar clauses to allow corporations to sue governments have been included in international trade agreements before, with disastrous effects. The Australian government is currently being sued by an American tobacco company for insisting that cigarettes be sold in plain packaging, and Uruguay is similarly suffering for implementing measures to discourage smoking. Ecuador was ordered to pay compensation of nearly two billion US dollars to Occidental Petroleum for cutting short its contract to extract oil when the company broke environmental regulations. Of course, this is all just money – it has no real value. But while countries retain an even partly capitalist system it has a great deal of invented value, and suing governments will mean restricting funds required to invest in public services and the well-being of the nation.

It was indeed fortunate that Britain's leaving the EU and the change of administration in the United States saw TTIP abandoned in 2016. But no sooner was it defeated than the similarly secretive CETA deal between the EU and Canada, with the same threats to society, democracy and the environment, was put on the agenda, one which would even duplicate TTIP by letting companies in the USA that trade in Canada sue European governments for enacting profit-harming policies[58]. Even if this Comprehensive Economic and Trade Agreement is rejected, other free trade agreements aiming to rip up environmental laws and hold caring governments to ransom could easily rear their heads in the near-future. The International Community has a clear duty when it comes to deals like TTIP, CETA and TPP. It must insist that the exact contents of these deals and what they will mean for governments and for people are made clear and open for all to see. With TTIP, the European Commission claimed that they would 'ensure products imported into the EU meet our high standards' and that 'EU governments fully maintain their right to adopt rules or laws to protect people and the environment [and] run public services however they wish'[59]. But this is not what the parts of the abandoned treaty that have been leaked reveal, nor, even if it is true, does the statement spell out how 'high standards' would be protected or guarantee that public services will not be put at risk by increased competition from the private sector. In the end, TTIP-like deals are intended to increase the profits of large multinational corporations – which is undoubtedly a bad thing. If negotiations and amendments changed it sufficiently to prevent this, they would have stopped pushing for it to be adopted in the first place. Therefore, we cannot trust that any form of 'amended' TTIP or CETA of the future will be good for the people of any country. The only way in which the public can know for sure is if any deal is made completely public, which is, after all, the only democratic thing to do. The International Community should not allow trade deals to take place until a full public consultation is held and public support has been ascertained.

5.3 'Costs and Benefits': The Monetary Approach to the Environment

All the major environmental problems we suffer from today have originated since the arrival of capitalism, and have come about in a period throughout which public and private policies of action have been under the influence of conventional, monetary-based, economic theory. Conventional economics teaches us to adopt a 'costs and benefits' approach to environmental problems. Under what we shall call a 'pure monetary' approach, these costs and benefits are always computed in monetary terms and decided by the market – the adherents of this approach consider any government interference on behalf of society to be counter-productive. When a particular cause of action is proposed

- the clearing of an area of forest for logging by a corporation, say, or an ordinary individual deciding to drive a polluting car – the actor involved is expected to weigh up the costs and benefits according to market prices.

So, to take the first example, say that a logging corporation has purchased an area of woodland from the government. The benefits to the corporation of logging the region will be the profit they are able to make from the wood. The costs will be to other people – those who use the wood for recreational purposes, for exercise or bird-watching for instance, or who live or work in the wood. Both the corporation and the other users of the wood value it for different reasons. But which values it more? The pure monetary approach says that the market will decide whether the benefits outweigh the costs: if these other users of the wood are willing to pay more to the corporation to preserve the wood than the corporation can make in selling logs, then the logging should not go ahead. If, however, the market price of the lumbered wood is greater than the total price the other users of the wood are willing to pay, the wood must be more valuable to the logging corporation than them, and it should be cut down.

This 'pure monetary' approach is essentially a form of utilitarianism: the maximum 'happiness' is favoured by taking the course of action that will, supposedly, allow the greatest 'value' to be extracted from the wood. But this 'value' does not include the recreational, spiritual and emotional value that the wood holds for the humans and other creatures that use it, a so-called 'experiential' value that is far too difficult to quantify. Instead, by measuring the benefits the wood can provide purely in monetary terms, and the amount that people are willing to pay to preserve it or exploit it, the proponents of this approach take into account only 'exchange value' – that is, the value in terms of goods and services that the wood can provide that have market prices, and which can therefore be exchanged for a quantifiable sum of money. That the wood might be irreplaceable to a particular person, let alone the animals that live in it and would certainly die were it to be destroyed, and might in this way provide a service that could not be 'exchanged' for any sum of money, is simply not possible under the pure monetary approach.

Now, in practice such pure, unfettered capitalism is rarely allowed to rule completely unchecked. There will usually be some government intervention, regulations (such as those forbidding the destruction of 'sites of scientific interest') and public consultation before major undertakings that affect the landscape take place. Therefore, there is some notion amongst society that the market is unable to properly value our resources and that checks and balances need to be applied. Nevertheless, in our capitalist world, the final decision still often comes down to money: regions of Amazonian rainforest have had to be bought by conservation charities in an attempt to protect them;

companies have almost (but not quite – yet) been allowed to drill for oil in African World Heritage Sites; companies are allowed to pollute rivers or the atmosphere so long as they pay some token amount in compensation. It was on this basis that carbon trading was invented (see above) in the hope that this would introduce the cost of carbon emissions into global markets and therefore discourage them.

Clearly, this approach is not working. The world continues to emit more and more greenhouse gasses, biodiversity is plummeting and areas of natural beauty are being destroyed. The oceans are filling up with plastic even as coastlines shrink and coral reefs are bleached. Industry and retailers, the producers and distributors of the superfluous capitalist goods that are driving this pollution, are not being prevented from causing tremendous damage to the environment we all share. Individuals – the 'consumers' – are not taking into account the cost of driving their cars, shopping for trinkets and gadgets or turning up their heating, and are continuing to do these things unabated. So there must be something wrong with the conventional economic approach: it isn't 'maximising the happiness' after all.

The adherents of pure capitalism would say that the problems are caused by government interference. If government departments that owned forests other public lands took always those actions that would maximise their profits, they say, by allowing the different parties who want to use these lands in mutually exclusive ways to compete for the ability to do so by bidding money, the most efficient use would result. In the Gulf of Mexico, for example, the right to fish, to extract oil (with the risk of an oil leak) and to enjoy the natural beauty of the area would initially be actioned off separately, because they are not necessarily mutually exclusive. If the oil well leaks, this will harm fish stocks and recreation potential, and the oil company will have to compensate the other users of the Gulf for the losses incurred, valued according to the market prices people were willing to pay to fish or to enjoy the area. Since money is assumed to be everyone's ultimate goal, this should satisfy everyone and happiness will be retained despite the disaster. If, for some reason, someone didn't want oil drilling to take place at all, they would have to outbid the oil company for the right to drill oil, then leave the permit unused; this would be an indication that they valued the absence of oil drilling more than the oil company valued the oil. A 'competitive, open and free market' decides what's best for everyone[60]. It's an approach inspired by one common (but arguably misguided) reading of the writings of Adam Smith, the eighteenth-century economic philosopher, to argue that an 'invisible hand' would direct a free market if everyone acted out of their own interests in the pursuit of money.

It isn't difficult to see the limitations of this approach, and in fact a fair reading of Smith reveals that he foresaw many potential problems, especially if 'cartels' of big businesses conspire to keep down wages and to prevent the public's concerns from interfering with their business. Wealth ceases to percolate to all levels of society and power becomes concentrated amongst the richest. In the above example, the main problem is that the animals that could be harmed by the drilling or the fishing have been ignored. It has been assumed that the oil company and recreational users who value the natural environment of the Gulf have an equal ability to compete with one another on the issue of whether or not to drill, and yet the fact that the oil company possesses overwhelmingly more money than any individual or nature conservation group is likely to have at their disposal is obvious. Other species of animal don't have money, so the extent to which they value their habitat doesn't enter the equation at all. In short, the true 'value' of the Gulf of Mexico, and all other natural environments for that matter, is not encompassed by the capitalist market. In such a market, only those factors that are immediately quantifiable in monetary terms are given a 'value', which is really a 'price'. Most of what is truly valuable on the Earth – clean air and water, a natural environment (our natural habitat) to have access to, and most of all the life itself of all conscious beings, which is of infinite worth to them – is ignored. The capitalist monetary way of assigning values is very crude; it only accounts for things that people have been conventionally willing to pay money for, even though most of the best things in life – which are often threatened by environmental destruction – are freely available in the absence of industrial development, and, because they can't be sold, are considered worthless. This is the most fundamental flaw with the pure monetary approach to managing environmental resources.

The second major flaw lies with utilitarianism itself. A utilitarian viewpoint focusses on taking whatever decision will maximise the overall happiness of the world, summed across everyone living, which sounds at first commendable. But this 'happiness' is measured, under the pure monetary approach, through money: happiness is maximised, it is assumed, if money-making is maximised, not necessarily with an equal distribution across society. This is clearly an inaccurate measure: it is obvious that a person can be happy without possessing much money or material wealth that can be 'valued' monetarily – think of a monk who spends his life content in meditation, study and prayer. It is equally obvious that somebody can have a great deal of money and not be happy – it is not unknown for some of the wealthiest in society to commit suicide. It is true that money can be used to purchase basic needs without which happiness would be very difficult to obtain, and that extra goods and experiences beyond these basics that under a capitalist system we have to pay for – trips to favourite places, books, televisions, parties and so on – can enrich our lives. In this way, money can be used to bring about happiness in a capitalist world. But this is no linear relationship, and indeed the happiest countries tend to be those that are the most equal, not those that are the most materially rich; capitalism and an emphasis on money reduce equality and therefore are unlikely to increase overall happiness. Economic growth can often occur for the richest and for the biggest companies in society, whilst the poorest remain unable to afford what they need. Therefore, trying to maximise overall happiness by maximising economic growth is disingenuous.

Even if it were not tied to money as its measure of happiness, however, utilitarianism possesses other ugly aspects. Firstly, it does not take into account any form of rights or duties, for human beings, other animals, future generations or any other group. The action that might result in the greatest overall happiness could involve killing a few individuals, or reducing them to a state of dire unhappiness. In a utilitarian system, such actions are justified if they lead (presumably indirectly) to greater happiness in others. The rights of those few individuals to life and freedom are simply ignored: they are sacrificed for the 'greater good'. Likewise, under a utilitarian approach, rainforests could be chopped down, rivers polluted or homes destroyed to extract oil, say, regardless of the rights of the people living in those houses or amongst that natural environment, let alone the animals making up that ecosystem. So long as the oil was used to make more people happy, the rights to life, habitat and livelihood of the people and other animals concerned would be ignored. Murder, theft, abuse, destruction – none of these are off-limits in a purely utilitarian ethical approach that acts in the name of the 'greater good'. Who should decide what this 'greater good' constitutes is not necessarily specified, but we can assume that in the capitalistic pure monetary approach it would be the market, and the course of action that rendered up the most overall profit. After all, if the oil company makes a huge amount of profit from the oil, a great number of people must have bought the oil and enjoyed using it. If more people were made happy by preserving the homes and ecosystems than by oil-derived products, they would outbid the oil company for the land and prevent the drilling.

A further problem, though, now becomes apparent: what about the rights and needs of future generations? Some would debate the notion that future generations can have 'rights'. They don't exist yet, so how can we possibly know what they'd want, or what they'd be able to cope with? Perhaps they'll invent new ways of dealing with whatever problems we leave them with, and its none of our responsibility to ensure that their future 'rights' are upheld. But realistically, it cannot be denied that future generations will have needs, and that these needs will be very similar to our own. Surely we have a duty, if we want our species to continue and for future generations to live joyfully, to consider these needs. If utilitarianism were applied consistently across time as well as space, to maximise the overall happiness we ought to provide the best possible world for countless future inhabitants to grow up in, and hardly consider the present happiness of its relatively few present-day inhabitants. But on the other hand, making people miserable now might make them reproduce less, reducing the future population which would reduce overall happiness – unless of course fewer people means more space for everyone, increasing each individuals' happiness by a compensatory amount. The truth is, we can't possibly know – indeed, we can't possibly calculate the overall loss or gain in happiness caused by any particular individual act or general policy. Including future generations within the utilitarian framework leads to a tangled and insoluble mess, which is why they are generally downplayed or ignored by the utilitarian, undermining the theory's very basis: its attempt to impartially increase happiness.

The pure monetary approach doesn't take into account future generations' needs at all: unless they have a prospective parent or other interested party willing to bid on their behalf, people who haven't been born yet don't have any money, so can't possibly express to the market the extent to which they would 'value' the preservation of the earth's resources and the natural environment. There might be countless millions of people who would treasure being able to visit the woodland in the future, far outweighing the number of people who will benefit from the oil extracted by drilling. But the pure monetary approach simply ignores them.

There is a further justification put forward to excuse focussing on the short-term and on people yet living, in addition to the flawed argument that we can't know what future generations would want. This argument goes that the decisions that we make – to drill or not to drill, to dam the river or leave it alone, to pump greenhouse gasses into the atmosphere or to ride a bicycle instead – will determine which people are alive in the future anyway. For example, if someone abandons their car and cycles to work, their life will be changed significantly relative to the alternative of continuing to drive. Perhaps, arriving at the office earlier, they'd meet the man of their dreams by chance, get to know them, marry and have children. But because they chose to cycle, they never meet this person, find someone else years later, marry and have different children. Every little change that we make – in terms of individual behaviour and government policy alike – has the potential to change the people who comprise the future world. When we think about it, we are each incredibly 'lucky' to be the people alive here and now at all. Even a different sperm from your father fertilising the same egg on the same occasion might have produced a different person.

In light of this, some people have argued that we don't have any responsibility to ensure that future people aren't harmed by our actions, because those people wouldn't exist at all if we hadn't acted thus. So whatever happens to future generations, they can't blame us, because without us doing what we choose to do, they wouldn't exist: someone else would. Therefore, the argument goes, we should maximise happiness now (and further argument can then begin over what that means in practice) and let the future sort itself out. Future generations shouldn't influence our decisions.

This argument is flawed on at least two levels. First and most obviously, by 'future generations' we don't usually mean only those who have not yet been born. There are also children and grandchildren already alive but too young to understand what we're doing to our environment or to have any say in stopping it. Ignoring future generations means ignoring these, and they are people whose future existence (barring a total catastrophe) is guaranteed: they won't be replaced by genetically different people because we changed our course of action. The environmental influences on their development will change, it is true, but we can ensure that these influences are as positive as possible by being as caring as possible, which means protecting the environment as well as each other.

More fundamentally, though, it shouldn't matter who exactly makes up the future, unborn population. If we leave the world in a mess from which they cannot easily recover, they will have every right to blame us. This is because 'lucky' is really the wrong word to use when we consider our personal existence on Earth. To say that we are 'lucky' implies that there is a huge bank of potential people waiting in the sky somewhere, and that we are the fortunate few from amongst these countless trillions to be actually brought into existence. In truth, of course, if we never existed we should never know that we'd never existed, and therefore wouldn't suffer for the fact. Being alive is not a sufficient criterion for somebody to consider themselves lucky. They are fortunate if they are brought into existence somewhere in which their needs can be satisfied and this life can contain joy; they are unfortunate if they are born into only conflict, malnutrition, disease and death. When we have before us the choice of two courses of action, one of which will harm the environment in the long-term more than the other, we do indeed face a choice between two future world populations. But one of these populations will be brought into existence in a state that is happier than the other. Is it better to create a less happy or a more happy group of people, given the choice? Clearly, the latter, so we should always take those actions that seem more likely to create future generations that will be able to meet their needs and have joy in their existences.

This point becomes very relevant when one tries to untangle the knot and make a consistent and logical attempt to extend the utilitarian approach to incorporate future generations within its consideration of maximal happiness. Quite simply, the approach snaps under its own weight. It yields patently ridiculous results. To maximise overall happiness, the population of the world should be maximised, so courses of action should be favoured that produce as many children as possible. Under this remit, we should each procreate as much as possible, because more people means more overall happiness, even if the happiness of individual people is very slight because they are born into an overpopulated world in which their needs cannot possibly be met, live in misery and die young. If the problem is looked at in another, equally utilitarian way, though, one that seeks to minimise suffering in the world, the result is opposite: everyone should be immediately killed, as quickly as possible, so that there is no one left to suffer. These are the only possible outcomes of applying the utilitarian approach to future generations, because there is no other way of maximising happiness or minimising suffering than by maximising or minimising the human population. Only when we reject the utilitarian approach of sacrificing everything in order to maximise the sum-total 'overall happiness' of society and instead seek to maximise the happiness of each individual can a more sensible policy line begin to emerge, one that encourages education and voluntary birth control to allow people to have the number of children that they'd prefer within sustainable communities. No blame can be apportioned on us by future people who do not exist as a result of such voluntary population control measures.

Utilitarianism also causes problems when it attempts to encompass other animals within its quest for the maximisation of happiness or minimisation of suffering. Conventional philosophy tended only to deal with humans' relationships towards one another, largely as a result of the medieval culture from which we emerged with industrialisation. This had been a culture in which, by-and-large, humans didn't seem so much of a threat to other species. There was habitat destruction, but the finite nature of the planet was often not understood, so it was always assumed that species would live on further afield even if they were wiped out locally. Animals were kept, of course, but in the smaller numbers embraced by present-day organic farmers rather than the huge herds of industrial mega-farms that are more likely to attract condemnation on ethical grounds. It would be in the owner's interests to keep the animal well-fed and happy for it to perform its work or produce milk or meat of high quality. With industrialisation, the pressure put on working animals grew, it was realised that hunting species to exhaustion in region after region for meat or fur couldn't go on indefinitely – the species would, in the end, run out of habitat – and gradually the notion that animals were being maltreated began to emerge.

In this way, the development of ethics towards non-human animals became increasingly necessary, but it was permitted only by the breakdown of another component of medieval culture: the notion that God had created man to be supreme amongst all of nature, and that the whole world existed to provide infinite resources for man's own use. This was the mainstream view of the medieval Catholic Church, and had been retained by many Protestant Christians, but began to fall away amongst both Christians and non-Christians alike in the twentieth century. We have always known that other animals can think, feel and suffer. But nowadays it is considered necessary by many people to articulate specific animal rights, or at least duties we owe to other animals, rather than only protecting them for the sake of their human uses. Some would extend these rights only to 'higher-order' thinkers such as chimps, dogs and birds, but this requires an arbitrary distinction to be drawn at the level at which suffering is considered possible to be perceived. Others would class all animals, including insects and others with less advanced brains, as possessing an equal right to life. Some would extend a 'reverence for life'[61] to all life-forms, including plants, bacteria and other primitive life. This doesn't mean that all forms of life should have equal 'rights': the human right to vote in a democracy certainly can't be extended to other species, and the sentient animal's right to life can't be applied to plants, bacteria or viruses, which we inevitably kill all the time and need to in order to live. But a utilitarian approach that acknowledged that animals, at least, have the capacity to feel happiness and suffering, would seek to increase the former or reduce the latter at all costs. This could mean, again, that individuals were sacrificed for the 'greater good' of overall animal happiness, and perhaps even that the human race would have to destroy itself in order to allow the rest of the animal kingdom to flourish. Utilitarianism, here again, produces unworkable solutions to ethical problems.

That is perhaps why the 'pure monetary' approach is based on a utilitarian view that takes into account neither future generations nor non-human animals, or any other form of life other than humans for that matter. This approach ignores all forms of inherent value – that is, value that we appreciate for its own sake, on which no monetary price can be placed – and assesses only 'useful' value – that is, the monetary value that an object is able to produce for its user. All things on Earth – from rainforests to factory workers, farm animals to man-made goods – are regarded as objects to be used or exchanged to make money. The theory underlying this is that an object that is most useful will make the most money and therefore produce the most happiness. Thus, a power station is very useful because it generates a lot of electricity that can be sold to make money. An individual human's life is only useful if that person produces a lot of things that can be sold or works in the service of selling something, and uses their money to buy lots more goods to keep the economy moving. A human who lives outside of the capitalist system - say, a traditional farmer producing food for the use of an African tribe without money - is worth nothing. A beautiful bird is worth only what its feathers can be sold for (or its song if it has one); a magnificent tree only what its wood will fetch. The intrinsic value in these beings, which is what people who enjoy the company of other people, the existence of a bird or the presence of a tree really hold dear, is ignored. That's why under the monetary system decisions are made that have disastrous effects on society present and future, on other animals and on the environment that we all share.

These decisions lie at the heart of all sorts of environmental crises, including those explored in the other chapters of this book.

Of course, the 'pure monetary' system is, thankfully, not in place anywhere in the world at the moment. Everywhere there are laws preventing particular boundaries being crossed in the name of making money. The problem is that these laws, whilst making certain actions off-limits – such as destroying heritage buildings or sites of scientific interest or subjecting animals of any kind to torture without grounds – do nothing to redirect the steamroller of capitalist 'progress' away from courses that make money and extract short-term values from our surroundings with no regard for what is intrinsically good and right in life. That's because they don't have as their core the intrinsic value of all the natural and man-made wonders of the Earth – including ourselves and all other animals, plants and lower life-forms. They don't guarantee different levels of rights to each group of life-forms, and they don't prevent money from being used as the measure of goodness, or the potential for making money from something from being the measure of its worth. Our laws don't impose public ownership of the public's natural and labour resources, and they therefore allow decisions that profoundly affect the environments in which we all live to be taken out of our hands. In other words, they don't reign in the monetary approach nearly as much as they need to for us to be able to come, collectively, to sensible decisions about environmental issues.

A Note on 'Ecosystem Services'

Human well-being is utterly dependent upon other species. So-called 'ecosystem services' benefit us in a wide variety of ways. Plants provision us with food, fuel, oxygen and chemicals; all sorts of species regulate our climate and waterways, pollinate our crops and protect us from disease. These things make existence possible. But this existence would be meaningless were it not for the aesthetic, recreational and spiritual benefits that we amongst the rest of nature's creations draw from the plethora of other life-forms that physically define our natural habitat. It is this inspirational aspect of the living world that makes life worthwhile.

Yet because this sort of benefit is difficult to quantify it is this most important service that is too often underplayed when the 'costs and benefits' of ecosystems are assessed. That can lead to decisions being made that have dire environmental consequences and consequently degrade the quality of life of local people and other animals for the sake of more quantifiable gains. So, for example, we witness the destruction of entire mountains to mine iron and the flooding of entire valleys to generate hydroelectricity in the Upper Guinea region[62] of Africa. We see the destruction of rainforest for soya plantations or beef pastures in Amazonia[63] and for palm oil in Malaysia and Indonesia[64]. And we observe an intensification of agriculture bringing pesticides and fertilisers to the industrialising world.

All this is done in the commendable name of 'raising people out of poverty'. But if 'poverty' is going to be tackled in its entirety, some of these policies need to be rethought. These 'developments' deal with the problem in a very narrow sense, aiming to harness nature to maximise its delivery of the easily quantifiable ecosystem services it can provide. The poor lack food, fuel, adequate shelter and protection from disease, and it's on delivering these needs that the projects focus when they claim to reduce 'poverty'. Mining and setting up smallholder farms where once was rainforest gives locals jobs and hence money, with which it is claimed that they will buy health and happiness. Intensive farming may rapidly boost the short-term yield of much-needed crops.

But these shallow improvements are surely short-lived. What will happen when the mountain is exhausted of iron, when three generations of oil palms have been planted on the same land and it can no longer support the crop, and when we run out of non-renewable fertilisers or pesticides kill off the pollinators that seventy-five per cent of our food crops rely upon? Will these people really have gained enough to continue to meet their needs from the iron and oil they've sold to a richer world greedy for luxuries or from the all-out abandonment of traditional agricultural practices? Or will they be left bereft, when the western multinationals have made their quick buck and fled, of the most important ecosystem 'service' and human need of them all – the inspirational wonder of the mountains, forests and pasture land that industrial rape has destroyed?

Of course, development doesn't have to be like this. Our aspiration as a species should be to allow everyone sustainable access to all the ecosystem services they need to live. But it's not enough to simply leave wild areas here and there amidst growing plantations, or to skirt around ecological 'hotspots' when building railways or mines. We need to do more: to recognise the intrinsic value in all animals, including people, and to respect their individual lives by halting habitat destruction and learning from traditional local practices alongside modern scientific expertise to draw the optimal benefit from the land we have already claimed. This could be achieved by curbing our consumption of nature's resources in the industrialised world, and instead sharing our time, effort and expertise with others around the planet. Because in the end we shouldn't be asking what 'services' we can draw from ecosystems or poor societies that possess tempting natural assets. Instead we should be viewing cultural diversity, biodiversity and individual lives as precious in themselves, and taking whatever steps we can to allow each of these to flourish.

5.4 Beyond the Capitalist Approach: Towards a Better Ethic

In light of what we have explored in this chapter, how can we create a better ethic on the basis of which to make environmental decisions in a society that truly benefits all? There is a place for utilitarianism, but only in a reformed and restricted sense. A helpful utilitarianism would recognise the existence of things that have intrinsic value to sentient beings as components in their well-being, and seek to maximise this well-being in each individual by protecting and giving us access to what we truly value and providing for our needs, as opposed to maximising supposed 'happiness' by increasing money-making. Equally essentially, it would be bounded by stringent and unbreakable principles. In maximising the well-being of all, the rights of none should be discarded. The best way to make ethical decisions that will be for the good of all is clearly to mix utilitarianism with another idea, that of deontology, which holds that we should act out of duty and in preservation of rights, but fails to provide us with a trajectory by which to increase general well-being. To an extent, such a mixture is what we have already: parliament passes laws, which act as deontological principles; companies and individuals then act within the framework of these laws (or sometimes outside it, if they are being unscrupulous) to maximise profit by utilitarian principles. But in some respects there needs to be more deontology: more rights (those of other animals and life-forms) need to be respected because of the intrinsic value that all forms of life contain regardless of their uses for mankind. Currently, laws can be very reactionary – smoking in enclosed public places was only banned in the UK decades after smoking (including passive smoking) was shown to endanger our health and carbon dioxide emissions are still allowed to pour from factories, power stations and cars. If our deontology were based on the rights of living beings, public smoking and greenhouse gas emissions, both of which cause great harm on all sorts of levels, would be outlawed as soon as these harms were realised.

'Rights' must, if they are to have any grounding in logic, be things that would be freely available to us in our natural surroundings and that we need access to in order to live a healthy life. These are things that the rest of society should not deny us access to, unless that access contravenes others' rights. So I should have a right to travel on foot across most of the land, since nobody created it and can claim monopoly over the 'right' to use it. But this right is waived when it comes against another's right to privacy, because I should lose little by skirting around somebody's private garden, whereas they would stand to lose more by my uninvited roaming across it. Or, if I were to commit a dangerous crime, I should forfeit my right to roam because I should have abused this right and used it to infringe upon others' rights, and would be likely to continue to do so were the state not to contain me. 'Rights' are a concept invented by humans and only applicable to human societies, in which people can choose to harm or to do good to one another and to members of other species. There is no duty upon other animals, which are not moral agents, to respect each other's rights: after all, they do not prevent other animals from living as they naturally would (given that it is 'natural' for prey to be killed by predators and so on). But humans, who have empowered ourselves into having a choice between many 'unnatural' actions through the founding of civilisations, do have this duty.

What 'rights' does each life-form on Earth have? This question needs to be addressed by societal consensus, informed but not exclusively determined by scientific observation. But science – which involves observing and experimenting with the world around us in order to better understand it – can certainly point us in the direction of a system of 'rights' that would be fair and conducive to the well-being of all those who have the capacity to feel emotion of any kind. For this capacity should surely be at the foundation of a fair system of rights. Any being that can feel pleasure and pain should have the right to live and to have at least access to their natural habitat, from which they can derive their needs, so that it is pleasure and not pain that they feel. This would include all humans and other animals. Non-sentient things, including plants, bacteria, fungi and non-living entities like rocks and buildings, do not have the right to life itself, but because they have intrinsic value to the sentient beings in that they shape our habitats and environments, they should nonetheless be protected where possible and only destroyed at need and with regret, in accordance with bounded utilitarian principles that seek to increase the well-being of those things that do have rights.

Thus, wiping out a deadly virus would not contravene its 'rights'; killing an individual animal would. Destroying the virus would be good for things that do have rights, and so should be attempted. There are of course provisos to this: a parasitic animal, or one that is attacking another animal, puts its own right to live and satisfy its needs up against that of its victim and its victim's right to what they need; the victim is justified in killing parasites that attack it because it needs to do so to live without pain. In the natural world, Predator and prey, victim and parasite are each part of each other's natural habitats. If the wolf is part of the natural habitat of the deer, then the deer has a 'right' to be hunted by wolves – this hunting is necessary to the deer to keep in check its population and the resources on which it draws, and to other species that rely on the same resources, which would be over-exploited by the deer were it not hunted. Hence, when it comes to animal rights, our duty should be to leave animals to exist in their own habitat, and to ensure that we leave enough of this habitat intact for them to do so. We should not cage, kill or experiment on wild animals.

Domesticated animals have different rights. Their 'natural habitat' is man-made, because their genetic profiles have been adapted that they might live with man. Hence, they still have the right to life, and to their basic needs – once born or hatched, a domesticated animal should not be killed or subjected to torture. But it can be caged or housed in ways that are conducive to its well-being: indeed, this is its right. The cow has a right to be kept safely in a field with enough to eat and drink, and to be milked if it has no calves, because it has evolved to do so. The dog has a right to its bed or kennel and the food that its master gives. We have brought these animals into the world and adapted their environments. Therefore we must not kill or experiment on them. Because all animals can feel pleasure and pain – whether wild or domesticated – the utilitarian arm of our societal ethics should mean that, in addition to not actively killing them, we should seek to increase animals' well-being. For wild animals, this means leaving them to live in their natural habitat wherever possible, rather than hunting them for non-essential purposes such as the pet trade. For domesticated animals, it means looking after them, and making their lives as happy and comfortable as possible. If this latter seems too much of a burden, we should not artificially create so many domesticated animals. These animals are essentially created to further our joy; once alive we have a duty to further their joy at the same time. But if they cease to further our joy we should not replace them; in their domesticated state non-human animals do not have a right to reproduce where this would infringe on the human right to satisfy our needs and the utilitarian goal of furthering our well-being. Therefore, we should actively control the reproduction of domesticated animals so as not to exceed the number that we can care for properly and happily.

Introducing rights for all sentient beings and recognising intrinsic value in entities of all kinds will help us to make better environmental policy decisions. Within the boundaries that these rights impose, a better driver of human activity than money and the pursuit of material-based 'happiness' is the pursuit of well-being for all sentient creatures. When it comes to rights, there can sometimes be no doubt about which is the correct decision: a decision that violates a conscious being's rights should never be taken. These rights, which would be decided by society as a whole, might include the right to life and to access to natural habitat and basic needs, for all animal species. For domesticated animals they extend to the right to be cared for and have their needs actively satisfied. To human beings, we can add to these rights the right to vote, to assemble and to access public goods and services. These public services would include education, healthcare, housing, policing and so on, insofar as they are within the limits of society's resources to provide. Rights derive from things we should naturally have access to – we are naturally able to assemble, to meet our basic needs, to support each other as a community and so on, so we should have rights to these things. But there should be no right to 'property': so long as these other rights are upheld, no person needs, nor would they naturally have 'property' of their own. Personal property certainly is useful and can increase our well-being, but we have no 'right' to it. Therefore, when ownership of such property infringes on another's rights, such as a wild animal's right to life, the right must be upheld and the property may need to be surrendered.

In a society in which power is shared amongst everyone, decisions should be made by a democratically elected or appointed government that presides over industries and services that are run on local scales for the benefit of the whole populace. Therefore, decisions that relate to the environment will be in the hands of the government, and by implication in the hands of the people, not in the hands of profit-hungry corporations. These decisions can then be made on the basis of a rights-based ethic: the fundamental rights of every conscious being – that is to say, every animal – should be clearly set out, and no decisions that contravene these rights should be made unless different individuals' rights come up against one another. Whether or not a decision would contravene such rights could be determined by appointed experts who would, say, evaluate how much habitat individuals of a particular wild animal species are likely to need in a given area for their population to be sustained. Furthermore, the intrinsic value of everything in our landscape, natural and man-made, must be taken into consideration. The knowledge of scientists and animal carers will be invoked to determine the value of natural resources to other animals, but the values that humans place in buildings, as opposed to other land uses, are subjective and differ from person to person, so can only be assessed by public consultation.

At the moment, planning applications are put up for public consultation, but the intrinsic values that people place in natural or man-made landscape features that could be endangered or destroyed by proposed developments are ignored; only objections based on the 'useful' value of these features – the tourism attracted by historic buildings and woodlands or the 'scientific interest' certain places have attached to them – or excessive strains that would be placed on local services were developments to go ahead are considered. People may find value in particular places that goes far beyond this. That's not to say that this intrinsic value to one particular person should automatically mean that a development of the place in question should not go ahead. But it should be genuinely taken into account, alongside the value that others hope to gain from the development. Provided that no (animal or human) rights will be violated by allowing the development to take place or not allowing it to take place, the decision should then be made using in accordance with the maximisation of well-being. The decision which will provide the most value – both intrinsic and useful value – overall can be assumed to be the best one, taking into account the legacy for future generations as well as the needs of the present one.

Some have argued that, in the interests of 'freedom' for each individual, governments should not direct what we do – indeed,, they should not intervene in our lives at all except to prevent one person or group from doing direct harm to another. With no government or law at all, even the staunchest libertarians and anarchists (who call for no government but not no laws) acknowledge, we could have no true freedom because we should live in constant fear of others lest they attack us in pursuit of some selfish gain. Therefore we need from the government at least some degree of security. But if we want true freedom – that is, the freedom to take choices that will make our lives meaningful and feel that we have a place within society, as well as the freedom from the destruction of our environment and social structures that we value and freedom from indirect oppression by others who have gathered resources to themselves and grown in power and dominance of their own accord, we need a government that does more than this: one that actively directs our lives and treats us as equals. So long as that government is truly democratic – its principles guided by the needs and desires of the people at large and concern for future generations and other species – such a government will not be a despotic enslaving power, but a liberating one. It will protect people and distribute society's resources and labour according to need and temperament. It will ensure that resources are used as efficiently as possible, but that efficiency of well-being – that is, maximising the well-being of as many people as possible – is prioritised over efficiency of economy – that is, making things as cheaply as possible with as little labour as possible, which may not always bring the most joy and fulfilment (for instance when automation denies people a job they enjoy doing) or be the most energy-efficient solution (for example when fuel-driven machines are used to replace people working on farms). After all, the economy of the country is only a means by which well-being is achieved – or is intended to be achieved – for all its inhabitants. It needs governmental direction to ensure that well-being, rather than 'value for money', is maximised; the 'invisible hand' of the market, driven by greed and perverted by corruption and collusion between the powerful as it is, cannot be trusted for this purpose.

The current paradigm that happiness is born of money and that 'lifting people out of poverty' by giving everyone more and more consumer goods and encouraging the whole world to be participants in the global capitalist market that can somehow be trusted to regulate our lives to give the optimal outcome is misguided. Prosperity is born of equality, not the absolute sum of a person's wealth. 'Equality' means equal access to the things that we value – both material needs such as food and shelter and spiritual needs such as people, communities, art, science, education and an healthy environment filled with diverse species of other animal and plant life. Our aim in policy, both on a local and global scale, should be to maximise this equality without contravening the fundamental rights possessed by each animal. Making policy decisions on the basis of 'costs and benefits' computed in monetary terms, when it is impossible to place accurate monetary 'costs' or 'benefits' on individual lives, communities, cultural works, and most of what we value, cannot possibly deliver this equality or prosperity. Money can be useful as a means for distributing resources; it should not be a driver of individual or governmental policy. The policies which we should follow, including those advocated in the second volume of this document, may not therefore be the most profitable or the most precipitous of material wealth in the world. After all, accruing material wealth for ourselves impoverishes others – be it people in poorer regions, other species or future generations of our own – and should not be done lightly. Rather, our policies should be based upon an ethical consideration of all beings with rights, and pragmatically and rationally seek to move our society and our planet in the direction of increasing equality and prosperity in a manner most caring towards all the beings – human and non-human – with whom we share this planet and whose existence gives to each of us an irreplaceable joy.

6. The Financial System

6.1 Banks

Under the capitalist system it was considered necessary to have banks - depositories in which members of the public can store their money in order that it might be safeguarded, accessed easily through use of a cheque or card without having to be carried about, and all the while accruing interest from that bank in return for the custom. Furthermore, under such a society dependent upon spending money, it became customary for individuals to obtain debts to the bank, so as to support the capitalist system upon which the bank depended, by borrowing money that they did not possess or, sometimes, have any prospect of paying back. Meanwhile, the bank would itself invest in various schemes, speculating - in effect, gambling - with large amounts of capital in order to obtain vast profits.

These are the institutions that we have allowed to dictate the course of our society, then: irresponsible gamblers whose business is simply to deal in money, and to accumulate it for themselves. Such trust has proved dangerous indeed. When either of these two systems - the banks' public and speculative arms - collapsed, through un-repayable loans and loss-making investments, a crisis would ensue whereby the survival of the bank would be called into question, and often it fell to the government to pay off the banks' debts to other financial institutions, in order to prevent a wider crisis from engulfing society, since the whole fabric of society had become dependent upon these holders and distributors of money.

Hence, the whole concept of profit-making banks leads to an unstable society, liable to sudden 'recessions' during which employment falls not because there are fewer jobs to do but simply because nobody can afford to pay for them, because the government is paying for the problems at the bank and ordinary people and small businesses are no longer able to borrow money from the bank. In reality, of course, the money invested by the bank is not their own, but is that deposited by ordinary people and wealthy investment funds. Meanwhile, a large swathe of other people are indebted to the bank, usually through mortgages, so that somehow the bank is viewed as 'owning' their houses, which clearly exist for the sole purpose of sheltering the people living there, and hence should by no means be in such unscrupulous hands. The owner of the house is deemed to be the one that has paid for it, rather than the person living there; this is a ludicrous situation that leads to the eviction of entire families from their homes in the worst cases, an unacceptable and disgraceful state of affairs.

In the end, we see that the currency brandied about by the banks, borrowed from and loaned to their customers, has no grounding in real commodities, as it should, but is simply allowed to pass back and forth between different accounts in the form of numbers on a computer. It is sometimes even created by financial institutions, an act technically illegal but not policed in the technological age, since governments have placed so much trust in these institutions and have come to fear them, as if it is the banks and the huge 'markets' that govern society, not our democratically elected officials. In truth, this surplus money, sloshing around from place to place without any connection to reality, is entirely unnecessary for the running of society and should be abolished.

Indeed, this surplus money and dependence upon it can, if it is allowed to, cause tremendous repercussions in the real world, simply by our imposing the unnatural and unnecessary rule that it is necessary to possess this money in order to obtain any product or service, and desirable to obtain as much of it as possible. We see this in the phenomenon of the 'financial crisis'. Such a 'crisis' occurs when institutions suddenly realise the non-existence of the funds on which they base their business, which leads to a loss of 'confidence' and a collapse of the entire charade upon which the financial system is based. The very fact that real-world consequences should result from a change in the confidence of investors is alarming: real, physical processes and constraints on resources are independent of the confidence of a few wealthy individuals, and it is these processes and constraints that represent the true limitations on our functioning as a society. Financial constraints, in the absence of physical constraints, should have no impact on what we can and cannot do.

The entire financial system based on these banks and investors, powerful simply because they have money rather than because they are elected by society at large, is nothing but a paper fortress. Grand and imposing it may seem from the outside, as it stands in might above us, dictating the course of events, but approach it and we see that its foundation is imaginary, its walls flimsy and is garrison empty of any real threat. This fortress is kept from blowing away in the wind only by the confidence of those that embrace it, holding sway over hearts and minds simply by the appearance of strength. Inherently, though, is not a viable means of running a prosperous society.

In truth, we need only one bank at the most, making no speculative investments – certainly not pumping resources into despotic and oppressive programmes, such as the arms trade, as banks were prone to do in the capitalist society – and needed to give no loans, but simply distributing the real, commodity-based currency we currently need to purchase goods and services fairly and evenly to the people of the country, who in return perform some service of their own for the good of society. We should use banks in accordance with their original purpose – as a convenience, to store money – rather than allowing them to become subverted into engines of greed, existing for the purpose of enriching the rich and enslaving the poor through provision of interest-heavy loans rather than gifts. We should use money in accordance with its original purpose – as a convenient means of exchange and method for the equal distribution of resources – rather than as a commodity to be hoarded for its own sake and equated to power, invested and inherited to provide certain members of society, truly no more entitled to a better life than anyone else, with more of this power than others. Ultimately, we should seek top abandon money altogether, for the reasons outlined in Chapter 2. Neither banks nor money should dictate the policies which govern our society, either domestically or in foreign relations; rather, it is they that should be subject to the control of a democratic society.

6.2 The Problem with Debt

There are two sorts of debt causing concern at present, personal debt and national debt, which have very different origins and implications and must be treated quite separately. With the abolition of money, of course, all debt could be eliminated entirely, which, as we shall see, could only be beneficial for everyone. In the meantime, it is imperative that governments do not confuse the two sorts of debt, as certain politicians of late have been wont to do, by for example equating the government in debt to a household with a large credit-card bill.

The existence of personal debt is a tragedy of our times. We all agree – or at least, all sensible people attest – that nobody should be homeless or starving, and that our children should not be without clothing and loving care. Why, then, do we force people to become indebted by means of a mortgage when obtaining a house, or drive them to seek loans in order to pay the rent at the same time as feeding and clothing their family? Surely we should give everyone – regardless of whether they work or need to seek 'benefits' – either enough money to buy the things to which they have a basic right (food, water, shelter and so on) or, better, simply give them these things, providing for the needs of all out of our common labour. Yet instead, ordinary people are forced to become 'indebted' to the biggest, most powerful of all capitalist corporations – the banks – or else to often unscrupulous 'pay day' lenders, to get what they need to live. Such an inexcusable situation arises only so that the richest can profit on the backs of the poorest – so that big business can profit from the needs of ordinary people. In the capitalist world where each person is judged by their 'success' in gaining monetary wealth, being in debt can be a source of shame. But it is not the indebted poor that should feel ashamed, rather the unscrupulous and greedy powers that have given them this debt.

Capitalism encourages needless and wasteful consumption by its very nature. When it comes to those luxury goods that are produced for the sake of the profit made by their production, which go beyond the needs of the people consuming them, those goods exist as a result of the capitalist system and it is therefore no tragedy if a person falls into the capitalist state of debt as a result of purchasing them, and is forced to relinquish them when they cannot pay back this debt. Somebody who accrues the latest mobile telephones, games consoles, excess furniture and mass-produced trinkets will not suffer, really, if forced to give these up. Since these goods are superfluous, this whole cycle is a needless waste of time, resources and energy and a distraction from much more meaningful things in life, and we are justified in criticising the capitalist system that creates it. But the phenomenon of debt in itself is not the problem here: it is the creation of too many goods and the manipulative use of advertising and peer pressure to encourage people to buy what they do not need and cannot afford. Repossessions of luxury goods would be nothing to be especially concerned about.

But excess luxury items are not the cause of the majority of personal debt today. Instead, it is for basic things that they cannot live without and in order to provide a happy home for themselves and their families that many people fall into debt. Rents and mortgages continue to rise; house prices are vastly above what most first-time buyers can afford, despite the fact that houses exist, fundamentally, for people to live in, not for builders and banks to profit from. Food and clothes for children have to be paid for on top of rents or mortgage repayments, and this is to say nothing of bills for electricity or fuel to keep houses liveable. Children may have free school education, but they need additional resources – not only stationary for school but books and access to the wider culture of our society – in order to have a wholesome education that must, under capitalism, also be paid for. Access to the internet and television, and the chance to go for a meal or a drink with friends may not be entirely essential to a person's physical existence, but for that existence to be happy enough to have any meaning at all it is important that everyone can have them, if they want them, from time to time.

For a person to become 'indebted' to a large corporation for meeting these needs is perverse. But because our society does not share out its useful work – leaving many people unemployed – and, though it requires of each of us money for almost everything, does not pay some people nearly as much as others, sections of our society find themselves in exactly this situation. If their fiscal situation then becomes yet worse – they become unemployed, for example, where before they had a low-paid job – they may find themselves unable to meet their debt repayments. In the current situation, this may lead to their electricity and water supply being cut off, their house repossessed by a bank that clearly doesn't need it nearly so much as they do, or the whole family being forced to resort to 'food-banks' provided by charities in order to feed themselves. All of this comes about because we choose to make ourselves indebted to each other – and, worse, the poor indebted to the rich and powerful – for goods and services instead of sharing our resources according to need.

The 'payday' lender has become, of late, a byword for exploitation of the needy. When, in the light of the 2007 'financial crisis' banks ceased to lend out money quite so readily to those deemed unable to pay it back, people who needed cash to pay their bills and feed their families were forced to turn to a third party, the loan company, to get it. Charging interest rates that sometimes reached into the thousands, these companies made millions out of the desperation of the poor, providing a short-term fix to money worries that soon escalated into a mountain of debt if repayments were not swiftly made. Following a barrage of condemnation from public-minded organisations as powerful as the Church of England, regulatory authorities are now clamping down on such abuses. UK payday companies have been forced to write off some debts after the Financial Conduct Authority found that they had failed to adequately assess the ability of the debtors to pay them back. But there is no use in shutting off this despicable industry that was for many people their last resort for obtaining credit without providing this credit by some other means. Nobody should be made indebted simply for living in the modern world. Nobody should be evicted from their only home. Everyone has to be given guaranteed access to what they need if our society is to be called at all functional or beneficial to its members, and the simplest way of doing this is to simply give every family a home and a ration of food and clothing and electricity regardless of their incomes. Then, the only debt that can be accrued is that spent on luxury items, and if those are repossessed by the greedy capitalists that sold them, no great harm will be done.

It is a slightly different matter when it comes to debt accrued by gambling or addiction, but only in terms of the cause, not the effect, of the debt, and the remedy required. No gambler or addict should be forced to give up their home or lose access to what they need to live. Though they may be at fault for 'wasting' their money, money is itself inherently worthless, and it is in the time they have spent away from friends, family, work and enjoyment of higher pleasures in life that they have really lost out. Gamblers and addicts therefore need extra help to cure them of the malady of addiction and rebuild higher purposes in their lives. The monetary debt they may have accrued should not prevent their having access to this, nor to their homes and sustenance. Again, it is only against the accruing of luxury items that their debt should be set, and then only when the provision of such luxuries remains within the private capitalist sphere. In a world without money, which would be a higher ideal, it would be impossible to fall into debt through gambling or addiction, and addiction to toxic substances would itself become more difficult, since there would no longer be any incentive for drug dealers and tobacco and alcohol companies or retailers to encourage increased consumption.

Whilst personal debt, at least as it stands today, is tragic, government debt is of no real concern. Governments can print money, borrow money, lend money – they have control over the worthless pieces of paper that they themselves imbue with 'value'. Except where countries have (often foolishly) surrendered control over their economies and adopted a currency in common with other jurisdictions, no bailiffs are going to come knocking if governments do not repay their debts. Capitalist markets and investors may 'lose confidence' in the government, that much is true. But unless you are a capitalist investor or shareholder and care about making monetary profit, that is of very little consequence. For in reality money was invented only to facilitate the government's oversight of the distribution of society's resources. It was invented at a time when the stability of society rested upon the existence of a privileged and moneyed elite that required some way of setting itself apart from the ordinary masses so that they might be kept subservient, and therefore wanted a way of controlling employment and trade. Now, though, technology has advanced sufficiently that governments do not need these 'magic coins', notes and numbers to arrange an efficient economy.

The government need only look at its inventory of resources, and at the number of people providing and requiring goods and services in each locality, to decide where action needs to be taken to shift the distribution of resources so that all needs are met and all can live prosperously. If doing so incurs monetary debt, that need be no obstacle at all, for the government doesn't need money at all. Therefore, instead of arguing about causes and blame, remedies and ramifications relating to the supposed 'travesty' of government debt as the capitalist political parties of today tend to do, we should simply shrug our shoulders. Most of the government's debt is owed to people within our own society. Most of it was accrued in bailing out banks. If those people aren't paid back, or if the banks simply collapse, no harm will come so long as the government continues to guide us in our work and distribute its fruits so that everyone is given what they need to lead a wholesome life.

6.3 Stock Markets and Bonds

When there is a demand for something in society, a company is set up to supply that demand. Customers pay the company money, and the company can therefore profit. But in order to develop to the extent where sufficient service can be provided for a profit to be made, the company will often require some investment of capital, on behalf of one of its owners, with which to purchase the necessary equipment, materials and labour. Once in profit, it can keep itself going, such that no further investment should be required. This is how, in the simplest form, a capitalist system of private provision of goods and services should function. The most economically efficient methods of producing all products of demand are favoured under this system, since each company seeks to maximise its profit and outcompete rivals by adopting the best possible mechanism (which may ignore environmental or social impacts that have not been economically evaluated). The fate of the company will depend on its ability to tailor its supply to match the demands of the market, and to advertise its own brand more effectively than its competitors.

But things are rarely this simple in the modern capitalist world. The owners of corporations become greedy for more profit, and for larger bonuses. They therefore seek to sell tiny amounts of their successful company to a new set of investors, who might be employees or members of the general public, in the form of stocks. In this way, the resources of many people are pooled, for use by the company to increase its profits. The stock buyers are then paid a proportion of these profits according to the extent of the shares they have bought, and, so long as the company continues to do well – because its product or service or brand is good enough to attract customers – all of these shareholders profit monetarily. The success of every company is measured by the price of its stocks, which can be bought and sold on the stock market. In this way, the stock market becomes a force of its own: through it, the strength of each corporation is measured, and, depending on whether the trend is to buy or sell shares, that corporation can find itself flying high or floundering based on this market's valuations. Hence, power over the entities running a capitalist society – the companies – is exerted not directly by the success of those companies in providing their service, and the preference of the customers who buy it (though this will undoubtedly have an impact on the perception of the company's strength) but rather by the confidence with which shareholders on the stock market view the company's future. Regardless of the real performance of the company, therefore, its success or failure can hinge on a mere rumour that sends the investors into excitement or despair.

It is this stock market, therefore, that gives rise to the concept of 'boom and bust', a cycle of rising and falling economic growth inherent to the capitalist system. Rather than human industries thriving because there is need for what they are providing, or ending because there are no longer sustainable resources available for them to continue – which would be reasonable factors to guide the course that society takes – the amount of 'economic activity' in each sector of society is dictated, under the capitalist system, by the confidence of rich individuals and conglomerates that influence the market in question. The world is currently experiencing a period of 'recession', not because of a true realisation that we have been extracting far too many resources over the past decades and creating far too many goods that we do not need – in effect, because modern industry is unprecedented in its wastefulness – but simply because the artificial 'bubble' of confidence that led investors in the stock market to believe that the value of their stocks was set to increase collapsed in 2007. When their confidence in the system is revived, economic growth will continue apace again, and, unfortunately, the trend towards increasing over-consumption will continue.

The stock-market crashes that are inherent within capitalism, though, can have profound effects. That is because, under capitalism, a large proportion of the goods and services that ordinary people need to live are controlled by private companies subject to the whim of market confidence, which means that these essential services are often cut back in a period of economic recession. Consumption by the richest in society, who are able to pay higher prices and weather the storm, continues apace whilst the needs of the poorest, who find themselves unemployed as companies seek to lay off workers to save money, are left suddenly unfulfilled. It is not that we no longer have the people or resources available to meet these needs: feeding, sheltering, clothing and educating everyone in society need not require us to exceed those resources that can be extracted sustainably. It is simply that, because the rich do not have confidence that they will profit by investing in the businesses that we leave to manage society, these businesses shrink to satisfy the demands only of the rich. The stock-market dictated system in therefore inherently unstable and certainly not conducive to the maintenance of a stable society.

Of course, no country in the world is under the grip of pure capitalism, in which a free market would reign supreme, allowing the ups and downs of stocks to utterly dictate the fortunes of the people. There would then be no protection for those at the bottom, whilst the rich would survive in a crisis simply through the money that they had managed to accumulate, which, in a purely capitalist society, would equate directly to access to resources and power. Such a condition would be one of lawlessness. Instead, in our society we have the government – a body representing the collective will of the people, at least in principle – in place to ensure that things do not get out of hand. Nationalised provision of goods and services should not be subject to market shocks: the government – that is to say, society itself – employs members of the populace to acquire the resources it needs, and to distribute these to those that need them in the general population. The monetary cost of doing this should not be important: if the government has the people and the resources to carry out actions required to produce prosperity, these should be done, regardless of the monetary cost. This is the basis of the current proposition: a situation in which all the basic needs of all the people are met, free of charge, by the people as a whole, in a cooperative and free coalition of human effort and reward.

But today we occupy neither of these positions. In today's world, the government must act as if it were itself some sort of large corporation, with a near-monopoly over certain 'markets' such as, in the UK at least, healthcare. It must charge the beneficiaries of its services –everyone in society – through taxation, then extend those services to all who need them in the populace. In this way, through progressive taxation that takes more from the rich than from the poor, some degree of rebalance is acquired whereby everyone has access to certain essential services and all are to some extent protected from the shocks of the stock market. Yet the system is flawed: for the rich are not willing to pay sufficient taxes to meet the demands of everyone, giving rise to a 'deficit', the excess of governmental spending over its income. Were money not to be taken into account when ensuring a good education, a home, and a good diet for all the people, this deficit would not exist and would not matter. But because the government is chained, like a capitalist corporation, to the requirements of monetary profit, the deficit becomes such a key concern in the minds of many politicians that it blinds out all others.

Paying off the deficit is, in effect, a way of making the poor pay their debt to the rich. For the money that the government spends in excess of its revenue from taxation is in the form of bonds, nothing more than money borrowed from other institutions rich enough to lend it. That society as a whole should have to be borrowing this magic invention – money – from a few powerful groups in order to function these days is preposterous; society should be in control of its money, not at its mercy. That any government should prioritise paying back these bonds rather than maintaining the prosperity of all is morally unjustifiable. The government cannot simply print more money to pay off its debts, as this option within a capitalist society would lead to inflation, soon making the currency worthless and ruining the savings of ordinary people whilst destroying the functionality of money, the purpose of which is to facilitate the trade of labour and goods between individuals.

Therefore, if a government wishes to reduce its deficit, it must raise taxes – which the rich will not allow it to do, for they warn that this will strangle the precious economic growth with which they hold the government in thrall and will entice them to leave the country in search of better wages – or cut public services. This latter option leaves the ordinary citizens who cannot afford private replacements short of good education, adequate protection from the police and good-quality healthcare. It therefore does exactly the opposite of what the government is put in place to do by the people: to provide them with these basic needs in as effective a way as possible given the labour force and natural resources available to society. Rather, it is the banks and the rich investors – already possessing far more money than they could ever need – that benefit, as some of the government's debts to them are paid off. In actual fact, of course, many of these debts are incurred by bailing out the banks themselves (see 'banks') due the collapse in value of their stocks in the stock market. This collapse itself, as we have seen, was produced in 2007 by mistakes the banks made, which led to investors no longer believing that those banks would continue to grow and profit.

The loss of confidence in this case began with the so-called sub-prime housing market. This was based on an initiative of private 'ownership' of houses, not in the sense that each person should automatically own the place in which they live, as is proposed here, but that people renting their property from councils or private landlords should purchase them, incurring sometimes very large mortgages in the process. The whole system developed out of a rise in property prices towards the end of the nineties and the first half of the naughties, giving rise to the misconception that to own property was the safest way of investing money, both in the case of mortgaging banks and of mortgage-less homeowners (see 'Housing'). When mortgages were sold to millions of people, predominantly in the United States, who couldn't afford to pay them off, and house prices tumbled below the debts they owed, the whole mechanism whereby banks had profited in the short-term by providing these unstable mortgages collapsed, and the interconnected global financial system that now pervades the capitalist world followed suit. Some banks, their positions on the stock markets crumbling, went bankrupt; others were supported by the tax-payer or rival institutions. The offshoot was that ordinary people who had had nothing to do with the unscrupulous dealings of these financial institutions came to suffer from government cuts and private company lay-offs. An unregulated sub-prime mortgage system and the greed of bankers eager for short-term profits created the crisis, but the fact that society was built on the foundations of the stock market was what allowed the damage to proliferate.

So, therefore, we must detach the provision of the true needs that must be satisfied to obtain a prosperous society from the ups and downs of the stock market. Luxury goods, perhaps, paid for out of wages for work done, could still be provided by independent corporations subject to such market forces. But the basic services of society must be nationalised, in full, so that they are provided to everyone regardless of monetary wealth, and irrespective of market forces. In this way, the power of the stock market to dictate the happiness of the citizens would be removed, and their wellbeing could be maintained at a constant level, by providing basic needs to the employed and the unemployed, the monetarily rich and poor alike. Such a society, in which the stock market had only a minor and unimportant role if it still existed at all, would allow everybody to become truly rich: rich in the experience of life, which could be obtained without pain; fed, sheltered, educated and provided for medicinally, irrespective of monetary wealth. The government bond should be abolished: instead the government should simply arrange labour and resources in accordance with need, and there should be no requirement for money to enter the equation in the public sector at all.

6.4 Insurance

One of the most curious aspects of a capitalist society is that citizens are required to obtain insurance against the impact of a natural or man-made disaster befalling their property, or else risk being left without home or support. Private insurance companies are paid by a large group of people, and are thereby able, though they do not know what will befall any individual policy-holder, to calculate the average payment they will need to make each day for the foreseeable future. They profit by taking more money in subscriptions than they pay out in the event of a disaster, and therefore it is in their interest to pay out as little as possible, composing confusing small-print on their policy documents specifically to confuse the customer, whose claim can then be declared invalid on the basis of some minor point or another that the claimant either didn't see or didn't understand. Why should a cooperative, prosperous society leave those who find themselves out of luck at the mercy of such unscrupulous corporations?

They need not, for there are two alternative systems of insurance: first, that everyone who chooses to pays towards a nationalised insurance scheme, run by the government, but this too would have to consider profit and loss when paying out to claimants. The second and better alternative is that the government simply provides housing and essential equipment repair or replacement free of charge or the need for insurance, as society pools its resources under the control of elected leaders to care for those who find themselves suddenly in need. Luxury items – such as cars that are not required as part of a job (and should therefore be phased out of a sustainable society anyway – see 'transport') might still be insured privately. But if an insurance company failed to meet the claimant's wants, the situation would not be a disastrous one because the government would still provide for the claimant's needs, those basic things that are truly needed to live a comfortable life.

Insurance companies can protect themselves further against the impact of a sudden natural disaster under the current system by in effect insuring themselves, so that other insurance companies bear some of the brunt of the calamity. But they also occasionally work in partnership with other private companies, or a state-run scheme, as was the case at the time of the 2005 Hurricane Katrina disaster in New Orleans. Here, wind damage was insured by private firms, but flood damage by the state, which led to the preposterous situation of people whose homes and livelihoods had been ruined by the storm being told that they could not claim on insurance because the damage was due to flooding, not to wind, irrespective of the fact that in many cases homes had been destroyed by the hurricane before the ensuing tidal wave arrived[65]. Such complications are another result of the heartless reality of the capitalist lust for profit.

It is clear that, throughout the capitalist world, insurance is big business. Television and radio channels are crammed with advertisements trying to persuade the public to ensure their houses, cars, even lives on what are claimed to be attractively cheap or comprehensive policies. Home insurance and car insurance are so widespread that to nationalise these (at least for cars that are essential for work) would seem a logical step, as it would illuminate the need for advertising, which is generally regarded as a necessary evil interrupting much more interesting broadcasts, and continue to provide peace of mind to the populace without the need for the stressful process of taking out an insurance policy. Furthermore, another fallacy of the private insurance business, the 'no-claims bonus', would be removed. This bonus, by offering a discounted rate of insurance to those who have not made a claim, aims specifically to prevent the making of claims for small calamities, and thus to save the insurance company money in the long-term. If insurance on all essential goods were free, and these essentials were freely provided by society for society, through the use of the government, the need for such discouragement could be avoided altogether, ensuring that houses and essential vehicles are kept in full working order at no loss to the user. After all, we all have an interest in maintaining the essential foundations that we need to live; in keeping the country's housing stock in good order and the transports that move goods and services around the country running.

There is no need at all for 'life insurance' in a cooperative society. This money-making scheme involves an individual paying an insurance company instalments over the course of their lifetime, in the event that, should they die, their family will receive financial compensation. Such a concept is based on the idea that money – a means of exchange for the distribution of non-essential goods – can somehow be used to replace a life; that the family of the deceased should be in need of the income of the deceased even after they are dead, and that this income was the most important aspect of the deceased's role within their family. If food, housing, energy, basic clothing, transport, education and health were all nationalised, there would be no need to thus 'compensate' a family for the death of a loved-one, as they would still have access to everything they needed to live. This would remove the need to levy the living lest they die.

Insurance, to conclude, is a phenomenon only required in a society based mainly on private enterprise, and is not necessary to – indeed inhibits – the wellbeing of a cooperative socialist state.

Risky Business

Still less necessary – for it is a dubious concept even amongst capitalist economists – is the idea of the 'hedge fund'. The hedge fund, a sort of 'futures market', developed in nineteenth-century America as a way of protecting farmers against low crop prices[66]. The fund would agree to purchase the grain from the farmer at an arranged price, no matter what the actual price of grain that year. The farmer might lose out if grain prices were high, but at least he would be guaranteed that, in the event that prices were low, he would still get enough money to earn a living from his farm. The farmer had 'securitised' himself, so to speak, by transferring the risk that grain prices will be low onto someone else – the hedge fund manager. But in capitalism, money is made by taking risks – this is why bankers and investors manage to obtain so much money, because they are rewarded for their willingness to risk it – so the farmer also loses the chance to make a lot more money should grain prices be high.

Nowadays, hedge funds have moved on entirely from protecting farmers to protecting investors from shocks within the stock market such as increases in interest rates or prices: a number of investors come together to put money into a hedge fund, which guarantees them a certain level of return on a particular investment the fund collectively makes, in theory, whatever happens. These funds provide insurance for large-scale financial risk-takers, removing some of that risk for a fee: nobody can enter into a hedge fund unless they have a minimum five or six figure sum with which to contribute towards it. Theoretically, it is this money that the hedge fund uses to pay out to its members if the market goes awry.

But the history of financial markets is a history of greed. Hedge funds exist, ultimately, to make money for those that set them up, through management fees and performance bonuses, and it is as a result of this that they have become notoriously untrustworthy when the market goes sour. It often turns out to be the case that the fund manager finds it impossible to meet the fund's obligations to all its investors, because, in their greed, they have allowed speculations that carry the possibility of very high losses to be hedged, hoping that, having collected the hedging fee, the market will go up, rather than down, and they will never have to pay out. At a time of financial crisis, therefore, many hedge funds tend to collapse, and only then does the truth about embezzled funds and volatile risks come out. The problem is that the investors that lose out when a hedge fund collapses – universities, pension funds, very large companies – provide important services to society, and their losses can affect a large number of ordinary people completely oblivious to their hedging strategies. Because hedge funds are not open to the public, they are often subject to much less strenuous regulations than other investment funds, allowing catastrophic losses to occur, and the 2008 recession was, in part, accelerated by poorly regulated high-risk funds that collapsed.

The encouragement of reckless risk-taking through the likes of hedge funds and insurance-rate 'swaps' by the financial world provides no clear benefit to society as a whole, and it is surely with some disbelief that we must greet the prospect that the people involved in such schemes are amongst the best-paid – and therefore, under capitalism, the most powerful – people on the planet. These were people who made millions simply by predicting how the market would behave, at a time when its behaviour was particularly stable and predictable. Many knew that a time would come when the funds would collapse; they simply hoped that this would be in the far future. Whilst the world's interest rates were low, riskier investments became increasingly tempting, and produced increasingly large profits[67]. But when the 'bubble' of financial prosperity burst, these were the people who felt the biggest fall, from unparalleled monetary success to outright failure. In the immediate future, it is likely that regulation within the capitalist system will increase and the sums amassed by hedge-fund managers will be less. However, allowing the capitalist system of boom and bust to continue will most likely mean that deregulation occurs again, in the future, and risky investments will again make certain individuals unjustifiably rich in money as they ride on the crest of another bubble. To prevent this from having a negative impact on society as a whole, the core essentials of the country – health, education, food and the like – must be entirely removed from stock market influences and the reach of the modern-day hedge-fund, through a process of bringing these industries into public ownership. Any risky investments made in the less essential markets still open to capitalist forces would then have little impact on any but the monetarily rich who chose to partake in such schemes. For the sake of their own long-term prosperity, it would be hoped that few did.

Cooperation and Competition

The capitalist world is based upon competition. There is always a race to be the cheapest, or the best-known, or indeed the highest-quality brand, so as to attract customers and make the most profit. Indeed, the financial system has been compared to the Darwinian struggle of Natural Selection, with more effective production, management and marketing strategies gradually winning out over lesser ones as companies thrive, adopt new practices, or go bust[68]. But at the same time, these competing entities are *companies*. They are dependent upon the cooperation of a group of people, big or small, who by joining their efforts together are able to achieve more than they could alone. In order to compete effectively, corporations need people with a wide range of skills, whatever their field of business is. So, just as businesses tend to 'grow' in market share and geographic spread, they also tend to grow in terms of workforce size, providing increasing levels of employment to local populations. Capitalism, in this way, encourages both cooperation and competition simultaneously; in some cases, rivals in the same field of business may even cooperate in order to ensure that that business is protected from ideas that could damage them all – cigarette companies collectively opposing claims linking smoking to cancer in the mid-twentieth century provide one example of this.

Yet this form of cooperation, as the cigarettes example shows, is not a positive one for society. It means that those with the most power – corporations composed of individuals who all have the profits of the company in mind – are able to exert control over the rest of society, even when the results of that control are harmful to the general wellbeing of that society. They do this by becoming so large that they employ a not insignificant proportion of the workforce and supply with goods or services a not insignificant proportion of the population. The individuals within these corporations, or the corporations in conjunction with one another, are then able to cooperate so as to maximise their own profits at the expense of those outside their own circle. When the employees of supermarkets cooperate to coerce the public into using their stores by participating in sales, or alliances of supermarkets cooperate to drive down prices, to the detriment of the smaller shops outside their circle of power, the same negative impact on society is obtained. The larger these corporations become, the greater the power they wield and the more likely they are to hold the populace under their own control. In the absence of the only corporation truly representing the will of the people (at least in theory), the government, these conglomerations would be able to twist society into functioning for the good of their own monetary profit, rather than the wellbeing of the majority of people.

Such corporations often justify their existence with evidence of the economic growth and employment they bring to the country. But employment for the sake of employment, as will be embellished upon elsewhere in this document, is not beneficial to society: only employment that improves the general wellbeing is to be celebrated. Employing workers to reduce their own power over how their country is run by using them to shore up such large businesses is not beneficial. Likewise, economic growth is not a good thing for its own sake: it is only beneficial if there are not enough resources being extracted to satisfy the needs of the population. In the case of our own society, the simultaneous social and environmental degradation recent decades have witnessed illustrate that there is more of a problem of over- than under-consumption of resources, and that, in fact, economic shrinkage is more desirable than economic growth, until a stable and sustainable level of extraction, innovation and production is reached.

Such a level can be obtained using small companies under the general direction of the government, and does not require large multinational corporations to achieve. Whilst it is true that such corporations have become large precisely because of evolutionary techniques not dissimilar (except that they are engineered by the mind of the man who learns from past mistakes rather than through random mutations) to Natural Selection, and might therefore be assumed to have maximised the efficiency of producing whatever goods or services they provide, it must be remembered that this evolution is geared towards maximising the profit of the company, not maximising the wellbeing of society. This is why the company, after all, is able to survive under a system whereby only those capable of weathering the storm of stock-market fluctuations can do so.

If small companies are left to their own devices, some will undoubtedly grow larger, therefore, in order to maximise economies of scale and outcompete their rivals with inferior business techniques. Only those that are capable of providing for some niche market that cannot profit from the use of such economies of scale are able to remain small and local enterprises. Farm shops that bring produce straight from the field to the shelf are one example of this. If the companies that want to grow were simply prevented from growing, and from competing, the result would indeed be that inefficient practices otherwise rooted out by evolutionary trends would be retained, to the detriment of the customers. That is why the government must oversee the running of each of the small, localised companies: to ensure that, once the best known way of providing particular goods or services to society is decided upon by society as a whole, that method is made well-known to all such providers. They may try out other methods, and indeed find one even better, but they must share their own and others' knowledge to bring about the best possible public service nationwide. That sort of public ownership – nationally overseen, but locally controlled and managed and adapted to the needs of local people, is the optimal way of running any business that serves us all.

The government will not consider simply monetary profit, which is not truly important to wellbeing, but rather will be at liberty to focus on environmental and social factors often neglected by conventional economics. The maintenance of multiple, localised companies allows some degree of differentiation and trials of alternative methods to develop, whilst the oversight of the government enables the best practices to be propagated through positively cooperative, rather than competitive, means and prevents the construction of corporations large enough to wield interests and powers of their own. This is how, in a socialist society, we can mitigate the competitive instincts of capitalism, and thus remove its cut-throat element that inherently requires the placing of one group – the successful – over another – the unsuccessful – and thus obtain a situation that is beneficial to all, without introducing the bureaucracy and inefficiency of direct state control of all industries and services.

This is an alternative model, but it is not one that, of course, will necessarily be adopted. There are many conservative influences that profit from the current system and thus seek to keep it in place. Furthermore, the entire capitalist structure – from insurance schemes to stock markets – is geared towards an element of competition which, although it may be harmful to those members of society that lose out, may also by its very nature be attractive to human beings. A capitalist society is treated much like a game. The taking of risks with money is considered enjoyable by many of those who do it, whether they are hedge-fund managers or simply ordinary people choosing where to spend their notes and coins. Do you support this shop, or the other? Which of the charities begging for money on the street should receive your aid? By what investment can your penny be turned into a pound? It may be that people actually enjoy the power that money gives them by means of such issues. Its very inherent worthlessness – as a human invention that we cannot eat, drink or (except in the most exceptional of circumstances) shelter under, perhaps taking the form of mere numbers on a balance sheet rather than actual physical material – makes money something with which we are prepared to gamble. We are not sorry to see it go in the short-term, if we know that our investment will bring benefits in the long-term. Therefore, contrary to common sense, it is often the case that people do seek money for its own sake, only indirectly liking it for what it can buy. To have a lot of money in the bank is to have 'won the game', so to speak, and most people would probably be reluctant to give up on the contents of the bank accounts even for the assurance that they would be kept fed, watered, sheltered and in good health for the rest of their lives. Removing the game of making money and the power with which it is spent would make the world a more boring place for some.

Therefore, the purpose of this document is not to propose a world that is necessarily without money. Such a world has existed before – prior to the settling down of our ancient ancestors to farm the land there was no such concept, and life revolved around hunting and gathering. But, although we certainly do not need money, unless we return to such hunting and gathering in order to satisfy our evolutionarily programmed thirst for adventure we still may want money to take the place of more natural forms of competition. It has been claimed that treating everyday activities in life as games makes us better at them, and it would seem that, indeed, we have invented money in order to provide us all with a game to play. Deep down, we like there to be winners and losers, haves and have-nots, so that we can appeal to our primeval need to be better than the rest in some form or another. Rewarding people for the work they do with money and giving jobs that are more difficult to get into higher salaries provides this impetus. So money itself is, in this day and age, actually a means of increasing our own wellbeing.

But that is not to say that the power of money should be allowed to trump all other considerations. It is our purpose here to show that the games of capitalism can be allowed to continue when it comes to the less essential facets of life – gadgets, luxuries – so long as they are not produced in quantities exceeding those that can be obtained sustainably. Meanwhile, the essentials of life – food, clothing, education – should be provided freely by society for society, with no need for money to taint them at all. This would mean that there were no losers and winners on the fundamental level, for all would have their basic needs provided for. But those that wished for a life filled with the adventure of money could still partake in it, by working and earning more to buy luxury goods, if those goods can be made sustainably (certainly they cannot in the volumes we currently produce them). Those that did not wish to play this game could do less work, or accept less pay for their work, and be satisfied still with all that they required. There would be no need for the ruthless competition that produces homelessness and hunger, for all would have a home and food. Competition for money would become like competition in sport. Participation in sport is not forced upon us, yet many do partake in it; likewise, participation in a full-time job would not be forced upon us in the socialist society, yet some would still choose to do it. This will be embellished upon in the chapter on employment. For now, we must simply conclude that the mechanisms of capitalism, though thrilling to some, are dangerous when applied to the basic needs of society. The stock market must not be allowed to rule over these needs.

6.5 Supply & Demand

Over the decades and centuries of capitalist domination in the industrialised world, aspects of life in which there is enjoyment – in one sense or another, some kind of 'demand' – have come to be controlled by larger and larger corporations, whose primary motive is to procure profit by supplying to satisfy that demand. Once, the stories we told each other, the music we made and the ancient works of art we produced were shared creations. They were perhaps simple by today's standards, and more difficult to reproduce beyond our immediate neighbours than works conveyed through modern media, but once publically aired they were free to be used by all as appropriate. Music marked as 'Traditional' survives to this day with no known author. Meanwhile, goods such as foodstuffs were procured locally and sold by individuals whose purpose was to fulfil a vital need in society, without any notion of 'growth' or expansion if their own small outlet to serve other communities and make greater profit. This was still the case up until the capitalist revolution of the nineteenth century, and indeed largely persisted in some industries until the commercialisation of capitalism that followed the Second World War, before which time the pursuit of profit above proficient supply was confined to a greater degree to the realms of heavy industry, manufacturing and finances.

But now, the commercialisation of aspects of ordinary people's lives has gathered pace considerably, so that in almost every sphere of need-fulfilment and entertainment, and all those inventions we have come to see as being necessary to the attainment of a healthy existence in the fundamentally foreign environment that is the modern world, there is an element of competition between opposing brands eager to supply our demands. The result of this can be an unhealthy excess of one commodity or another, to the detriment of our minds and bodies and the planet as a whole, because it is in the interests of these players to create artificial demand – to convince us to purchase things in excess of what we would otherwise desire.

The ability of producers and retailers to persuade us to buy more and more, and to buy from them as opposed to their competitors, is strengthened as these companies become larger and larger. By out-competing smaller providers, mergers and takeovers, all of which are encouraged by the cold, cruel rules of capitalist 'development', smaller groups get stamped out entirely by larger ones, until an increasingly small number of companies obtains an increasingly dominant control over all things that we hold in any way dear, and therefore provide a demand for. From supermarkets to clothes manufacturers to film studios, by far the biggest proportion of the demand is supplied by the big businesses drawing in colossal sums of money.

This is problematic because, although we live in a democratic society, the small group of companies that dominate each aspect of our culture are not in any true sense democratic. It is they that ultimately decide which books we can read, which information we hear about, what sorts of products we can use – through what they offer us to buy. The capitalist society may appear superficially to be awash with choice, but in reality it is one in which a few individuals at the 'top' dictate the flow of ideas and resources and control the implementation of inventions within society to suit their own ends. This differs from a feudal hierarchy in one key respect: the corporations are not single individuals or families, but are composed of a body of employees and a board of shareholders, who are each in different ways just as much the victims as the perpetrators of such antidemocratic perversions of their own freedoms.

The employees are exploited, being made to work for the best part of their lives doing jobs that are not necessarily purposeful or good for society in the long term, designed as they are more for the profit of the company than for the wellbeing of society. Sometimes, especially in fast-food outlets, mega-farms and supermarkets, they are paid much less than the 'living wage' necessary to acquire the material resources needed for a decent life in a capitalist society. They may become trapped doing poorly-paid jobs, permanently treated as if they were temporary, disposable workers by their employers. The shareholders, meanwhile, waste their lives worrying about making the business as profitable as possible so that they can grow their hordes of worthless riches.

Public ownership of the companies that supply our natural demands as a society would, of course, eliminate these problems. It would also obviate the need for relentless advertising, branding and waste of that kind that larger producers currently use to try and out-do each other and draw in customers. Big businesses put huge sums of money into creating 'brands' for themselves, so desperate are they to assure custom by metaphorically branding themselves onto our lives, so that we become used to using them. Potential customers are encouraged to buy form the big brands rather than other, cheap or better, goods providers simply because of the aura that surrounds their logo. This aura can be enhanced through celebrity endorsement, a positive concept that the company has attached to itself through advertising, or the sponsorship of some popular event or television programme. Such sponsorship indeed can and often does lead to the hijacking of the entire event to suit the purposes of the company: placards sporting company logos are often attached to stadia used for popular sporting events, and sponsors' stickers are plastered over sportspeople's kit, even though these are of no benefit to either the players or the spectators.

Such advertisements have existed for many decades – beginning with the painting of company logos onto factories and chimneys in the nineteenth century – but with the progression of capitalism they have become ever-more dominant, and ever-more subtle. Where once advertising was largely a form of bragging, trying to highlight the benefits of the goods and services one company was trying to sell over those of its rivals, nowadays it is used to manipulate the public, to encourage them to desire what they would otherwise not want at all. Instead of relying on existing demand and trying to be the one to supply it, nowadays profits are multiplied by creating artificial demand. A soft drinks manufacturer will, for instance, produce an advertisement that makes the viewer thirsty; a supermarket will show souped-up videos of delicious meals to make us want to eat – and more importantly, want to eat what they're selling. A mobile telephone manufacturer will try to convince us that it their latest model will enhance our lives. An entire industry has grown up in the last few years to exploit social media to make advertising still more subtle, tailoring adverts on webpages to suit the exact temperament of the user.

Even as they seek to propel their images out into the world, to achieve the 'brand recognition' that will secure them so much custom, most companies are not subscribers to the old maxim 'no publicity is bad publicity'. Some major advertisers have sought to 'capitalise' on the movement against manipulative ads that has arisen amongst an increasingly aware public, by producing adverts that parody themselves, trying to seem to be on the same side as the public and thus winning over still more custom. Yet at the same time they are eager to avoid the uncontrolled usage of the very brands and logos that they have designed to lodge deep in the minds of all beholders. These corporations want to have things both ways: they want to become so integral to people's lives that they are able to control them and exploit them, to extract as much money as possible. But at the same time they don't want their brand name to be used without permission in the paper and internet publications that some such people create, lest they be in any way besmirched. When trademarked musical jingles are republished elsewhere, or the company's name is explicitly mentioned in a negative piece of journalism (as in the famous 'McLibel' case launched by McDonalds against those criticising its fast food) they are quick to sue for copyright or trademark infringement or for libel. In this way, these companies prevent the public from discussing them openly and freely, even though they have by their very own actions made themselves to be so important to their customers. How can a state in which we are not allowed to speak publically about those that govern our desires and actions be called free?

So it is that our world is manipulated not by the will of the majority of its inhabitants but by that of a small group of large conglomerations that have fewer and fewer actual employees, often subcontracting their work to temporary workers' agencies and exporting more laborious manufacturing tasks to poorer countries where labour is cheap and working conditions much worse. They try to appear 'ethical' and 'green' to their customers in the industrialised world, while their dirty social and environmental practices are carried out far away where nobody who 'matters' to their profit margin can see. The goods they produce – from the latest designer trainers to tacky toys to grossly unhealthy soft drinks – are often far from essential, and could be replaced by fewer, more sustainably produced and healthier alternatives were the public able to demand only what they genuinely wanted, freed from the relentless stream of adverts that pollute today's world and from the consumerist general attitude that such companies have fostered, driving us all to consume more and more to no particular purpose. By allowing big businesses to proliferate and control the industries that matter to us, we allow them to work together to create false demands and meet them with damaging means of supply, something that can only be harmful to ourselves and to the generations that follow us.

7. Towards a New Economics

We have now explored some of the many ways in which capitalism is destroying our planet and holding back our society. This chapter will move beyond this exploration of the current state of affairs, attempting to propose a new economics that will avoid these problems caused by a dependence upon money, and bring about a better future for all. To this end, the chapter ends with a series of 'Action Points', by following which, it is hoped, we can bring about a transition towards a better way of doing things - the New Economics. The ways in which this new economics will transform the wider economy, from agriculture to energy, politics to foreign relations, will be explored in the second volume of this book.

7.1 Work, Rest and Play

What is the purpose of the work that we do? Do we work for the sake of the goods that we manufacture and the services we provide to each other? In one sense, we do: insofar as we need food, houses, clothes and so on we need people to work to produce these things; a desire for good health, clean streets and means of travel leads us to depend upon people who provide these services. But in reality, although work has to be done to meet some of the needs that we have as humans, the majority of the work that we do is not related to these basic needs at all. Through modern technology, the basic needs of our society are met by just a small proportion of the workforce. And even for the minority of today's population - and the majority of our forebears - engaging in the production or dissemination of food and other necessities, it is not the end products themselves that are the real motivation for their work. The farmer does not grow crops because he likes his bread. Instead, he does so for one of two broad reasons: either he is enthralled to capitalism, and delights in making money by selling the grain; or he takes delight in seeing the needs of others satisfied through his efforts - a useful job well done with real benefits for society.

These two motivations are what drive all that we do in our work in a capitalist society. It may be that we take joy in our work, driven by the innate desire in all humans to live purposeful lives, spending our time and effort in doing something that will be of benefit to our fellows and will bring about joy and happiness. The work may be arduous - even tedious - at times, it may cause us stress and worry or take us far from our families and homes. But it gives us a sense of satisfaction and allows us to make the most of our talents and traits, and we feel that those small sacrifices are worthwhile for the benefit that we are bringing. This sort of work – a true vocation – is work that we delight in and enjoy, and can be difficult to distinguish from 'play'. It's the sort of work we've been doing for millennia, since before the dawn of civilisation, when we hunted, gathered, manufactured tools and began to create works of art. All these things involved us utilising our surroundings to provide for each other's needs and to entertain our fellows. The peasants that made up the majority of the population in past societies worked hard, often doing weary, arduous and unenviable labour for long periods of time, buoyed on by the satisfaction that they were serving one another and God by providing the produce on which everyone would feast on the rest-days. That was their purpose in living: to provide for one another and sustain each other in life. Each would do as much work as they felt was necessary for this. Their motivation for work was primarily a social one.

Work regarded in this sense can go far beyond the 'day job' that we spend much of our time doing. It extends to hobbies that bring ourselves or others joy – pictures we paint, books we read, produce we grow, plays we put on and even sometimes cultural events we attend – in our 'spare time'. Certainly, acts of good will to others – volunteering, helping out, spending time with people – are very good and worthwhile examples of 'work' in this sense. Whenever we are actively engaged in some purposeful task that will be of benefit, we are 'working'; the rest of the time we are 'resting'.

But the industrial revolution and the dawn of capitalism brought a second dimension to the nature of work, one which is far divorced from a love for life and a willingness to serve and enjoy one another. It was under capitalism that the individualist motivation for labour was forged. Forced into factories to do menial work into which they could bring no creativity or imagination, slaving to produce goods that were often superfluous to need and served rather as luxuries either for the rich or for their own consumerist lower classes that capitalism was bringing into being, the majority of people in the industrial age seldom saw work as a delight. Work became something to be endured, something that one would be timed whilst doing and paid for accordingly. Work became a means of earning money, which could in turn be spent on the material goods the capitalist world was churning out rather than on items that were truly enriching. In this way, the development of capitalism shifted the purpose in life away from serving one another and towards lining our own pockets and crowding our own lives with consumer goods. In the capitalist world, work – for which one is paid – is far detached from play – which one must pay money to enjoy. Things that we do but are not paid for are not regarded as work; things that we do not pay to do are not regarded as play. Such things do not help to grow the monetary economy because no money changes hands, and are therefore frowned upon as frivolous and unimportant. There is little time for 'rest' at all.

When put in such stark terms, it is not difficult to see the problem with money when it comes to our working lives. If we are to spend most of our lives following a particular vocation, it ought to be one that we enjoy and cherish, and that brings benefit to society. It should not be so meaningless and purposeless that we do it only for money, and have to seek meaning in life by buying superfluous goods and cheap entertainment. Work needs to be reclaimed as a creative, imaginative and uplifting pursuit, sometimes difficult but always worthwhile, and indistinguishable from play. Only then can we obtain satisfaction in our lives, satisfying a higher need for fulfilment – 'actualisation' as Abraham Maslow puts it – that is too often overlooked amidst the drudgery of today's workplace. No longer are the majority of people imprisoned in factories. Most people are now employed in the so-called 'service economy', helping companies to provide goods and services that we either don't really need at all or that would be better provided by nationalised industries that focus on benefits to society rather than profits for the shareholders. There is not such a clear distinction as the above portrayal might suggest between the monetary and more fulfilling motivations behind work. Most people in work, it is probable, do have at least some degree of satisfaction with their job and feel – rightly or wrongly – that they are making a positive contribution to society of some kind. But the capitalist ethos about work still persists, in that the workforce is paid by the hour, workers are often far detached – in offices – from the people who will use the goods and services they help to provide, and work is seen as necessary only insofar as it is a means to make money. Some people are genuinely able to follow the career path of their choice, and find their work rewarding of its own accord. But in the capitalist world, they remain a fortunate few. Most are still driven by the wheels of production and consumption, money-making and spending that capitalism set in motion first in what is now the industrialised world and continues to construct as it spreads into every corner of the globe.

7.2 The New Slavery: The Reality of 'Development'

When the future world looks back on the twentieth and twenty-first centuries, they will see a time of great political change in Africa, Asia and South America, when the clutch of the old Empires fell and new, independent states arose to usher in a new period of transformation across these parts of the world. But what they will see, at least up to the present time, is not a development from misery in poverty to new-found riches and prosperity. So far, the story is one of societies often subjugated and shaken out of kilter by colonial regimes that have, under independent governments, gone in many cases from bad to worse. Industrialisation, and the monetary enrichment of the upper classes of 'developing' countries across the globe, has led already to increased levels of environmental and social exploitation, and only served to further decay the individual traditions and overall wellbeing of such a large swathe of the human population (see 'developing devastation'). By far the most concerning feature of this supposed 'development', a word which hides such realities as urbanisation, globalisation and cultural erosion, is the spread of such inhumane and appalling living and working conditions for the lower classes – themselves invented by the importing of western values – from the Philippines to China, as have not been seen since the early decades of the nineteenth century in Europe and North America. This capitalist 'modernisation' of entire countries, which serves only to profit the multinational corporations that fund it and the governments that encourage it, creates a new form of slavery that can often be akin to the conditions endured by people living under such tyrannical regimes as Stalinist Russia or Mao's China.

The difference is that this new form of oppression of the lower orders of society, defined here as those who endure the lowest standards of living, comes not as a result of the deranged vision of some power-hungry political leader or class. It arises from the desire of western companies, limited by the regulations and finite market size of their home countries, to expand their business enterprises into all corners of the globe and export the labour required to construct their products to the places where labour is cheapest, so as to maximise profit. Secondarily, it arises from the aspiration of the upper classes within the 'developing' countries towards what they perceive as a superior quality of life enjoyed in the west. The terrible means – children slaving in sweat-shops, forests devastated by logging and precious landscapes and homes swept aside for the concrete and steel of 'modern'-style architectural complexes – are seen as necessary steps towards the promised end result, a western-style standard of living for all, and the perceived state of happiness and well-being that will accompany such a shift. As this document goes to prove, the notion that the western lifestyle is necessarily superior to that of other nations is no more than a myth, and the widespread adoption of imported technologies to transform as-yet 'undeveloped' parts of the globe would have devastating consequences. But even disregarding the futility of the ends hoped to result from the globalisation of our planet, no promise of future contentment can ever justify the huge pains to which the least powerful and most desperate of the world's citizens are forced to endure in the name of 'development'. Furthermore, there is no indication that this promise of western lifestyles for all will be fulfilled, even if it were to be desirable: the more fundamental motivation is profit, dressed up as 'development'.

7. A New Economics

The proliferation of sweatshops

In the latter half of the twentieth century, large companies in Europe and North America began to realise that, rather than concentrating on producing a product themselves that could be sold, by virtue of its perceived quality or low price, to the domestic market, more money could be made in outsourcing the production of trainers, toys or whatever to factories in the 'Third World', where labour was cheaper and regulations laxer. Here, they knew, governments were eager to transform their countries into new manifestations of the industrial west, which was seen as a more progressive and more desirable place to live. After all, it was the industrial west that had been able to colonise and dominate the rest of the globe during the imperial years of the nineteenth century: surely this, they reasoned, must mean that the western technology and social structure was superior, and must be emulated. Hence, these governments came to focus on the same measure by which the capitalist western world gauged its own success: monetary wealth, and GDP. Increase these, they reasoned, and the quality of life must improve. In this way, they came to offer tax breaks, lax laws and other incentives to actively encourage the development of factories in their countries that could produce goods for the big western corporations to sell to customers in North America and Europe and also to the richer people in those very parts of the globe where the new factories were based. The companies themselves would gain from a much lower cost-base for their products, and could focus their efforts, instead of on production, on the development of brands to stamp themselves into the mind of the 'consumer'. What would mark them out from their competitors would not be the quality of the gadgets or clothes they were selling, but rather the prominence of the logo on the finished product (see 'supply and demand').

So it was that the modern-day 'sweatshop' was born. Hidden in deregulated zones in countries such as China, the Philippines and Vietnam, it still exists. Workers are prevented from farming the land their families have tended for centuries as newly established urban sprawl covers over the fields. To earn the money to feed their families, they are hence forced, with little education either academically or in manual skills, to enrol in low-skill posts at huge factories, where the parts for a whole variety of different end products may be assembled in different buildings. Here they often work for twelve to sixteen hours a day, even those as young as fourteen in some cases, for barely enough pay to get by. Many risk losing their job altogether if they refuse to work overtime for little if any added bonus, and their breaks are short and closely controlled by the factory owners. This is a life, lived out for six or seven days a week, of nothing but tedious work and exhausted sleep, a life surely far less desirable than the rural lifestyle it has replaced, and, what's more, a life of uncertainty: after months of enslavement at the grindstone, workers may find that, the factory's latest contract having been fulfilled, they are left for weeks with no work at all.

This tortuous system has much in common with the production lines of the early nineteenth century in Europe and North America, when the nowadays so-called 'developed' nations were still undergoing a period of industrialisation and regulatory laws regarding child labour, working hours and minimum wages were still to be imposed. This has led some economists to come to the grossly inhumane assertion that the concern is not with there being too many sweatshops in the world today, but too few[69]. Their argument is that, since the western world is, in their view, so much superior to the other cultures existent around the globe, and since such factories were apparently necessary to the industrialisation that proved key to the development of this world out of its medieval agrarian roots, so must the construction of these houses of suffering be necessary to the 'development' of the poorer nations of today. Furthermore, of course, the existence of sweat-shops is beneficial to the creation of the global capitalism that such economists seek to obtain, in that it supplies the most goods from one part of the world for the least possible cost to another, and in this way represents a triumph of the free market over national boundaries.

But these goods themselves are far from essential to the well-being of society; nor are their extortionately low production costs passed on to the monetarily wealthy customers who buy them from the likes of Disney, Gap and Nike. When workers in the factories of Asia are shown the prices for which the garments that they spend hour after hour stitching for pittance are sold, their response is one of disbelief and despair. Typical wages for the production of an item of clothing in the sweatshops are just 0.01 per cent of the sales price, with most of the profit going not to the sweatshop owner that produces it but to the corporation that contracts out the sweatshop. Wages are typically far below the living wage required to satisfy a family's needs[70].

Bringing About Change

In the late nineteen-nineties, the world began to wake up to the appalling human rights abuses that were being carried out by the big brands, and voices calling on us all to criticise and boycott those companies deemed to be responsible became increasingly vocal. In the USA, United Students Against Sweatshops was founded in 1997, and other, older organisations such as People & Planet in the UK, founded in 1969, have for many years now led campaigns against sweatshops. But for every company exposed and shunned for exploiting the poor and desperate, and every promise that is made to end this or that exposed malpractice within the production process, it is likely that many more abuses continue unknown to the western 'consumer'. The problem lies not with specific companies and their practices, but with the system as a whole. So long as the western 'consumer' is encouraged to buy excessive quantities of mass-produced goods at the lowest possible prices – which are only possible to achieve using near-slave labour – harsh working conditions and long hours will continue to be a reality for those who manufacture these goods. Sweatshops will only be fully eradicated when the richer world becomes prepared to pay more money for their clothes and gadgets, and to replace them less often. Or, when capitalism is disposed with entirely, and local communities are re-empowered to supply one another with their own needs.

The best way for us all to live is to allow each community to decide on the best policies for themselves locally, country by country and region by region. Corporations based in one part of the world should simply not be doing business in another. It is not democratic to say that a company or trade organisation meeting in London can decide on the best working conditions for people slaving away in China. Both the factories for production of goods and the sellers of those products should be located within the country in which the product is sold, so as to ensure that a fair level of control is given to local people over their own industries. This is a vision that needs to brought to reality worldwide: dissolving the division between 'rich' and 'poor', we must allow every country and every distinct community with each country to develop in its own way and serve its own people, at the same time respecting other communities with other ways of life. It makes neither social nor environmental sense to produce goods far from where they are to be used and with no input from those who are to use them. Rather than enslaving other countries to suit our own consumerist lifestyles, we must empower them, providing the technological expertise and material basis on which to sustain themselves. This would entail truly positive development. What is classed as 'development' today is too often nothing of the sort.

7.3 Employment & Division of Labour

In July 2014, unemployment stood at 2.2 million in the United Kingdom, which represents a vast number of people out of work. The majority of these have the ability to work, and could work, if only they were given a share contributing to the life and achievements of our society. Unemployment has, of course, always been a critical issue in politics. But too often it is reduced in the wrong way, and the jobs produced are not useful, fulfilling to the worker or sustainable. We need to look at employment holistically, considering what it is that we as a society want to be done, at who is capable of doing it, and at how we can, in light of this, best share out the work that there is. We should never provide jobs for the sake of jobs: jobs that do more harm than good for society and for the environment, such as building houses where they are not needed or advertising products that people wouldn't otherwise need are not usefully contributing to the prosperity of our people. The focus of job creation should be on the sustainable, important jobs that need doing to achieve and maintain our future prosperity, not to destroy it. Initiatives such as the Green Jobs Alliance in London have already made a start towards achieving this aim[71], but much more needs to be done.

Divide the Load, Share the Rewards

The first thing we need to consider as a society is what jobs we want to be done. There are some jobs that involve sustaining us all, providing the basic needs of life: these are jobs in agriculture, in building and in distributing goods that we need. There are jobs that provide essential services: transportation, education, healthcare, policing, electricity, water and fire-fighting. There are jobs that move things forward in the arts, sports, science, technology, humanities, religion and politics; these are the jobs that allow everyone in society to pursue its ultimate goals ('The Goal of Humanity and Society'). There are also jobs that provide more specialised goods and services – producing and selling electrical equipment, for example – that enable people to have some luxury in their lives, if we can afford it. These are all valuable jobs, and we as a society should decide the share of our workforce that we want to be involved in each of these, in different capacities. Each sector involves more manual jobs – working in the fields or on the shop floor – and more managerial ones – overseeing a university department or running a business for distributing shoes, say, to where they are needed. Every person working in all these jobs – from the prime minister to the policeman, the doctor to the bus driver, the bin-man to the baker – should receive, automatically, the entitlement to a fair ration of food, electricity, housing and everything else that they need. People in these jobs may choose to work for longer than the basic requirement (which we shall discuss below), to bring extra benefit to society, but this does not change the ration of expendable goods that they require and should not warrant them any additional access to services that ought to be accessible equally to all.

There are some jobs that are currently done but which are excluded from all of these categories. Marketers, advertisers, investment bankers, professional investors, professional gamblers, managers of gambling shops and so on. All these are jobs that serve the monetary interests of the people doing them or the companies employing them (i.e. they 'make money') but which provide no specific good to society. These jobs we should not seek to encourage, and there should be no targets for the numbers of people occupying them. People will be free to pursue these jobs if they want – we should not consider banning gambling, say, or even marketing – but they won't be given a ration from the state for doing so. In other words, when all other jobs and businesses are publically organised (and localised, as we shall discuss below), these jobs will remain in the ghostly 'private sector' and the people doing them will earn only money, not rations. In a world where money is recognised as worthless and is not needed to obtain the goods and services we want and need, such jobs would be seen for what they truly are: also utterly worthless. But their children would still, surely, be educated in the same schools and they would be treated in the same hospitals and protected by the same police and firefighters as everyone else, for anything else would constitute a lack of compassion on the part of society.

Once the worthwhile jobs have been decided, we next need to decide the most sustainable way of allocating people and resources to each sector of the workforce, to get out as much of the end products as we need in an environmentally friendly manner. We may decide, for example, that we need far more people working in agriculture, so that some degree of de-mechanisation can be brought about to reduce greenhouse gas emissions. Such 'basic needs' jobs will require some minimum number of people to fill, which should be considered first. Next, we shall come to the essential services jobs. We shall have to decide how many police, firefighters and so on we need and have the resources to sustain in each district at each time of the day. Third will be the 'ultimate goals' jobs and the 'specialised goods and services' jobs, which will be lumped together because each of them is more expendable than the other jobs, and there is more leeway for reducing or increasing the numbers of people we employ in these sectors as we see fit. We may decide that computers should be produced in the UK, rather than through what amounts to slave-labour abroad, so that although we need far fewer than the capitalist corporations have encouraged us to buy, the number of people in the UK working to produce them should increase. We may desire for there to be more actors, say, because there isn't enough theatre in a given region. Or perhaps it would be good to have more tennis players. But if these jobs are not filled, no disaster will result. We can't put specific figures on the number of jobs we want to be available in each of these sectors: we can simply say 'ought to be increased', 'ought to be decreased' and so on.

After all these considerations, we shall be left with a list of jobs that must be filled in each of the first two sectors – basic needs and essential services – and a list of jobs we'd like to fill in the remaining two. Some of these jobs will require qualifications, whilst others will not. But pay for these jobs should not depend on the qualifications required, because this might imply that the doctor was somehow a more important or deserving person than the bin-man, just because he or she is more qualified. The same basic ration should be given to every person showing themselves to be doing useful work for society: there should be no place for a meritocratic judgement of who is more or less worthy than others. However, access to these more managerial or skilled jobs will of course still be restricted to those who have gone through a university course or apprenticeship in training for such positions, not because such people are 'better' or 'more deserving' but simply because, on a purely practical basis, they are better qualified through their training to do these particular jobs well. They will, presumably, have chosen to do this training because they enjoy that job, just as other people will have chosen not to do the training because they have no desire to follow such a vocation. The advantage of having qualifications would therefore be a greater choice of jobs and possibly the opportunity to perform a variety of fulfilling jobs at the same time.

Before anyone is allocated to any vacant positions in the workforce, the number of essential jobs available must be divided by the total size of the workforce. It is hoped that the resulting fraction will be considerably less than unity. This is the fraction of the workforce that would be employed to meet our basic needs and essential services if everyone employed worked for twenty-four hours each day and everyone else was unemployed. Or, it is the rough fraction of each week that *everyone* is required to work if *everyone* is employed doing essential jobs and *nobody* is unemployed. This is the amount of time per week that any given person of working age and ability will be recommended to work in order to gain their 'ration' of basic needs – food, water, housing (which we shall discuss in a later chapter, but most people should be able to remain in their current homes were we suddenly to change to this system of employment), use of public transport to within a set distance of work and home, admission to all libraries and museums, access to all television and radio broadcasts and so on.

The fraction thus computed will be communicated to everybody, to make it clear how much work per week it is absolutely necessary as a bare minimum for us all to do, were we all to work in essential jobs. Having space for some people to do all the other jobs that are useful to society – the 'ultimate goal' and 'specialised goods and services' jobs – will therefore rely upon some people doing more than the minimum requirement of work in the more essential jobs, or in everyone doing less-essential jobs on top of the essential ones. So, whilst everyone would know the approximate minimum number of hours that they were expected to work in a week, because this number would be very low compared to today's typical working week, most people would choose to do some sort of work over and above this. It is in our human nature, after all, to want to be serving others in some way, living meaningful and purposeful lives and making use of our time. That is why even in today's society many people volunteer – helping the needy or putting on events for others to enjoy, for example – or pursue 'hobbies' such as painting, writing, acting and crafting that can be just as useful as their paid jobs outside their official 'working hours'. Therefore, people should be able to share their time and creativity with others in ways other than would be involved in their official 'job' if they so choose. There are a huge number of ways in which we can each be productive. Primary amongst these is a job that has not officially been treated as such at all in the past – that is, caring for one another, and spending time with our friends, family and loved ones, a job that every person should find plenty of time for in their lives if those lives are to be meaningful and joy and peace are to abound.

If everyone had a job they enjoyed and obtained fulfilment from, though, many people might choose to work for more than the bare minimum number of hours in that particular vocation rather than necessarily pursuing other avenues. Therefore, although such a minimum would have to be computed to provide a basic guide, the idea of measuring working hours could be largely dispensed with. It was only with the dawn of industry and the factories that people began to be paid for their time by measuring the number of hours they worked each day – only then did we begin to sell our time as a commodity and lose this most precious gift. Moving into the factories allowed families to increase their revenues and escape material poverty at home because the wages in nineteenth-century factories were good, at least for men, and women and children could be employed too (albeit in more menial jobs) to bring in extra income. But in return for this revenue, people were enslaved in the factories, giving up the best parts of all their days to their busy 'work', which was not fulfilling and useful work at all but involved the drudgery of operating machinery to make excessive quantities of goods for the factory owners to sell. The workers would seldom have time to enjoy the fruits of their labours – the money they brought in – for which they had sold their time, and with it their very lives.

But we do not today face the same desperate situation of poverty and uncertainty in the countryside and penury in the city. We have the resources to give everyone a happy life without the need for excessive hours of work. It would be much more logical and precipitous of far more happiness to abandon the invented notion of selling our time, to cast off the idea of the 'working day' with its fixed hours, and instead return to valuing our work by what we actually produce. Picture two people painting vases. One person might work quickly, creating a not especially delicate pattern that is nonetheless very pleasing to the eye. The second might work more slowly, pausing to consider the details of each part of the pattern they are producing, exerting less physical effort per minute but creating a more elaborate finished work. In the end, though, the final products are equally beautiful, despite their different styles, and equally useful to society.

It should not matter that one artist 'spent' more time than the other. In fact, we should not even measure the amount of time for which each person works – only the quality and quantity of the output they produce. Being rewarded for what we do, rather than how long we spend busily 'doing', will free us to work joyfully and creatively and to use our days to their full potential by doing each type of work we pursue at the times most convenient rather than inventing work to do to fill a specified number of hours or cutting short our labours when a little more time would have been beneficial. An individual who finds it useful may still measure the amount of time for which they work at a particular job, of course, and set themselves targets to ensure that the amount of work they want to do gets done. But there should be no edict from above concerning anything but the bare minimum recommended number of hours to work.

Nobody needs to be compelled to work, because for the vast majority some form of work is necessary for a fulfilling life, and will be sought of its own accord. But what about those who are currently unemployed and refuse the job they are allocated? Should they be denied their basic ration? Certainly not. They will need to eat and drink, to have shelter and access to transport, museums and broadcasts, just as everyone else. Denying them these things would hardly make them more useful to society in the future, in any case: doing so would make them less thoughtful, less educated and more embittered. If somebody genuinely does not wish to do any kind of work whatsoever, that does not render them a valueless person in themselves, and they will no doubt be capable still of providing much love and meaning for others.

Therefore everyone, regardless of which official job – or none – that they perform, should be supported by society to have all that they need in life. We should hold basic goods such as food and water in common, allowing people to take as much food as they need (for there will be no incentive to hoard when we know our needs will always be met). The clothing we produce should be given to those who need it, theirs to keep until they no longer have need of it or it wears out and is replaced. Luxuries such as electricity should be shared out according to however much can be sustainably produced, and gadgets such as computers and televisions should be available on a use-by-use loan within each local community to be shared and communally maintained. Each person should automatically own the house that they live in, and be able to arrange a swap if they need to move by applying to the government. Healthcare, policing, public transport, broadcast media and the like should all be free for all to use. Everyone (or almost everyone) contributes, through their job or jobs, to the provision of these goods and services, and everyone should be able to benefit from them. There will therefore be no need to pay people with money, for there will be nothing left to buy except inherently worthless trinkets such as silver and gold ornaments that have no inherent value.

For money, as we have already seen, has no practical or sentimental value in itself; money if it exists at all should only provide added extras necessary only to make life a little more interesting if their deliverance is ethical and sustainable. There is no need to pass it on to anyone else. Property, though, may need to be inherited: children may still be living with a parent who dies, in which case it makes sense for them to inherit the house; they may move into a dead parent's house out of sentimentality, inheriting that one and giving up their own. We may treasure dead relatives' or friends' goods as reminders of the person we have lost, and such items might therefore be bequeathed to us by will. There is nothing wrong with this; this is not a sign of capitalist greed, but of nostalgia and love for a lost companion.

Of course, for society to run efficiently, the work that needs to be done cannot simply be left for people to do on an ad-hoc basis, but must be apportioned appropriately. This should be done on a local, not national, basis for most kinds of jobs, to ensure that most people do not have to travel far for work and to take into account the different needs of different communities. Though everyone should be able to choose their main profession and useful hobbies, and no-one need be bound by strict working hours, we will each need to register our profession with the local government and may be asked to spend some small amount of time helping to do essential jobs that the local government has identified to be unpopular. Jobs that currently go undervalued but are of immense importance, such as care for a long-term sick loved one or young child, should be included as a (perhaps temporary) career option.

This is how it might work. Once it has been calculated which jobs need to be done and roughly how many people will be needed to do them each, all the jobs that need doing can be advertised to everyone in society. Each person would first be given the opportunity, when this scheme was first set up, to continue in the job that they currently hold, but under a new public ownership and on a revised contract whereby they were only required to work the basic minimum number of hours society had agreed upon, and only if this job was still deemed to be useful in a post-capitalist world. This would leave some of the 'basic needs' and 'essential goods and services' jobs unfilled, because many of the jobs people currently do fall into other categories and the number of hours worked per person would have decreased, plus some people might not want to continue doing a job they found to be unpleasant and unfulfilling. The currently unemployed, and those that had left their jobs, would then be offered these jobs to choose from if qualified. If they did not choose a job themselves, they would be allocated one of these jobs automatically according to their location and qualification.

This may well still leave some of the 'basic needs' and 'essential goods and services' jobs unfilled, so everyone would then be offered the opportunity to apply to do extra work to fill portions of these positions. Some people might end up, thereby, doing two very different jobs – twenty hours per week organising an art gallery, and another five hours working in the fields, for example – if they so chose. Most would probably choose to do a bit of extra work on top of their main job. Everyone would have plenty of leisure time, though: the amount of extra work possible would be capped so that nobody could work more than, say, forty hours per week or whatever was deemed necessary by society. It may not be possible to work for this long if there was not enough useful work to be done to fill it; it would not be fair to allow one applicant ten hours of extra work and deny it to another, equally qualified, one, so that each would have to be satisfied with a job-share doing five hours each, for example. This may in practice mean that the cap on maximum working hours per week per person is brought down to a lower level than the maximum deemed acceptable by society, to make the distribution of extra work fair for all who want it.

This alternative system is rather different to the one we have at present, but is advantageous in many ways to everyone in society. It frees us of our attachment to money, and of the hierarchy whereby some people are 'valued' more highly than others and given greater pay. It removes everyone from want of their basic needs and of access to our societies cultural achievements. It means that we divide the work that we do have between as many people as possible, which might mean each person working less than five days a week or less than eight hours per day, but guarantees everybody some form of employment, usually in the area in which they want to work and have gathered expertise. This fair division of work is as vital as the fair division of resources.

If any fair society finds that, with all basic needs met and the rest of the jobs in society allocated according to desire, the artistic, scientific and manual talents of the populace exceed the amount of full-time work to be done, surely there are two options that might be taken. First, one part of the population may work full-time by today's standards (i.e. forty hours per week) or part-time, doing all the work that is required, and able to exert their skills usefully, but with only a limited amount of spare time in which to relax, pursue hobbies and do other, unpaid work – such as creative tasks and volunteering – which enrich the overall experience of their lives. The other part of society would have its basic needs catered for, under a fair socialist system, but would be left solely to pursue these activities in the absence of a clear, paid role, something which is undesirable both for themselves – because they would lack a clear direction in life and sense of worth – and for the rest, who would feel that they had to work harder and may come to resent the unemployed. This is essentially what we have now, but would have a better welfare system supporting the unemployed.

The alternative is the system presented above. In that system, everyone who wants to be employed is employed and everyone has leisure-time. Everyone has equal access to the resources they need to live in return. This is a system of cooperation and equality, not of 'us-and-them' division, competition or meritocracy. A person who has more 'merit' – more qualifications – will have a wider choice of jobs, but not a higher salary. Everyone doing a job in any of the four categories is of equal importance to society, and is valued equally. The fact that any one person may do more than one job, cutting across the different categories, will mean that everyone has the opportunity for a wider range of experiences than is presently possible. Income inequality, meanwhile, will be abolished.

Localising Jobs

If ours is to become a truly sustainable society in the long-term, we need to find ways of alleviating the social as well as environmental degradation that decades of consumerist culture have created. One of the qualities that society has lost is a feeling of belonging to one's local community, and amidst capitalist competition a sense of common endeavour has sadly declined. If this feeling is to be restored, it is important that local economies are resurrected from the graveyard state that big business has so often abandoned them to, so that local people are able to provide local goods and services again, with each person playing their own role in a cohesive social structure.

There are many roles within local communities that have fallen out of use, but which were actually quite important to this feeling of community. In a country through which we all travel less, staying in our local environs (be they cities, towns or villages) more to reduce fuel consumption, it will be necessary to re-establish some of these local jobs. They fall under all four brackets of the employment map. The local production of clothes, an 'essential service', has been largely destroyed by cheap imports from Asia which, in a more sustainable world, will have to cease. Local artisans and craftsman will be encouraged to make essential and a few non-essential goods in place of cheap Chinese imports and clothes produced in sweat-shops. We have already mentioned the computing and electronic technology industry: those computers and 'phones that we need to be produced or repaired should be worked on locally to the users. We won't need nearly so many of these in a more sustainable society because they can be shared. The 'personal computer' and the idea of having a car and a 'phone for every person, replaced after as little as a year, were invented by capitalist corporations keen to profit from the waste produced by making and selling an unnecessarily large amount of these goods. We should share the ones we have now, and use the surplus for spare parts so that not many more will need to be produced from scratch over the coming years. So every community might be envisaged to have its own electrical engineer as well as its own baker, grocer, vehicle mechanic and so on.

They should also have their own policeman and doctor, something that used to be the case but has fallen foul of budget-cuts and excessive travel. The move needs to be away from big, nationwide businesses with huge warehouse-style stores. Goods should be produced and distributed (or sold in the case of luxury items) on a local scale, with small-scale businesses overseen and provided with resources but not controlled by the local government, in publically owned industries that allow local innovation and variation to thrive. This will require more jobs (which is why it was less profitable for big businesses to pursue such local autonomy and small outlets) but will provide more cohesive communities and should involve less pollution as people will no longer need to drive or take public transport to reach the goods and services that they need.

Farmers are one particularly important example. Vital to the restoration of not only sustainability but also pride in British agriculture will be the localisation of food production, so that the local farmers produce food, first and foremost, for the consumption of people in the neighbouring villages, towns and cities. The practise of transporting fresh food across the country by lorry is not only unnecessarily polluting in itself, and a burden on our roads, but also destroys our connection to the people that grow our food, one of our most basic needs, and hence destroys some of that community grounding that we need for our emotional well-being. Worse still than transporting food across the country is importing it from abroad. If meat consumption is scaled down and the amount of food that we waste is reduced, we should be able to raise the proportion of food grown in this country far above its current level of around sixty per cent. Eventually, all the food-types that can be grown in this country sustainably (not bananas or chocolate but most of our cereals and vegetables) should be produced locally to the consumer. The vast amount of energy wastage associated with food imports and the destructive effect of forcing poorer countries to become dependent upon exports to the rich world rather than nurturing a sustainable prosperity for themselves could thereby be avoided. It may mean having certain foods only in season, but there is nothing fundamentally unpalatable about such a perfectly natural state of affairs.

Useful Employment

We all possess some desire to make something useful of our lives: why should we not, after all, seek to use this long amount of time we are given – seconds, minutes and hours adding to days uncounted over the course of an average life – to some end? But there can be a great difference between what is truly useful employment – that is, work that brings fulfilment, comfort or satisfaction of needs to ourselves and others – and what is valued by the capitalist society. So many of the things that we truly enjoy involve labour and effort and produce great benefit to others too, and are rewarding for that very reason. Yet, unless they involve the production of commodities that can be sold for the use or enjoyment of somebody else – unless they can be used to make money – they are not counted as 'useful' to the capitalist economy.

So it is that many activities that occupy a meaningful place in our lives – gardening, cooking, painting, walking, practising a musical instrument, playing sport and even caring for loved ones or needy strangers – are counted as 'hobbies' and relegated to the side-lines of our existence, outside 'working hours', even though they bring ourselves and others great joy and, in many cases, material benefit. One who quite happily carries out all these tasks all day long, interacting with and benefiting with others around them, may well be counted as 'unemployed' simply because they do not earn money for doing so. Thus, we are all driven to prioritise over those tasks that are truly meaningful to us 'proper work' that may provide far less benefit to society, but which accumulates wealth for corporations and contributes more measurably to economic growth. This is why capitalism is so ecologically destructive and constitutes a plague upon the well-being of society: in its reckless pursuit of growth it drives forward those things that make money, even when doing so has an undesirable outcome for everyone. It causes us to do bad work, all too often, and prevents us from doing good.

An important component of the new economics of work in a money-less society would therefore be to reduce the number of hours that each person is expected to spend in 'full-time' paid employment per week in return for the same benefits of access to goods and services. Not only would this allow jobs to be shared out amongst all people, it would also give everyone time to pursue equally important activities aside from their main occupation. With useful or enjoyable work shared between everyone eager to do something useful (that is, nearly everyone) and not-useful, unenjoyable work abolished, the currently unemployed would be freed from the scourge of feeling a lack of fulfilment and ability to contribute, whilst those currently in full time employment would be released time to make the most of in other ways.

Work that people do outside their main work, as a hobby or out of willingness to help as they are able, can have benefits of many kinds for wider society. Having more time outside work means that all will have time to spend volunteering or practising a skill; time to conserve the environment we all share; time to walk rather than drive to work, and meet people along the way; time to visit the sick and the elderly; time to paint, write or make music; time to explore the world around us – these are all things that we value in life, and which our aspirations for are part of the reason for our founding and participating in human societies in the first place. How many times do people of working age put off this or that ambition until after they retire? All too often, they find themselves after retirement age no longer fit enough to do what they had hoped to do, or die before they get the chance. In a happy, prosperous society, surely it should be our ambition that everyone should be able to make the most of their lives, when they are young and healthy as well as when they are old and frail, and none of our years should be taken from us by pointlessly toiling from 9 until 5 at a job in which we do not find fulfilment. There may well be some people who love the job that they do and find that it enables them to serve society in the best way that they can, to the extent that they have little desire to engage in other activities and would rather dedicate all or most of their lives to that work. These people are very fortunate in their vocation, and the option to do so should always be open to them. But nobody should feel compelled to spend the majority of their active hours working at a single task, as for many their efforts are better exerted elsewhere for some of the time.

We did not, when we invented the social structures – including the capitalist financial system and economic infrastructure – and technologies used to today, envisage that they would simply lead to a world in which half of us can live and work in soulless buildings, slavishly performing sometimes pointless tasks, whilst the other half live in poverty or unemployment. There is no reason that the benefits of today's world, which our forebears strove with such effort to bring about but which are now enjoyed to excess by some and denied to others, cannot be shared out equally. We can do better than this. We can easily create a society in which everyone can enjoy employment, the opportunity to engage in art, science, leisure, experience of the natural world and other fulfilling components of human culture, and have all their material needs satisfied. The only thing that prevents us from doing this in today's world is that both work and material wealth are distributed far too unevenly, and our environment and well-being both suffer as a result.

It is clear, then, that a paradigm shift has to take place in how we define what is 'useful' work to be applauded – and we should not reward only formal work. But this can only come about if we adopt a new economics, to be explored in greater detail later in this chapter, in which the workers – that is, all of us – themselves, rather than profit-seeking corporations, provide employment to themselves. In other words, there must be public ownership of local organisations, with wages paid in the form of access to local goods and services, provided according to want and need. Organising ourselves as a workforce and delivering services must be carried out on a local scale to avoid unnecessary bureaucracy, and to encourage us all to engage with those around us and build up supportive, sustainable communities. Power must remain in the hands of all people, not big national organisations – be they publically or privately run – which is the motivating idea of democratic government in the first place, with innovation driven by the needs and ingenuity of the people, rather than the patently ineffectual profit motive.

In this way, not only can people's lives be directly improved a great deal, but much wastage of effort and resources can be avoided: goods and services will be supplied only in quantities sufficient to meet the genuine wants and needs of each other, rather than being manufactured in copious quantities to satisfy an artificial demand that has to be drummed up through advertising. Localism will, at the same time, imbue us with a sense of community that our forebears held but that we have latterly lost: a sense that we are not just competing individuals, but rather are an interdependent communal body in which each has his or her own part to play. The local baker, farmer, plumber, accountant, librarian, teacher, shopkeeper and so on all have their place within a local economy, know each other, and provide useful services to a prosperous community together. Perhaps not everyone will be involved in local jobs – there will still be some national organisational and media jobs, for example, that should not be localised – and they may well look different in the town to in the country, but each locality will be able to decide for itself what jobs were useful to do, and who is best placed to share in doing each.

In order for the work we do to provide the maximum social benefit and to be environmentally sustainable, it is quite likely that many of our current working practices will have to be redesigned. Often, this will involve resorting to more labour-intensive methods: walking to work and practicing organic farming methods are both examples of this. This may lessen 'labour efficiency' as measured in a traditional capitalist way, but the drive for greater such efficiency has been in many cases only an excuse to over-use energy-intensive and potentially destructive technological developments which, though useful where properly employed, have often been used to excess where not strictly necessary and have enabled the rich to lay off employees by automating jobs or extending the hours a person is able to work. The car is an example: it is useful for transporting goods between specific locations, but it is only the capitalist urge for 'growth' and fast-as-possible travel for work and leisure that has led to its use by so many people on a daily basis where walking would actually be much better in the long run, despite taking longer out of the working day.

If we can create a system of employment that is equitable in all its rewards under sometimes more labour-intensive but always safe, environmentally sustainable and sensible methods of working, ours will be a freer, happier society with brighter long-term prospects. This will require the removal of capitalistic desire for economic growth, individual competition and big business dominance. But it will free us all from our current state of slavery to profit – and the endless call to work, spend accumulate replace and generally waste more and more. Peace and prosperity will come, should we choose to foster them, when we set equity rather than consumption as our primary collective goal.

7.4 The Trouble with Taxation

It might at first seem curious, to minds so heavily entrenched in the money-led concepts of capitalism as ours are, for a work espousing government-led equalisation of society to label taxation as 'troublesome'. Indeed, within a predominantly capitalist system the continual redistribution of monetary wealth from the working population and especially from the richest to serve the common needs of society is essential for the upkeep of health and well-being, for the poorest and unemployed in particular. Taxation in these circumstances promotes a greater degree of equality within a hierarchical system, which in turn leads to prosperity.

But this only holds true within a capitalist system that, as we have seen, entails needless unhappiness as a result of an inescapable hierarchy that places some people above others in material wealth, power and respect, favouring the cold coin over the warm heart in its judgement of worthiness and at the same time stripping our planet of many of its life-giving resources. Taxation is necessary in such a fundamentally discriminatory society, to add a touch of kindness in support of those on the losing side in a constant competition for wealth and power. But it is only a temporary stop-gap: it will not in and of itself dissolve hierarchies or fundamentally change the nature of society. Taxation is based on the power of the purse, moving money around to effect superficial changes but not in any lasting way delivering more power into the hands of the poor. In a society that is truly freed of inequality, where all are able to perform jobs that are to them meaningful and every person is respected equally, there will be no need to have money to have power, and therefore there will be no need for taxation, so despised by rich and poor alike, to take place.

In a socialist society, there may exist money, and there may exist amongst some of the populace a desire for money, but there will be no need for money, and hence no place for taxation. Nutritious food, shelter, transport, health, education and all the other basic staples of life will be free for all to enjoy, with no hierarchy or exchange of currency. Money will become a curiosity, a pretty thing that some may covet or desire but which there is certainly no practical benefit to obtaining. Therefore, the monetarily rich who are infatuated by money may keep it: they will be no 'richer' in the real sense than anybody else, for it will not affect their capacity to live or to acquire those things that they want or need. Money will have become worthless, stripped of its power to purchase anything except, perhaps, a few pointless material luxuries that nobody needs and which do not provide any real benefit. It will cease to be much of an aim in a person's life to make money, which would become merely a facilitator of trade in non-essential goods such as jewellery and ornaments that most people neither want nor need. There will be no need to construct markets and speculate because nobody will prize millions and billions of pounds as being especially important: these supposedly vast sums will be exposed for what they really are, merely worthless numbers on computer screens.

So, if money is retained at all, in a socialist society it will be demoted to a luxury good in itself that is only worth bartering for other equally pointless luxury goods, coveted only for the beauty of the notes or the coins by those who delight in such things, and certainly there will be little need to mint any more than is currently in circulation. Goods with any real use would be made for the good of society, not for monetary profit, and would therefore be entirely divorced from monetary valuation. Hence, with money no longer important in our lives, it will be no longer necessary to redistribute it through taxation. The provision of free goods and services, which do not have to be paid for because the workers producing them are not paid either, but all simply hold the common fruits of their labours in common ownership, will be sufficient for a stable and prosperous society. In the short term, whilst we are still transitioning towards this ideal society, taxation of the richest should be increased, because money is still connected with power and the fulfilment of material needs. But in the longer term, as this connection degrades and public and private ownership of property gradually become one and the same, money will cease to represent real wealth and its redistribution will no longer be necessary. Money will cease to represent power or prestige: it will only represent itself, and nobody should be especially concerned about the uneven distribution of a few pieces of nickel and scraps of paper bearing the image of Her Majesty, beautiful as they may be as an historical curiosity once so important but latterly abandoned in favour of reason and prosperity.

7.5 New Economics

In the capitalist world, economics is all about money. People work to accrue money, and they 'support the economy' by spending this money on goods and services, the deliverance of which keeps others in work. A 'booming economy' is one of growing production, growing consumption, and more and more money builds up in the bank accounts of the rich. Big business flourishes, stamping out small enterprises in the name of financial efficiency. Everybody has a duty to earn and spend, keeping the capitalist megalith moving; the unemployed are frowned upon and lambasted for their inadequacy. Everybody is in constant competition to gather money and, with it, material wealth. Every individual or family must fend for itself. An inability to afford modern luxuries is counted as failure, and the price of basic needs such as houses and nutritional food rises as the rich become richer, so that even in a society of abundance, those unfortunate enough not to have well-paid jobs are made poor. The economics of money is an economics of inequality.

Historically, money has only ever stood in the way of a true economic prosperity. It was invented by the proud and the powerful to quantify their supposed superiority, used by the wealthy to extract and utilise resources from the poor. The allure of a gold coin – something which is, in itself, actually useless and should therefore be practically worthless – was used to gather up the fruits of the labourers for the powerful to use to enrich their own lives or to wage wars and found new institutions. In an economy without money where one item was exchanged for another, it would be more difficult to accumulate wealth, and for a central authority to be able to exercise power and coordinate society through the control of resources: every person would have only what they could produce themselves to barter with. But by placing a value on worthless pieces of metal, and tricking everyone into believing that these pieces were worth having, the chieftain could use this metal to buy up material things with comparatively little effort and establish his authority. Money was, at one stage, essential for the establishment of a safe and stable society. But it was all based on an illusion, one which established inequality at the very heart of the economy. Money is therefore at the heart of the rising inequality that we witness in the world today.

But we have moved on beyond the need for there to be rich and poor for society to function. The new economics will not be one of inequality or competition, because it will not be one of money. In today's world, we do not need to frighten or trick the populace into obeying a more wealthy leadership for there to be stability and security. We may invest power in our leaders, but we need not grant them access to more personal wealth and resources than anyone else. We now possess the technology and the understanding to build a society on cooperation, and for this we do not need money.

The new economics will be one in which production and consumption of material goods and services is carried out only in order to provide for the wants and needs of the people in each local community. Communities would be self-sufficient, each employing people skilled in every skill and craft necessary for healthy and fulfilled lives to be lived. There would be a local farmer, policeman, doctor or nurse, shopkeeper, carpenter, teacher, electrician and so on, every one of them playing a meaningful role within the community. Indeed, every single person would have just such a meaningful role, which they would choose according to their ability and desire. Each of these should be supported by the community, everyone sharing the fruits of their labour and benefiting from those of everybody else. If, by chance, there was no work for one or more of these people to do on a given day in that particular place, they would not be compelled to use up resources in working just for the sake of it. Perhaps they would choose to do some voluntary work or help out where work needed to be done; if not, they would be free to pursue other delights – to read about arts and sciences, enjoy entertainments, appreciate nature or play games for example. They should not be denied their ration based on their failure to do a day's work: the labourer cannot be blamed for having no labour to do. Indeed, it may be that at other times they have to work much longer than others because they have much work to do. Working hours must not be fixed in an economy that is healthy and prosperous for all: they should be chosen pragmatically according to the work that needs to be done, the number of people doing it and the need for each of them to remain healthy and happy. The tyranny of the clock that came about with the industrial revolution will be abolished.

Some might say that such a localised economy, with separate people in each place providing local services, is less efficient than what we have today. But they would be looking at efficiency in the wrong way. It may cost less money today to provide services on-mass on a national scale, and to deploy servicemen and goods deliverymen from centralised offices and depots in motor-vehicles. But this is only because the emissions from the fuel required to run those vehicles, the damage done to the environment by other travel required when amenities are placed a long way from the residences of the people that use them and the emotional strains associated with a lack of community support have not been properly costed. Further, more people would be employed in a localised economy precisely because of its apparent 'inefficiency'. But this can only be a good thing: the system of work will be all the more truly 'efficient' in a real sense because it will give a greater number of people employment, meaning and purpose in their lives. It is only because the physical and emotional health 'costs' of unemployment are not taken into account in today's notions of economic efficiency that this is not realised by proponents of a small, centralised workforce.

Without money to facilitate trade, some might suppose that the new economy will relapse to a 'barter' economy: one in which items are traded directly between people according to their own surpluses and desires. But this will not be the case. Rather, it will be a 'sharing' economy. There will be no need to barter because there will be no need for private possession of property beyond the items that each person needs about themselves (that is, their clothing, a watch and so on) or within their own homes to make those homes comfortable. The craftspeople who manufacture clothes, furniture, utensils and the like will produce as many as there are people with need of them; there will be no need to produce any more until they require replacement, in which case they can be manufactured on request: there is no need to trade and barter, since everyone provides the fruits of their labour to the rest of the community to use. Some items that we have in our houses today – washing machines, say, and televisions – would be better kept in a communal storage facility where they could either be used (as in a laundrette for the case of the washing machine) or borrowed (as for the television) when somebody has need of them, and made available to everyone else to use afterwards. Should there prove to be more demand than the number of these devices available can supply, it would simply be a case of devising a rota system or manufacturing more, depending on the will of the community and the resources available to them. This would be a more pleasant system than one that requires each person to trade money or goods to obtain such devices for their private use, taking upon themselves the risk that the device will fail and their trade will have been wasted. In the sharing economy, the machines will be maintained by a local expert and everyone can be sure that they have access to the most appropriate technology available. One need not envy another's television, for everyone will share all the televisions.

The creation of such an economy will, inevitably, be a gradual process. All the amenities that people require access to will have to be put in place in every village and every city or town district, so that communities of ideally one hundred and fifty people at most will share access to these. This number represents the maximum number of people that we can truly know personally at a single time according to research, and the maximum size of the tribes that we have evolutionarily become accustomed to living in as a species. It is a sufficient size for there to be at least one person specialising in each service essential to the community, though perhaps some specialists – piano tuners, say – will be less numerous than one per community, and might serve a whole set of communities reachable within walking distance. But to spread out these specialists appropriately, it may be necessary for some people to either change profession or move district, or for the sizes of the communities to be initially larger so as to encompass a larger residential area. Only gradually will the size of communities be reduced to the ideal level as people of different professions move around appropriately and their spread becomes more even. Such a spread would have to be consciously encouraged – though not of course enforced – by the central government, which would be responsible for providing training for all professions (probably through apprenticeships to existing professionals) and advice on where to live and work to individuals and couples. The government itself, of course, would continue to be elected at the level of the constituency, which would consist of a large number of communities grouped together to ensure that the number of MPs in parliament remains manageable.

The new economics will be one of sharing and compassion, of strong local communities and a place for everyone. It may be unconventional, in a world fixated by capital and competition, but it is far from unnatural. For, we have to ask ourselves, what is the purpose of the economy in the first instance? Why do we make things, and deliver services to one another? It is to sustain the life of every being in our society, and to foster joy amongst all people. Why should it be that a person needs to 'earn' their way to life and sustenance? If the joy of every person is just as important as the joy of every other, and of the same quality and desirability, and this joy rests upon the fulfilment of that person's needs, why should it be that any individual is denied access to anything that they need to live? The economy should first and foremost, provide food, shelter, clothing, education, healthcare, warmth and respect for every one of society's members, regardless of their origin, wealth and standing. Therefore, it is not sensible to create rankings amongst ourselves by apportioning more or less of a quantitative substance – that is, money – to each person and to deny to some the fruits of the economy that others receive in abundance. To share the fruits of our labour amongst everyone in each community – to ensure that everyone has what they need to live and enjoy life– must be our aim in the work that we do. That our current economic system fails to do this is attested to by the thousands of homeless people on our streets and hungry families queuing and foodbanks or evicted from their homes. Such pains are not illustrative of failings on their parts. They are illustrative of failings in an economy of inequality that ranks the well-being of the more fortunate, inexplicably, above that of the less fortunate. The new economics will redress this problem. The new economics will bring about prosperity for all.

7.6 'Cryptocurrency'

In August 2008, without fanfare, the domain name 'bitcoin.org' was registered. This was to be the beginning of a new phase in the history of money, one in which currency – which has always evolved to match the technology of the day (see Chapter 2) – finally embraced the digital age. 'Bitcoin' was the first, and remains by far the most popular, 'cryptocurrency': a currency whose value rests entirely on the cryptographic mathematical methods used to produce and transfer it.

Money had long before this ceased to have any real-world value, but a cryptocurrency goes one step further. It has no physical counterpart whatsoever, no governmental control or oversight and no centralised 'bank' in which to store it. With several million people already using such currencies, storing them in their 'digital wallets' and using them to purchase real-world items, some have predicted that cryptocurrencies will be the new face of online capitalism. Others have criticised such currencies as little better than scams, leading people to waste their computer power and conventional money generating worthless digital 'coins' whose use is nothing but a fad. But conventional currencies are, nowadays, equally worthless, gaining value only through public perception of their worth and trust of those issuing them. If people perceive bitcoins or any other digital currency to be of worth, and trust the means by which they are produced and distributed, there is no reason why cryptocurrencies could not become the money of the future.

Could cryptocurrencies solve some of the problems inherent in conventional currencies, and allow a more sustainable, friendlier form of capitalism to be developed? Hardly. In fact, like the technological advantages that capitalism has seized upon before it, the rise in cryptocurrency only promises to make it more pernicious, less sustainable and more unequal even than it is at present. Why this is the case we shall analyse shortly, but first it is worth taking a few lines to define exactly what constitutes a cryptocurrency, and how such currencies work.

The first modern cryptocurrency, Bitcoin, was introduced by its inventor, the mysterious Satoshi Nakamoto in a paper published online in 2009, a few months after the launch of 'bitcoin.org'. The idea of a digital currency based on electronic cryptography by then dated back a quarter of a century, but this was to be the first decentralised form of cryptocurrency, free from control by a central bank, and the first that would be widely bought-into across the world. Formally, a cryptocurrency is considered to be one that does not require a central governing authority to prescribe its value or facilitate its trade; whose ownership can only be proven using cryptographic methods (see below); and for which information about who owns how much and how more can be 'mined' are stored across the whole 'chain' of computers owned and run by those who use the currency, not restricted to any one locality but spread across the globe. This makes it impossible for any one person or organisation – even the currency's founders – to change or manipulate this information, or for any government to control the currency's value or flow.

A cryptocurrency of this kind is such that it is constantly being created at a formerly prescribed (at the currency's inception) and publically known rate. This creation is carried out by the entire cryptocurrency network all at the same time – that is to say, by all computers that are linked on the currency's 'block-chain'. Each computer in the chain 'mines' for currency by solving difficult mathematical problems, and are given a share of the currency set to be created per second according to their ability to do so. If there was only one computer on the chain, it would receive all the new currency; with multiple computers, a more powerful computer that solves more of the problems faster has a greater share of the currency created per second. The problems solved are cryptographic ones, involving the factorisation of very large numbers for example, required to validate bitcoin transactions, and the 'mined' currency is a form of reward given to a user for investing their computer processing power in carrying out this validation. When a user 'mines' new currency by investing processing power to carry out the required calculation, their new 'block' of currency is added to the block-chain, with that user as the owner, only if they can provide 'proof of work' in the form of the form of the correct solution to the cryptographic problem that they have solved.

The rate of currency creation is usually continually decreased, so that eventually a cap of the total quantity of the cryptocurrency will be achieved. This is done by making the problems that miners have to solve more and more difficult. The block-chain holds a record of how much currency each member possesses and at what rate their 'wallet' contents are increasing, information that is shared across all computers in the chain so that it cannot be centrally controlled, amended or deleted by any one user or group of users – which is what enables the currency to be completely decentralised. The information is encrypted, hence the term 'crypto-currency'. Each user of the currency will have a public key and a private key corresponding to that user; the public key is seen by everyone on the block chain and is required to validate transactions of cryptocurrency, but in order to withdraw cryptocurrency from a given account and transfer it elsewhere, the private key is also required. A public key can be easily generated from the user's private key, but carrying out the calculation in the opposite direction, to correctly work out the private key given the public key, is technologically unfeasible.

This is the same trick used by banks to allow online transactions of 'real' money between private accounts: the public key will be a very large number, which is by definition difficult to factorise – that is to say, to find a particular pair of smaller numbers that multiply together to make that large number. The private key consists of these two factors. Given any two numbers of, say, 4 digits in length, any computer can easily multiply them together to form an 8 digit number, the public key. But given this number, even the most powerful computers in the world would struggle to work out what those factors were, and might take days, weeks, years, or an indefinite amount of time to factorise a very large number: the only known method is to go through all the possible combinations one by one. Human brains exhibit the same asymmetry: I could ask you to multiply 84 by 57 in your head or on paper, and you would, quickly or slowly, eventually come up with 4788. But if I'd asked you instead to tell me all the factors of 4788, you will find it a considerably more difficult task.

The above description is by no means an exhaustive account of the workings of cryptocurrencies, and we shall not go into the differences between them, or the particular features of the most popular, 'bitcoin', that have made its use so relatively widespread. But what this short introduction may illustrate is just how complicated cryptocurrencies really are, and what enormous resources and advanced infrastructure are required to launch and maintain them. They are, in effect, very clever computer programs designed to generate virtual 'wealth' for their wealthy users that is acknowledged by everyone on the block-chain, just as real-world money is an invention designed to allow the already wealthy to increase their standing by investing this money in order to create more.

What, then, is the problem with cryptocurrency, and why would its widespread use lead to a yet more ugly form of capitalism than what we have at present? Cryptocurrencies suffer from two big drawbacks, practical and theoretical. The practical problem lies with the 'proof of work' – the mining. What mining for cryptocurrency essentially entails is large numbers of very powerful computers gobbling up vast resources and releasing huge quantities of heat, simply to carry out very difficult calculations whose answers are of no interest whatsoever, other than to prove that the calculation has been carried out. Computers devour electricity, and sustainable ways of generating electricity are in short supply – so much so that the world is powered almost entirely by burning fossil fuels. Even if sustainable renewable ways of generating electricity can be utilised much more widely, it is unlikely that the world can afford to waste vast quantities of this electricity carrying out meaningless calculations, and we are far from reaching the stage where all our homes, hospitals and businesses can generate all their electricity renewably. This means that cryptocurrency mining is already having a direct detrimental impact on our environment, by contributing to greenhouse gas emissions and the associated climatic change, or else is drawing away renewable resources that could otherwise have been deployed elsewhere, with the same overall effect. Its environmental footprint is little better than the real-world mining for gold, nickel and silver required for real-world coins. By the end of 2017, up to 4 gigawatts electricity was being wasted on bitcoin mining alone, which is on the same order as the electricity use of the real-world global banking sector. More cryptocurrency use will mean more emissions, if mining continues in its current form.

Of course, in an age where climatic change has at least passed through everybody's consciousness, efforts have been made to change this. One idea is to change from the 'proof of work' principle for mining cryptocurrency to 'proof of stake', whereby a miner proves they have significant enough resources invested to warrant being assigned new currency, without actually having to carry out any calculations and mine it. This, though, is not likely to be taken up with any confidence by cryptocurrency users, and even if it were it would simply mean that the wealthiest in the cryptocurrency world would be able to get more wealth by showing off how much they have already in the physical world, which hardly bodes well for a fair society. This brings us on to the more fundamental problem with cryptocurrency, its implications for society as a whole.

We have already seen how the use of conventional money has become a fallacy, in that conventional money has for a long time been essentially worthless. To enable swifter and more convenient use of currency, and therefore stimulate further economic growth, it is stored in the form of numbers on computer systems and generated out of thin air by banks whenever they make loans, to further their own interests. But at least in principle it can be converted into notes – or better still, coins – that have at least some tangible value. This is not true of cryptocurrency. Generated, accumulated and transferred entirely online, and 'mined' through an entirely arbitrary process involving the carrying out of pointless work, it has no inherent practical value whatsoever. This means that for those best able to manipulate the mechanism for generating it, cryptocurrency offers yet easier means of accumulating vast quantities of money. The process of wealth accumulating in the hands of the wealthy that has already been taking place from a global perspective under the existing capitalist system would only be accentuated, hence, by the widespread adoption of cryptocurrencies.

This problem is made yet worse by the very feature of cryptocurrencies that are their chief advertisement – the fact that they are devoid of any central control. Although no form of capitalism is good for society, it is demonstrably true that decreasing the regulation of finances by governments makes things worse for the majority by encouraging the social and environmental degradation that capitalism can so easily give rise to. If we are to use currency to govern our affairs, the best authority to control it is a democratically accountable, benevolent government, not an impenetrable computer algorithm that ordinary people cannot understand, nor the whims and wishes of the wealthiest. To switch our monetary transactions to an unregulated, uncontrollable, intangible and invisible currency can hardly be expected to be beneficial when it comes to ensuring that the needs of the people are met and the system is fair for all. It would only make existing injustices and inefficiencies worse.

Furthermore, relying on a currency that exists entirely on the internet is a far more dangerous move than it is often imagined to be. Since the widespread roll-out of the internet some quarter of a century ago, the tacit assumption among nearly everybody appears to have been that the internet is essentially infallible. After all, with so many machines being linked together, across different institutions, homes and businesses as well as within individual data centres, surely the potential for the system to fail through the fault of any one machine is removed. But the internet is a new and in fact potentially very fragile invention. It is true that the failure of individual computers is unlikely to cause the internet as a whole any trouble, although it could cause havoc for somebody suddenly stuck without any means to survive in a money-driven society if their computer crashed. Yet if some unexpected or extreme event – very bad weather, natural disaster, political upheaval or even excessively large solar flare – were to occur, the electricity supply to millions of computers or data centres could be cut, or the infrastructure carrying the internet around large regions of the globe destroyed, causing widespread havoc. Malicious agents – be they warring states or rogue individuals – could also conceivably develop software capable of jamming, deleting or stealing information from large portions of the internet.

The technology is simply not tried and tested sufficiently for us to be sure that such large-scale disruption could not take place, and we should not regard ourselves as being at all certain that the internet we use today will not crash catastrophically tomorrow. For this reason, it is important not to allow our lives to become in any way dependent on having an internet connection. The recent development of internet banking, and the use of computers to distribute even physical currency, is therefore dangerous; using a cryptocurrency, or any other kind of digital-only currency, to facilitate all transactions online could be a very foolish mistake indeed.

What would a society whose interactions were based around cryptocurrency look like? Probably, it would be a society yet more unequal, more misguided and less environmentally sustainable than the capitalist one we endure today. Control of the lubricant of the economy – money – would not be in the hands of an accountable government able to guide its distribution; the already wealthy would be in a still better position to grow their wealth; and the whole thing would be even more dependent upon using electricity-hungry devices and plastic cards to transfer currency. The ability to opt-out of digital means of living and working, which are such recent inventions yet already are becoming all too prevalent in today's world, would disappear entirely, as would the ability to rely upon an analogue backup if computerised systems and communication networks crashed. It would become almost impossible to avoid the use of electricity in one's day-to-day life and work, since the economy would be locked in to the use of the computer and the internet, and society would be much more vulnerable to the potential disaster caused were such manmade and fallible systems to crash, whether by accident or through malicious intent.

Many people today already suffer grief because services they need to access, such as benefits payments, are made available only online, and they either struggle to use computers or find that their machine or internet connection is faulty. With a digital cryptocurrency, it is difficult to see there being any kind of physical-world alternative that one could recourse to in the event of such problems, which could lead to hardship for many and even life-threatening situations when, in a money-based world, people cannot access the savings or benefits that they need to live.

Of course, it is in practice unlikely that the whole financial system of most countries, or indeed the world as a whole, would be converted to use a cryptocurrency, exactly because of the lack of sovereign control associated with such currencies, control that most governments would be rightly loathe to give up. But aside from the issue of regulation, all of the above arguments also apply to a much more feasible but almost as dangerous alternative that we have already begun to move towards, the cashless society. Already card payments, online or in shops, have overtaken cash payments as the primary means of monetary exchange in the United Kingdom[72] with the help of new 'contactless' payments that avoid the need to enter pin numbers. If such a trend were to continue, it is far from inconceivable that a government of the near future would seek to save money by abolishing notes altogether and switching to an entirely digital currency, with all the same drawbacks as a cryptocurrency save for the lack of overall control. This, too, would therefore undoubtedly be a mistake that would serve to heighten many of the problems our society and our world as a whole already face. It would, of course, be much better to do without money at all, a situation rather to be brought about by decoupling it from the economy through a gradual and carefully organised means than by waiting for an internet outage to bring down the whole digital monetary economy in one foul swoop. But if we must have money, let us at least keep it grounded in the physical world, not in the intangible aether of 'cyberspace'.

7.7 Action Points

To create a New Economics, there are a number of things that we can do straight away, if we cooperate as a society under a sympathetic government. The transformation from a society dominated by money may be extensive and revolutionary, but it need not be difficult nor painful. The following Action Points are intended as a starting point from which this transformation of the economy might begin.

1. Prevent private profit-making corporations from operating across more than one country
2. Ban imports of clothes, gadgets and other goods from abroad
3. Discourage the purchase of more of these goods than is strictly necessary for the enjoyment of life: rather, encourage 'make do and mend' and the manufacture of long-lasting, high-quality wares made with sustainably-sourced materials

4. Reinvigorate local-scale goods-manufacturing and crafts by providing training to the currently unemployed and others who may wish to become craftspeople
5. Set up a repair clinic in every community to help people to fix broken items
6. Set up distribution networks to bring goods to the people who need them
7. Provide aid and expertise to poorer countries, sending out ambassadors to help struggling communities to develop the skills that they want and need elsewhere
8. Set up training programmes to enable anyone who so desires to learn how to practice a particular trade that will be of benefit to their community
9. Provide guaranteed access to food, housing, amenities and public services to everybody, so that nobody needs to pay for these things through wages
10. Set up an employment advice network that can advise everyone as to which jobs need doing and how they can train to do the job that they are best suited to
11. Through local councils, distribute jobs that nobody wants to do amongst everyone of working age and ability, so that everyone does these jobs for a few hours per week
12. Instate paternity or maternity leave for the first five years of every child's life
13. Localise jobs to maximise benefit to the community and communal cohesiveness
14. In the short term, increase taxation of the wealthiest to redistribute this money to where the need is greater
15. In the longer-term, having abolished payment for food, housing, public services and all other utilities and amenities that bring life, health or happiness, and having made all goods in common, abolish taxation altogether
16. Provide goods and services for everyone to share unilaterally in each community, so that work is done out of the passion of the worker and a desire to provide for the rest of society, not for money
17. Abolish banks and cease printing money, given that it is no longer necessary
18. Strengthen local economies through training and distribution of jobs, so that each contains the people and resources needed for everyone in that society to enjoy a happy life

Further details of what a new society with a new, non-capitalist economics, might look like today, and Action Points to transform all necessary aspects of our present society in line with this, will be explored in the second volume of this, my exploration of The Problem with Money.

Tobias Thornes
17ʰ August 2017

Notes to the Text

This list of references is intended to provide places where additional information may be located to complement the corresponding points made in the text. It is by no means an exhaustive bibliography.

[1] *BBC News,* 'Mourners Mark Tsunami Anniversary' (26th December 2005)

[2] UNESCO, 'Surviving a Tsunami' booklet: *Surviving Traditions* (p.5)

[3] UNESCO, 'Surviving a Tsunami' booklet: *Evacuation Strategies* (p.15)

[4] Ferguson, Niall: *The Ascent of Money* (Penguin, 2009), chapter 1

[5] Encyclopaedia Britannica, 1962 vol.15 p.694

[6] Ferguson, Niall: *The Ascent of Money* (Penguin, 2009), chapter 1

[7] Usury Laws Repeal Bill, 1854

[8] Ferguson, Niall: *The Ascent of Money* (Penguin, 2009), chapter 2

[9] Heine, Heinrich: *Ludwig Borne: eine Denkschrift* (Ludwig Borne: A Memorial), 1841

[10] Nef, John: *Not One, but Two Industrial Revolutions* from *The Industrial Revolution in Britain* (D C Heath & Co., Boston, 1958, ed. Philip A Taylor) ch.2

[11] Marx, Karl: *The Communist Manifesto* (1848)

[12] Hammond, John & Hammond, Barbara: *The Town Labourer 1760-1832 The New Civilisation* (1918), p.8

[13] Mantoux, Paul: *The Destruction of the Peasant Village* (1928) from *The Industrial Revolution in Britain* (D C Heath & Co., Boston, 1958, ed. Philip A Taylor) ch.8

[14] Chambers, Jonathan: *Enclosures and the Rural Population* from *The Industrial Revolution in Britain* (D C Heath & Co., Boston, 1958, ed. Philip A Taylor) ch.9

[15] Hammond, John & Hammond, Barbara: *The Rise of Modern Industry* (Methuen & Co., London, 1925) ch.12-13

[16] Ashton, Thomas: *The Industrial Revolution* (Oxford University Press, London, 1948)

[17] Rostow, Walt Whitman: *British Economy of the Nineteenth Century* (Clarendon Press, Oxford, 1948)

[18] Moore-Bridger, Benedict: *City Trader wins more than £1m by Gambling on Scottish No Vote* (London Evening Standard, 22nd September 2014) available from http://www.standard.co.uk/news/london/city-trader-wins-more-than-1m-by-gambling-on-scottish-no-vote-9749631.html (accessed 25th September 2014)

[19] Marcuse, Herbert: *Eros and Civilisation* (1955)

[20] Brooke-Hitching, Edward: *The Phantom Atlas* (Simon and Schuster, 2016)

[21] *Rubber Mountain* from *New Scientist* (19th May 2012, pp.24-25)

[22] European Commission: *Science for Environment Policy In-Depth Report: Plastic Waste: Ecological and Human Health Impacts*, available from
http://ec.europa.eu/environment/integration/research/newsalert/pdf/IR1_en.pdf (modified November 2011)

[23] Reed, Christina: *Dawn of the Plasticene* from *New Scientist* (31st January 2015, pp.28-32)

[24] Derraik, J G B: *The Pollution of the Marine Environment by Plastic Debris: A Review* (Marine Pollution Bulletin 44:842-852, 2002)

[25] Moore, C J et al: *A Comparison of Plastic and Plankton in the North Pacific Central Gyre* (Marine Pollution Bulletin 42:1297-1300, December 2001)

[26] Reed, Christina: *Dawn of the Plasticene* from *New Scientist* (31st January 2015, p.31)

[27] Kartar et al: *Polystyrene Spherules in the Severn Estuary – a Progress Report* (Marine Pollution Bulletin 7:52, 1976)

[28] Department for Environment, Food and Rural Affairs: *Statistics on Waste Managed by Local Authorities in England in 2013-2014* available from https://www.gov.uk/government/uploads/system/uploads/attachment_data/file/375945/Statistics_Notice_Nov_2014_Final__3_.pdf (modified 18th November 2014)

[29] The Ocean Cleanup Project: information available from www.theoceancleanup.com (accessed 16th March 2015)

[30] Raloff, Janet: *How Plastic We've Become* (*Science News*, January 2008), available from https://www.sciencenews.org/blog/food-thought/how-plastic-weve-become

[31] Davies, Emma and Sanderson, Katherine: *Toxic Shockers: Key Chemicals to Look Out For* (*New Scientist* 26th November 2014)

[32] Ibid.

[33] Carslaw, David: *Oxford Street – Highest NO2 Concentrations in the World?* (London Air, King's College London) available from http://www.londonair.org.uk/london/asp/news.asp?NewsId=OxfordStHighNO2 (modified 10th July 2014, accessed 18th August 2016)

[34] Neslen, Arthur: *UK Faces European Court over Coal Plant Emissions* (The Guardian, March 2015)

[35] Stone, John: *Air Pollution to Blame for 60,000 Early Deaths per Year, Government to be Warned* (The Independent, November 2014)

[36] Allen, J et al: *Early Postnatal Exposure to Ultrafine Particulate Matter Air Pollution: Persistent Ventriculomegaly, Neurochemical Disruption, and Glial Activation Preferentially in Male Mice* (Environmental Health Perspectives 122:9, September 2014)

[37] United Nations Department of Economic and Social Affairs: *World Urbanisation Prospects* (2014 revision highlights, available from http://esa.un.org/unpd/wup/Highlights/WUP2014-Highlights.pdf)

[38] Tans, Pieter & Keeling, Ralph: *Trends in Atmospheric Carbon Dioxide* (NOAA/ESRL and the Scripps Institution of Oceanography) available from http://www.esrl.noaa.gov/gmd/ccgg/trends/index.html (accessed 23rd October 2014)

[39] CDIAC: *8000-year Ice-core Records of Atmospheric Carbon Dioxide*, available from http://cdiac.ornl.gov/trends/co2/ice_core_co2.html (accessed 23rd October 2014)

[40] Weertman, Johannes: *Milankovitch Solar Radiation Variations and Ice Age Ice Sheet Sizes* (Nature 261:17-20, May 1976)

[41] Gray, Lesley et al: *Solar Influences on Climate* (Reviews of Geophysics 48, October 2010)

[42] Tett, Simon F B et al: *Estimation of Natural and Anthropogenic Contributions to Climate Change* (Journal of Geophysical Research: Atmospheres 107:D16, August 2002)

[43] Williams, Caroline: *Golden Opportunity* from *New Scientist* (18th October 2014, pp. 40-42)

[44] *New Scientist* 1st June 2013, p.16

[45] BBC World Service radio: *Science in Action* (25th July 2013)

[46] Asafu-Adjaye et al: *An Ecomodernist Manifesto* (2015), available from http://www.ecomodernism.org

[47] *The Ecologist*, May 2011

[48] Hansen, J et al: *Assessing "Dangerous Climate Change": Required Reduction of Carbon Emissions to protect Young People, Future Generations and Nature* (PLOS ONE 8:12, December 2013)

[49] Carbon Tax Center: *Where Carbon is Taxed* (accessed 27th June 2015, available from http://www.carbontax.org/where-carbon-is-taxed/)

[50] Pearce, Fred: *Into the Wild* (New Scientist, 23rd May 2015, p.24)

[51] *Shell preps for 4deg C Rise* (New Scientist 23rd May 2015, p.6)

[52] Mofor Linus; Nuttall, Peter & Newell, Alison: *Renewable Energy Options for Shipping* (International Renewable Energy Agency Technology Brief, 2015)

[53] Lee, David S et al.: *Aviation and Global Climate Change in the 21st Century* (Atmospheric Environment 43:3520-3537, 2009)

[54] Darby, Megan: *UN Shipping Chief Warns Against Emissions Cap* (*Climate Home* 28th September 2015, available from http://www.climatechangenews.com/2015/09/28/un-shipping-chief-warns-against-emissions-cap/)

[55] Boden, T A, Marland G & Andres, R J: *Global, Regional and National Fossil-Fuel CO2 Emissions* (Carbon Dioxide Information Analysis Center, Oak Ridge National Laboratory)

[56] Bhaskar, R N: *What Chinese dam on Brahmaputra Means to India* from *Daily News India* (27th November 2014)

[57] MacKenzie, Deborah: *Antibiotic-Resistant Superbugs Now a Global Epidemic* (*New Scientist* 30th April 2014, available from https://www.newscientist.com/article/dn25498-antibiotic-resistant-superbugs-now-a-global-epidemic)

[58] Dearn, Mark: *The Canadian Trade Deal which will Let In TTIP by the Back Door* (accessed 6th December 2016, available from http://www.politics.co.uk/comment-analysis/2016/09/01/canadian-trade-deal-will-let-in-ttip-by-the-back-door)

[59] European Commision: *Transatlantic Trade and Investment Partnership* (accessed 7th May 2015, available from http://ec.europa.eu/trade/policy/in-focus/ttip/about-ttip/)

[60] DesJardins, Joseph: *Environmental Ethics: An Introduction to Environmental Philosophy* (5th Edition, Wordsworth, 2013) ch.3

[61] Schweitzer, Albert: *Out of my Life and Thought*

[62] Boyes, Steve: *Iron Mountain: "Net Positive Impact after Mine Closure"* from National Geographic (modified February 2014), available from http://voices.nationalgeographic.com/2014/02/21/iron-mountain-net-positive-impact-after-mine-closure-part-2-of-2/

[63] Martinelli, L. A. et al: *Commodities for Export Still Threaten Rainforest in Brazil* (Nature 467:271, September 2010)

[64] Edwards, D. P. et al: *Wildlife-friendly Oil Palm Plantations Fail to Protect Biodiversity Effectively* (Conservation Letters 3:236-242, August 2010)

[65] Ferguson, Niall: *The Ascent of Money* (Penguin, 2009) p.120

[66] Ferguson, Niall: *The Ascent of Money* (Penguin, 2009) p.226

[67] Elsinger, Jesse: *The Hedge Fund Collapse* from *Upstart* (modified 12th June 2012), available from http://upstart.bizjournals.com/views/columns/wall-street/2008/11/11/Collapsing-Hedge-Fund-Industry.html

[68] Ferguson, Niall: *The Ascent of Money* (Penguin, 2009) p.351

[69] Sachs, Jeffrey

[70] Klein, Naomi: *No Logo*

[71] Howarth, Lorna: *Green Jobs for London's Young People* magazine (September 2012) p.21

---

[72] Kollewe, Julia: *UK Debit Cards Transactions Overtake Cash for the First Time* (The Guardian online, modified 18th June 2018, available from https://www.theguardian.com/business/2018/jun/18/uk-debit-cards-transactions-overtake-cash-for-the-first-time)